The Woman

A Guide to Becoming Elegant
By Eunice J. Leong

Table of Contents

Copyright

Other books by the author:

Secrets of elegance
The Finest Class

For more information, please visit www.elegantwoman.org

Introduction

Dearest reader,

A warm hello and welcome! Thank you so much for taking this journey with me. I look forward to going through the pages of this book with you. Before we get started, I would like to share a few things that will hopefully encourage you to set off on your own personal journey in pursuit of elegance.

How Did This Book Come About?

When I left home at eighteen, I soon realized that the only way to successfully integrate into my new and unfamiliar surroundings was to begin my own personal journey of self-discovery. I had to quickly learn how to become a more refined woman, to grow in self-reliance, and to develop better poise. I wanted to find a system to document my notes along the way, given that my bulging diaries were no longer a practical option. So, I created a blog as a means of journaling my thoughts and findings. This proved to be a successful channel; a place where I could share my journey with the world and gain valuable feedback from readers.

My blog grew to be a fairly large project, and finally the call came for it to be turned into a book. You may read more about my story on my site: www.elegantwoman.org

Before we move on, there are a few things I would like to share with you. First of all, I need to point out that I am not the 'elegant woman'. I'm not perfect. I haven't arrived – yet! But I am enjoying the journey as I strive to become the person I've always wanted to be. Having done extensive research on the subject of elegance for over ten years, I believe that I've gained some authority on elegance and living graciously. It is important to note that there is no such thing as the 'perfectly' elegant woman, so please try to avoid getting into passionate debates about who is elegant and who is not. There are principles of elegance, which I share with you in this book, but nothing is set in stone. It can be a good idea to aspire to be as elegant as "so-and-so", but don't let that limit you in your quest for change. There is more to elegance than one type of look, manner, hairstyle, and so on.

There are many different types of elegance in this world. These differences are to be admired and celebrated! I encourage you to personalize your own elegant style, to work on becoming the kind of elegant woman you would like to grow into.

There is also more to a woman than simply being labeled as 'elegant'. Let elegance be one of the many good qualities you possess. While living a sophisticated lifestyle may be what you aspire to, let your legacy be, "she was an elegant woman who made a difference in her world".

Always here cheering you on,

Eunice

P.s. In the book, when it says, "Read more about *a subject* on www.elegantwoman.org". It means you can type in the <u>words in *italic* into the search box</u> on my website to locate the article. Now let us begin.

Who Is the Elegant Woman?

What does it mean to be elegant? I often asked myself this question and it is a question that is asked by women the world over.

Welcome to *The Elegant Woman*, a guide for women who are striving to attain qualities of timeless style, grace, and poise. This book is based on my personal insights into the art of refinement and living graciously, a dream shared by many. So just how did this book and its associated website come to pass? Well, I've wanted a creative channel where I could record my findings on the art of living elegantly; somewhere to log my personal discoveries as I strived to become the woman I have always dreamed of being. Elegantwoman.org became a result of those efforts and subsequently, it became this book. While 'How to be an elegant woman' is my theme, it merely serves as a framework on matters of a woman's heart. Like most women, I am particularly interested in achieving elegance in the following areas:

Areas of Elegance

- Self Confidence
- Relationships
- Elegant Living, Elegant Lifestyle
- Beauty, Personal Grooming, Dressing
- Manners and Etiquette
- Home Décor
- Social Ease, Entertaining Elegantly
- Personal Refinement

Note: Personal refinement includes education and ambitions, such as the education of travel, food, wine, and so on. I love to draw lessons from elegant women every day in my continual pursuit of refinement.

A Tribute to Elegant Women

When it comes to running my everyday life, I try to live as elegantly as possible. Although perfection is an unrealistic goal, I focus instead on making progress. After all, it is the journey that counts! All of my findings and experiences are shared here in this book.

1. The Definition of Elegance

"Our words reveal our refinements; they tell the discerning listener of the company we have kept; they are the hallmarks of education and culture." ~ Dale Carnegie

Let us first look at the definition of elegance. If you browse through dictionaries, you'll realize that there are many definitions of elegance. Some apply to engineering, some may describe style, and others may equate elegance with a way to quantify a procedure. These variations show that elegance means different things to people. For instance, think about what elegance means to you right now. What comes to your head when you think of an elegant woman? What is your definition of elegance?

When I thought about this, my personal definition of a truly elegant woman is someone who is gracious and exhibits gracious behavior. Yet, when you look more deeply into the meaning and definition of 'Elegant' and 'Elegance'(see words in bold), it is clear that there is much more elegance than graciousness.

Now, take out a highlighter or any colored pen and highlight/circle/underline your favorite adjectives used to describe elegant from the list below. You'll see some of my favorites in bold.

Elegant & Elegance Defined:

Adjective
1. Tastefully fine or luxurious in dress, style, design, furnishings, etc.
2. Gracefully refined and dignified, as in tastes, habits, or literary style: a fine young gentleman.

3. Graceful in form or movement: wave of the hand.
4. Appropriate to refined taste: a man devoted to elegant pursuits.
5. Excellent; fine; superior: an absolutely fine wine.
6. (Of scientific, technical, or mathematical theories, solutions, etc.). Gracefully concise and simple; admirably succinct.

Synonyms: 1. See **fine**. 2. **polished**, 3. **courtly**

Related Words:

Adjective: beautiful, tasteful

Synonyms: Affected, appropriate, apt, aristocratic, artistic, august, **chic**, choice, **classic**, clever, comely, courtly, **cultivated**, **cultured**, dainty, delicate, dignified, effective, **exquisite**, fancy, fashionable, **fine**, **genteel**, **graceful**, grand, handsome, ingenious, luxurious, majestic, modish, neat, nice, noble, opulent, ornamented, ornate, ostentatious, overdone, polished, rare, recherché, **refined**, rich, select, simple, stately, stuffy, stylish, stylized, sumptuous, superior, turgid, **well-bred**

Origins of the word: Characterized by or exhibiting refined, tasteful beauty of manner, form, or style.
Webster's definition: El"e*gant\, a. [L. elegans, -antis; akin to *eligere* to pick out, choose, select: cf. F. ['e]l['e]gant. See Elect]
1. Very choice, and hence, pleasing to good taste; characterized by grace, propriety, and refinement, and

the absence of everything offensive; exciting admiration and approbation by symmetry, completeness, freedom from blemish, and the like; graceful; tasteful and highly attractive; as, manners; style of composition; a speaker; a structure. A more diligent cultivation of literature. ~ Prescott.

2. Exercising a nice choice; discriminating beauty or sensitive to beauty; taste.

Synonyms: Tasteful; polished; graceful; refined; comely; handsome; richly ornamental.

Adjective:

1. Refined and tasteful in appearance or behavior or style; "fine handwriting"; "a fine dark suit"; "she was fine to her fingertips";

2. Suggesting taste, ease, and wealth;

3. Displaying effortless beauty and simplicity in movement or execution; "an elegant dancer"; "an elegant mathematical solution -- simple and precise".

WordNet 3.0, 2006 by Princeton University
adj. [common; from mathematical usage]

Combining simplicity, power, and a certain ineffable grace of design. Higher praise than 'clever', 'winning', or even cuspy.

"**Engineering elegance**" — The French aviator, adventurer, and author Antoine de Saint-Exupéry, probably best known for his classic children's book, *The Little Prince*, was also an aircraft designer. He gave us perhaps the best definition of engineering elegance when he said:

"A designer knows he has achieved perfection not when there is nothing left to add, but when there is nothing left to take away."

If you can, meditate on these words. That means, pick a word or a string of words from your favorites list and then think about them. For instance, '...not when there is nothing left to add, but when there is nothing left to take away.' Try to find out more about what it means, think about how it applies.

If you pick a word, such as "fine", try to think about as many images or scenarios in your head that model the description. This will help you increase your awareness and consciousness of elegance. This is an exercise you can do anytime, and a few minutes of meditating on elegance here and there will go a long way to helping you reach your goals. Now on to Chapter 2, which will help demystify the elegant woman's confidence.

2. An Elegant Woman's Confidence

The Secrets of Elegant Self Confidence, Poise, and Gracefulness

Let me start by sharing this wonderful quote by Genevieve Antoine Dariaux (a French fashion guru and an inspiration to women):

"To be elegant is first of all to know oneself, and to know oneself well requires a certain amount of reflection and intelligence."

There are two acknowledged stages to becoming elegant. It all begins by embracing and developing the inner self, because true elegance starts from within. In other words, turning into a refined woman (as opposed to being that way naturally), is all about working on yourself from the inside out.

Most people know, or at least know of, someone who is deemed elegant. She may be a celebrity of high repute, or perhaps it's that popular girl who seems to have it all together. Then again, it might be the one with the designer clothes and collection of iconic handbags. Or perhaps it's the well-dressed lady who is always articulate and poised. Whoever it is, she may well be the person you have always longed to be like.

My idol has always been Audrey Hepburn. She is among the top of my list of role models and women to watch. Audrey Hepburn was undoubtedly one of the paragons of twentieth century elegance, leading the way in defining what growing into an elegant woman actually signified. There have also been several women who I've met during my lifetime, where I've thought, 'I want to be her when I'm older.' Or perhaps more precisely, 'I want to be just like her!'

We attempt to pursue this potential, this craving for self-improvement, in various ways. When we're able, we might buy the kinds of things that exhibit grace. We dress our best and carry designer branded bags believing we are as elegant as the model in the fashion spread. But to be honest, none of this superficial investment can make us truly elegant. So, with that question in mind, I've tried to get this phenomenon down to an exact science.

Who is the elegant woman? Why is she the way she is, and how can she be so different from those of us who are not elegant even though we strive to be? Well, people are individuals. We are all unique in our own way and possess distinct characteristics. Some women will be naturally elegant whereas others can become more elegant" through training and mindfulness. There will also be those who are not able to emit the air of sophistication without the necessary knowledge no matter how hard they try. That's just the nature of being human. Though there are many types of elegant women, at the crux of it all, they share similar qualities.

Dictionary.com defines an elegant woman as one who is pleasingly graceful and stylish in both her appearance and manner. But a truly elegant woman is so much more.

Acquiring an Elegant Self-Confidence

So where do we start if we want to learn the foundation of how to become elegant?

It begins by increasing and maintaining a new confidence that is rooted in the principles of elegance. I call this an elegant self-confidence. I like to think of it as a kind of decisive confidence that is a cut above the rest.

When a woman is confident in an elegant way, she shines without being aggressive or arrogant. A confident woman is definitely nobody's doormat, yet there is a certain ease with this acquired quality of elegance, one that is quite rare and beautiful.

So let's explore this quality of elegant confidence in more detail.

My personal theory is that there are two stages of acquiring elegant confidence. These can be loosely characterized as internal and external qualities. The first stage is to work on your internal personae. Examples of our internal identity include our heart and mind, thoughts, beliefs, ideas, attitudes, perspectives, and so on.

The second stage would be to work on external qualities, such as personal grooming and deportment (which relates to mannerisms), such as the way you walk and move, your posture, poise, the way you speak and sound, and the way you dress.

To establish an authentic and unwavering elegance, you'll need to build a strong foundation of internal qualities first.

In the Bible, Jesus says, "You blind *Pharisee, cleanse first that which is within the cup and platter that the outside of them may be clean also." (Matthew 23:26) [1]

It is only when your internal qualities are set (and they are strong and just), that building external qualities of elegance can begin. Having good internal virtues also makes improving external elegance a whole lot easier. Even if you make mistakes on the outside, they are less important because your true elegance from within shines through and consequently dominates your genuine persona.

Kindness Rules

There are many definitions of elegance, as we explored in Chapter One. For me personally, my own version of elegance is defined as "graciousness in action." To me, an elegant woman is a gracious woman.

---

[1] *The Pharisees were hypocrites and fakes.

Genuine graciousness is difficult to fake and also difficult to sustain. True elegance in a woman means she is gracious throughout (from the inside out). There isn't a tipping point where she becomes otherwise, meaning she is as she is. This is authentic elegance. She is being herself and not pretending to be anyone else. For instance, she is not the kind of person that will shove others out of her way on a crowded train due to her impatience. Some women might try to look and sound elegant, but then behave badly when no one is looking. The mask of pretense eventually cracks and the true personality becomes exposed.

How to Be Gracious?

You are gracious when you make a genuine effort to love others. True graciousness means that you value and appreciate others for who they are; it is when you treat everyone the same, regardless of social status, looks, speech, cultural backgrounds, education, and so on.

Do not save your best behaviors for certain groups only. Genuinely care and put all others first instead of talking only about yourself. Listen to people and let them talk about what's going on in their lives. Be mindful that the best conversationalists in the world are those who listen a lot and say very little.

When Audrey Hepburn was growing up, she recalled her mother telling her that "I, I, I..." is boring. Hence, she was raised to consider putting others before herself.

When you are genuinely gracious, something happens internally that affects your outward behavior. You'll start to carry yourself better and move with an elegant self-confidence. Women of elegance intuitively know what to do and say without having to pause for thought; they know the appropriate behavior in any given situation.

Be Your Authentic Self

Secondly, as cliché as it may sound, to be elegant, you have got to be authentic. That means you have to try being you, whoever that happens to be. In other words, you need to be real and not 'pretend' (a common shortcoming in many of us). Being fake is a hard habit to break once it becomes a part of someone, but those who are able to portray themselves as they really are tend to be a much happier bunch overall.

Inauthentic Elegance

I've seen friends try to be elegant by wearing pearl necklaces, social climbing, becoming food connoisseurs, showing branded bags like Prada, and a multitude of other external things used to portray an air of elegance.
There is absolutely nothing wrong with any of the above. These women are only trying to fit in and enjoy life, but it's not what you might call 'authentic effort'. It's definitely not true elegance, that's for sure.
      A woman like this may appear elegant on the outside, and seem familiar with all those elaborate things in life that are there to impress, but she's far from elegant in reality. Unless she has developed her graciousness, her facade will wear off when she least expects it, like say in a fit of anger. Or you may see her sponging off others. In a spontaneous outburst, she might raise her voice at sales staff and cause a scene, be rude to a doorman, or generally bad-mouth others to anyone who cares to listen.
      To be as 'real' as possible to yourself, and true to others, you'll need to be more self-aware. This is very doable, but it does require practice.

To Gain Self-Confidence, Get to Know Yourself Better

Many of us think we know ourselves pretty well. The truth is that a lot of us don't know ourselves nearly as well as we think we do. Over time, I came to realize just how little I knew about myself. For example, I realized this when I found myself repeatedly spending money buying something "that is just not me", investing time and money in things that I'm not good at, forcing myself to do something I really didn't want to do, and the list goes on, and on, and on.

We usually can't help it. Sometimes we'll buy an item because something or someone has subconsciously influenced us to do so. Other times we aspire to be someone or something we're not.

All this is normal social behavior, but that doesn't make it rational. If you have made, and continue to make, such mistakes, fear not! I mean, who hasn't bought something only to think afterwards how ridiculous that purchase was? The solution to such atypical behavior is that we have to fine-tune our self-awareness.

Here are some other typical examples of areas where you might be applying pretense and not authentic elegance:

- Putting on airs and graces.
- Doing something only because you think it will make you look rich, elegant, or sophisticated in the eyes of others.
- Trying to impress somebody for selfish gain.
- Doing something odd or wrong simply to protect your image.

The root meaning of the word "Elegant" is authenticity. It is the key to unlocking genuine self-confidence. To know your true self is one of the fundamental steps for obtaining personal security and self-esteem, which is an invaluable trait.

Many women have secret struggles with self-confidence and self-esteem. There are countless root causes for this issue, far too many to discuss here. While I am no psychologist, I do think it's best to keep things simple in order to gain a better understanding of elegance.

After all the research I've done, I truly believe that gaining elegant self-confidence has an awful lot to do with authenticity. It's a matter of discovering who you are and what God has given you with regards to talents, aptitudes, aspirations, and dreams. Knowing what you possess gives a sense of clarity and purpose to your life. Discover your unique qualities, and you will soon realize that you have a job to hone and take your attributes out into the world to help others. Or as that wise old adage goes: "You can't keep it unless you give it away".

How Does One Become Authentic?

- One place to start is by taking a personal inventory.
- Take some time to discover your likes and dislikes.
- Discover your strengths and talents. What about your dreams (goals)? You have them for a reason.
- What inspires you?
- What is within your grasp? What can you do? Assess the opportunities around you.
- What do you like doing? What do you dislike doing?
- Are there more ways to increase the number of activities that you like doing?
- Are there more opportunities for you to do things that make use of your strengths?

Likewise, let's take a look at the list of things you dislike doing. Why are you doing them? Is there a way to minimize those activities?

Sometimes we feel that we don't have a choice, or we might be doing things for the wrong reason. This self-analysis exercise allows you to become more conscious of your decisions.

Don't do anything because you fear what people think of you. Likewise, doing something to impress others does not result in long-term happiness. Doing what you like and love is truly being your authentic self.

In summary, when you work on those internal questions with open-mindedness and honesty, you are embarking on a journey of self-discovery. This will drive you to become a better version of yourself. You'll also get rid of 'impurities' along the way, and the consequence of that is you'll not waste time, money, and effort on those things that don't matter.

Refining yourself to your fullest potential is attaining elegance.

You may no longer have time for low self-confidence. You may suddenly wake up and realize you know a lot more about something than you thought. You begin to embrace elegance with a passion, and speak with modest pride and self-respect.

To be true to ourselves is to be authentic. We become comfortable in our own skin. We can stop being self-conscious and focus on others. This is the basis of an elegant, gracious woman. It is indeed the beginning of elegant self-confidence.

Now you're ready for the next steps!

3. An Immaculate Appearance

A Higher Standard of Grooming

A timeless quote on style: When Christian Dior was asked, "What is the key to good dressing?" He said this…

"There is no key! If there was it would be too easy, rich women could buy the key and all their fashion worries would be over! But simplicity, grooming, and good taste — the three fundamentals of fashion — cannot be bought. But they can be learned, by rich and poor alike."

For example, how does Audrey Hepburn look so timeless? How do designs become classic? We take a look at fashion, its influences, and nail down styles that never go out. The basic principles of achieving a beautiful, elegant look that is timeless are actually quite simple. There is, of course, a more sophisticated elegance, a taste you will develop over time, but for starters, we will stick to simple clean lines and focus on quality. (**Note:** You don't need to go out and spend a ton of money. An elegant woman is more materially-restrained than most realize.)

There is always something very cohesive, rounded, soft, subtle, an ethereal look even, about a woman who is elegant. It's a look that appears effortless, and perfectly gentle.

Elegant Style Principles

The look of a timeless, elegant woman includes the following points:
- Clean

- Neat
- Graceful in appearance
- Quality clothing
- A pleasant appearance and expression
- Dresses appropriately, according to the occasion
- Prefers timeless, classic styles

How Is Your Personal Grooming?

The first steps to achieving a timeless, elegant style, is to pay attention to your personal grooming (this means a lifestyle change for many!). Remember, the important thing here is not to become overwhelmed. These are just baby steps that are simple and subtle changes.

It is impossible for someone to be elegant if they're not immaculately groomed. With that in mind, here are the basics of good grooming:

Skin Care, Makeup, Hair

At the bare minimum it is important to have a clean face, manicured (or clean and tidy) nails, and to smell fresh (from having regular baths, not from perfume). Wear fresh clothes at all times. Clothing makes a huge difference in how you feel and smell!

Develop your own customized skin care regime, and stick with a hair-care routine that you know brings out the best in your locks. Keep it simple; pay attention to which products serve you well. Be disciplined about your selections and avoid the temptation to become fickle and try every brand in the store once you've established your skin and hair care choices.

You may be wondering what I mean by 'customized?' Well, it simply means experimenting and finding those things that work best for YOU personally, and not what the media hype tries to convince you to buy. You see, the beauty products your friends use, or the skin care range being plugged on the shopping channel, may or may not work for you. We're all very different and this is why you need to experiment independently.

As for makeup, unless you need lots of it for work, try not to have too much clutter in your cosmetic arsenal. Maintain your look always by keeping it fresh and updated. Go for a more natural look during the daytime and a more dramatic appearance after dark.

She Is Neat and Clean

A truly timeless look is always freshly laundered, neat, and in place. I love how the following quote describes this concept:

"For all her chic thinness, she had an almost breakfast-cereal air of health, a soap and lemon on cleanness, a rough pink darkening on her cheeks." – Truman Capote, Breakfast at Tiffany's.

Why do I emphasize neat and clean? Well, it's because I've met women that are neat but are not clean, and vice versa. As for me, I tend to be clean but not necessarily neat. I'm sure there are a lot of you reading here that can relate to this.

Whatever your tendencies, remember you have to be both neat and clean. You don't have to worry about being perfect, so long as you make an effort to be spotless and tidy more often than not. Remember, our journey is all about progress, not perfection! By following these suggestions, you are being good to yourself. So, as often as you can, do your very best to turn both neatness and cleanliness into a habit.

Personal Grooming for an Elegant Woman

To achieve an elegant look, one has to value personal grooming.

Groom (VT): To tend carefully as to person and dress; make neat or tidy.

Self-grooming is not about vanity. In fact, proper grooming takes the 'spotlight' away from you. You will not attract attention by having someone think, 'Gosh, she looks so pale', or cringe inwardly at the sight of dirty and unkempt fingernails. Personal grooming is about presenting yourself in the best possible light. It portrays to other people that you are someone who cares about themselves in a positive way.

Someone once said, "The cornerstone of elegance must be represented by a bar of soap." Maybe from a bygone age, a bar of soap was all she had. Today we have help from many places, friends, beauty counters, and magazines, to name but a few means. It is simply impossible to not know at least a little about personal grooming.

Bad personal grooming can be spotted a mile away. Some examples are unconcealed red patches on the face, clothes that are not ironed, dirty fingernails or chipped nail polish, a run in the stockings, a dirty or scuffed shoe, untidy hair, sloppy makeup, a weak collar, bad designer knockoffs, faded clothes, etc.

The Mirror Test

Perform a mirrored self-examination test. Take some time to look over yourself in the mirror. This is an exercise in constructive self-criticism.

The Breakdown 'MUST-Do's' of Personal Grooming:

Face and Good Skin

A person with good personal grooming always seems to have a clear, even complexion. If you do not have good skin, establish a skin care regime that works for you. Other basic good skin care tips are to wear sunscreen, exercise regularly, sleep well, and drink plenty of water. Naturally, we all have moments in our lives when we are battling with a few zits. A good concealer helps mask those imperfections. Covering up is important as a spotty face is distracting.

Dental Hygiene

Maintaining beautifully white teeth does wonders for having a great smile. Do not scrimp on a good toothbrush and toothpaste. Also, make it a habit to see your dentist every six months. The investment is worth it, especially as the years roll on! If you can afford it, get your teeth professionally whitened every couple of years. Alternatively, there are plenty of teeth whitening products out there that can be applied at home, but use them with caution! Too much whitening can cause abrasion on the enamel of your teeth, and eventually produce the reverse effect.

Do not rely on breath mints to make your breath smell pleasant. Regular flossing and brushing is the foundation of a clean smelling breath..

Removal of Facial Hair

Hair around the lips must be removed at all times. Eyebrows should be shaped about once every six weeks and maintained weekly.

Makeup

Aim for a fresh, healthy appearance. Learn to do your make up elegantly and with complete confidence. It should be applied evenly and be free of smudges. Wear heavier make up in the evening, such as bolder eyeliner strokes. Learn how via make-up video tutorials. My recommendation: http://www.youtube.com/user/lisaeldridgedot com

Elegant Hair

Personal grooming for hair means it should be clean, neat, tidy, and elegantly styled. You should wash your hair every other day. Good hair etiquette means not scratching your head, combing your hair, or attempting to tie your hair in public places. Find a hairstyle that suits the shape of your face. Also consider your lifestyle when choosing a cut. If you have a fairly busy schedule, opt for a low maintenance hairdo.

A medium length coiffure is the most versatile. You can wear it up or down, straighten it out or curl it up. You can tie it up in a casual pony tail or leave it as it is. This is for those who enjoy doing their hair. You may look on my website for some ideas. If you wear a different color to your natural hair, be sure to get your roots treated regularly.

Body - Exercise and Posture

You can tell when a woman applies personal grooming to her body by the way she looks and carries herself. Certain exercises affect your core muscles and give you good posture. That reason alone is enough to engage in exercise! I know when I'm not getting enough physical training because I noticeably start to slouch. My stomach muscles become weak as well.

When you exercise, you build your self-esteem and confidence at the same time. This is because you feel good about yourself, what you're doing, and why you're doing it. You feel better when you can shop for the clothes you want to wear and not be restricted to only those clothes that you can fit into.

Pay attention to your gestures and movements. Move with grace. Have someone videotape you, or take up some ballroom or ballet lessons as a method to help improve movement and posture. We will talk more about this in detail in a later chapter.

Hair Removal

Occasionally I have girls write to me saying how their mothers never taught them about personal grooming, and therefore lack the skills. Fret not, as I've always believed that your desires will teach you whatever you want to know. In general, hair from your legs, underarms, and bikini lines should be removed at all times. You might need to address your upper thighs and arms too, that's if your natural body hair tends to be long and dark.

For your face as mentioned earlier, any visible hair on the upper lip should be removed, and the eyebrows need to be shaped to suit your look.

Nails

Personal grooming for nails means they should always be clean and nicely shaped. Ideally, your nails should be polished or buffed, or coated with a clear protective base. Whether nails should be long or short depends on your lifestyle and preferred look.

Dirty fingernails are a rude shock, not to mention potentially harmful to health. The most elegant look is the French manicure, because it's clean, neat and healthy. Oh, and don't forget your toenails.

Dressing Elegantly

The final word on personal grooming is to just state the obvious in that dressing well is imperative. Dressing elegantly and appropriately can't be stressed enough. We'll definitely talk about how to dress elegantly in more detail in the coming chapters.

Anti-Aging Skin Care Tips

This section covers the very basics of anti-aging skin care tips, and ones that I use personally. It's a 'must read' for elegant ladies and skincare beginners.

I've always believed that the foundation to an elegant appearance is good clear skin. Of course, hair and makeup, along with all the rest of it, are also important. However, when you find something that works for your skin, it makes it much easier to maintain an elegant appearance!

There is a plethora of material written about skin care, but I'm writing this article for the woman who is finding herself overwhelmed and lacking any real direction. In other words, she is at ground zero. Don't worry though; this is nothing to be ashamed of. I myself didn't have anyone to show me the way. There was no older sister to guide me, and my mother belonged to the soap and water generation.

Since the advancement of aesthetics (branch of philosophy that deals with the nature and expression of beauty), research has proven that there are much better things for good skin care than plain soap and water. I myself have read a fair share of books and articles, and have tried and tested some of the techniques suggested. Below is the shortlist of the most basic ones.

The Three Basic Anti-aging Skin Care Tips

1. Watch what you eat.
2. Adopt a good skincare routine.
3. Take vitamins and supplements.

Watch What You Eat

It is a true statement, "You are what you eat". If I could summarize, it would be to 'eat fresh'. I'm not a nutritionist, but please eat according to your body type and lifestyle. There are many books you can read up on healthy eating.

Skin Care Routine

This is what I want to focus on. You will need some basic products. Some women swear by twelve steps and use a stack of products, but this system should be tried and tested on your own because we're all very different.

Step 1: Use a cleanser

Some call it facial wash, but it's the same thing. There are many different types. If you are new to a face care routine, try a mild one. Read labels. Any cleanser you use should say 'mild' or 'gentle' or 'for sensitive skin'. Usually, these are the ones you wash off with plain water.

Step 2: Use a toner

If you are purchasing a toner for the first time, buy the same brand as your cleanser and get some cotton wool while you're at it. Dab some toner on the cotton ball and swipe every area of your face gently.

Step 3: Use a serum

Serums come in day and night form. Of course, some can be used for both day and night. They are basically concentrated beauty creams that used to be exclusive to beauty salons.

Step 4: Facial moisturizer

There are also day and night moisturizers, but I use just use one all-purpose moisturizer to keep things simple.

Night Time Routine and Exfoliating

If you wear makeup, you've got to get a makeup remover to ensure all traces of it are removed before bed. You should also get an exfoliating lotion or a brush/sponge, to ensure you get rid of dead skin cells once a week.

Vitamins and Supplements

At the very least, take one multivitamin daily. I don't think what we eat today is sufficient for getting all the necessary nutrients, no matter how hard we try. The food we consume is not what it used to be, that's for sure! You can also visit a nutritionist for more advice (money well spent).

Other Anti-Aging Skin Care Tips

- Sleep early, sleep well, and sleep enough!
- Drink lots of purified water.
- Try to breathe in good, clean, fresh air. If you live in the city, get an air purifier.
- Change your pillowcases often.
- Sleep facing the ceiling.
- Go for a facial once a month.
- Get plenty of exercise.
- Use facial masks at home as much as possible.

If you've got some extra cash, read and research into some aesthetic beauty devices, both for home treatment, or at the salon, such as the TALIKA Paris Light DUO.

- Avoid the sun. Wear sun screen.
- Avoid sugar as much as you can.

Have fun with this. Do your own beauty research and find your own anti-aging skincare tips and secrets.

4. The Art of Elegant Style

"Elegance is refusal" ~ *Coco Chanel*

How is it that women like Audrey Hepburn, Grace Kelly, Natalie Portman, and other elegant women manage to stay so timelessly beautiful and essentially stylish?

The first principle for attaining a style that is considered elegant and timeless is, as Coco Chanel stated, learning how to refuse. Yes, you have to learn to refuse your way to elegance. This is the 101 on how to achieve an unfading classic style.

What she means is that you refuse to accept and blindly follow every trend that is out there. Fashion is fickle, to say the least. A trend may be in today and out tomorrow. Also, most of us do not have the fortunate versatility (that only a few rare women possess) to pull off every latest trend. You know the type; they are the ones that look great in all colors, any hairstyle, and fit into all types of clothes with ease. They don't have to think too much, nor do they have to reject any fashion trend. These women are just able to pull it off and look good no matter what.

As for the rest of us, well, we have to work hard to find those classic styles that suit us. These are ones that make us look our very best. Our style changes will be minimal, if at all, and introduced gradually, just to keep our look updated, albeit in a subtle way.

Fundamentals of Good Dressing and Style

The fundamentals of good dressing begin by knowing your face shape, body shape, skin tone, and your colors. They also include learning about what types of clothing fit you well, and what designs are the most flattering on you. The fundamentals of 'Good Dressing' and attaining an elegant, timeless style, begin with a couple of self-awareness exercises.

Imagine Your Life in a Movie

Try to imagine watching yourself in a movie. Stand back and observe your lifestyle. Where are the places you frequent? Who do you meet? How do you get around, by bicycle, train, car, on foot? Reflect, too, on the kinds of activities you pursue the most?

Do you stay home and cook a lot? What about employment, do you work in an office? Are you someone that goes to the gym regularly? Maybe you're taking care of children most of the day?

As you become more aware of the lifestyle you lead, you'll be better informed when doing a wardrobe edit and therefore able to properly plan and buy only what you need.

Self-Analysis: Do You Know What Is Good for You?

The fundamentals of good dressing are the fruits of self-examination. Just to recap, that means knowing your face shape, body shape, skin tone, colors that compliment you, fits that flatter you, and equally important, those that do not. Come to realize what you need and what you can afford. Once you know 'you', then, and only then, can you search and shop diligently.

If in doubt, stay close to simplicity. Ensure that whatever you buy is not too tight. If possible, try it on for size and fit. See if you can move, stand, and sit without ruining the shape of the clothes.

Think about your existing wardrobe when you make purchases. Know what you need and be aware of what you already have too much or too many of. As mentioned previously, be mindful of your lifestyle and ensure that you have enough range to dress well for every occasion in your current routine (giving priority to the activities that take up the bulk of your life).

Avoid clothes that you cannot see yourself actually wearing. Make sure that the garments you buy suit your personality too. Some of you reading here might have a more forgiving budget for clothes, in which case you may well be able to afford to take bigger risks with the items you purchase.

Being constantly attentive is a great way for you to reinvent yourself. We need reinvention in our style and looks from time to time, especially as we age! Taking risks with an item of clothing, or going for a style that you've never tried before, is a great way to add a little spark of inspiration to your regular wardrobe. You may need more time to 'break the outfit in', testing it with various pieces you already have, but, if you get it right, it will be pleasantly gratifying.

Also, by taking the occasional gamble, you won't ever be accused of being boring, out-of-date, or stuck in your ways. The very worst thing that can happen is that you have to admit defeat and accept that your gamble was not a look that suits you after all. Who knows, maybe you'll be able to have a good laugh at the pictures a couple of years later.

Finally, in order to maintain an efficient, working, and lovely wardrobe, it's important to remember to do a **wardrobe edit** from time to time. I would advise you to edit your wardrobe every three months or so. We'll be covering this more in later chapters. Remember to take good care of your clothes. As Christian Dior says, *"You cannot be well groomed if your clothes are not well cared for"*.

Personalize Any Dress That You Buy or Make

This is the fun part. You are a creative individual, and this is the place to really express your personality! Think carefully about how you would like to stand out in an elegant and subtle way.

For instance, have you thought about adding a bejeweled brooch of a swan, or perhaps a pin of a satin rose? Maybe you can add a matching colored headband? Or maybe bangles are more your thing? Then again, you might be a stickler for rose-colored pearls.

Everyone's unique in their own way, and we live in times of abundant accessories. It's always interesting to see what accessories women pick to express their style.

My belief is, as long as your choices blend well with your outfit, you should go for it. However, be careful not to overdo it when using accessories. When there's too much going on, you run the risk of resembling a human Christmas tree or looking like someone that is trying far too hard to be stylish. Too many accessories also make an outfit look fussy.

Maybe you're like me, with a lack of flair for accessorizing. Fret not, as the suggestion is to keep your accessories simple and minimal. That is still part of being elegant!

The Art of Color - Fill Your Wardrobe with Basic Colors First

Unless you can afford to have a large wardrobe, it is important that you fill it with only those colors you are happy to wear without hesitation.

If you love white and wear it often, then fill your wardrobe with many white garments, or perhaps various shades of white that you like. If you have not yet ascertained the colors that are most flattering to your complexion, then play safe and choose earth tones or neutral colors. You can always dress them up or down with accessories. But do make sure you get color charted sooner rather than later (Google this if you don't know what it means).

Dressing According to One's Age

While most people fight against aging in an attempt to look younger than they really are, there is a trend where some try to look too young. There is only so much youth you can fake without looking completely ridiculous.
It's not unusual in Western societies to see beautiful, grown-up women looking absolutely bizarre by wearing the most inappropriate clothing, often items more suited for teenagers.

It's equally as silly to see very young girls trying to look too adult by dressing too grown-up, especially those who wear stilettos and an overload of makeup.

There are some women who totally refuse to accept the transition into womanhood. They still dress as they did when they were teenagers, irrespective of their age. Some even dress in the fashions of the current teenage trends and behave like them too! This is distasteful behavior for mature women. And family members that are close to these individuals often suffer a great deal of mockery and embarrassment, particularly the kids if they have any.

A young girl should dress in girlish styles up until around the age of fifteen. Sixteen and up, she and her mom can go shopping together for slightly less 'childlike' styles. It's an age where she will inevitably want to learn more about applying make-up, although at such a young age, perhaps the subtle use of lipstick is most appropriate.

At eighteen, she can learn the full makeup regime and start to wear heels. In my opinion, a girl should only opt for full makeup for formal occasions, like weddings. Being in her youth, she can get by happily with tinted moisturizer, groomed eyebrows, and lighter shades of lipstick.

At twenty-one, she is considered an adult. She should dress and behave like one too, that's if she's to start adult life on the right foot. It will be her decision concerning the amount and type of makeup to wear. Her choices in clothes will reflect on her lifestyle.

A lot of how young females evolve into womanhood depends on their cultural background. In some places, like Europe for example, it's considered repulsive to have an adult female trying to look too young and trendy for her years.

In Asia, many women appear ageless, that is, they look the same age year in and year out, particularly up until around middle-age. It's quite difficult trying to figure out their actual age. It is also more accepting in many Asian countries for a woman to dress in girlish styles, or less mature styles, even though she may not be that young.

In North America, dressing styles are more liberal than in Europe. However, dressing too trendy or too young may not work in the less liberal towns and cities.

Until a girl becomes an adult, she really ought to stay away from excessive luxury goods or from looking "too rich". Attempting to look too mature too soon is unbecoming, loud, and makes her look older than her years, or like a spoiled brat. My personal thought on this is that I feel girls should not indulge in high-end luxury goods until the age of 25, and even then only if it's compatible to her lifestyle, otherwise she comes across as pretentious, inauthentic, and inelegant.

There is also a difference between how a single and married woman dresses.

Also, when a woman gets to be over 50, her body, hair, and skin changes. She may begin to wear clothes that cover her knees and neck. She will look for more comfortable, practical clothing, but without compromising her style. My very elegant 75-year-old aunt wears long sleeve silk dresses to cover her aging neck, knobby knees and bony arms. She is one of my biggest inspirations for dressing elegantly as an older lady.

Colors

Limit your clothing collection to just a few colors at the beginning, especially if you are doing a major edit of your wardrobe or are building one from scratch. Fill those racks and shelves with staples.

Fail-proof colors include: White, ivory, black, navy blue, gray, beige, and khaki. You're probably thinking that all sounds a little dull, right? Don't worry, think of them as a canvas from where you can sprinkle your personality with the use of accessories and splashes of color.

The next colors to consider, in limited quantities (and only if those colors suit you), are reds, yellows, turquoise, and pastels.

Once you've sorted out the above, you might want try adding a couple of prints to your collections. If you do, always buy polka dots before any other pattern! You may well be one of those women that wear prints with finesse, just like one of my really elegant friends. If this is you, then you must go ahead and wear printed designs if that's what you love to do. It has to be said, though, very few people wear prints in a stylish way, which is why I don't usually recommend this approach for beginners.

There is no single fashion rule on this, but I've always felt that black is too harsh for the morning or early afternoon. Try to restrict black clothing for early evening wear or nights. However, if you're just starting out and you don't have a big budget for clothes, at the very least, have one classic black dress in your collection. You can wear it in various ways with the use of accessories. (Think shawls, brooches, necklaces, bracelets, and so on.)

That's pretty much what Audrey Hepburn did in the movie *Breakfast at Tiffany's*. She had one black cocktail dress, one black gown, and a beige coat. But she accessorized, and did it very well too!

In terms of daytime wardrobe, white is always a great choice of color for morning and early afternoon. In fact, it works well at night, too. It is also the perfect canvas for accessorizing, simply because white works well with just about anything. Pay attention to the fabric though, because only some materials are good for daytime, namely cottons, whereas silks are more suited for nights.

The 'color rules' apply to footwear too. For your shoes and bags, you should also begin acquiring basic colors such as beige, chocolate brown, navy blue, and black. And of course, it's very wise to add one pair of classic red shoes to your footwear collection. By the way, the color rules above also relate to coats.

As basic as the colors of your clothing may be, it's always a good idea to add a little change sometimes. You can always introduce a little sparkle, a fresh splash of new color every once in a while, or an on-trend blouse, dress, or shoe style in order to spruce things up a bit. People do exactly this with their hairstyles from time to time, and clothes should be no different.

Change is central to beauty. This is why people renovate and revamp their look periodically. I once knew a lady who wore yellow every single day. She looked ridiculous! Use colors that are not under 'basics' as accents to add a little chic to your outfit.

Point to remember: When putting an outfit together, don't forget the color of your hair and your makeup.

Many fashion designers recommend not wearing more than two colors in one outfit. I don't quite follow that rule, but I do understand where they're coming from!

Your Basic Outfits: The Workhorses of Your Wardrobe

When buying clothes, always remember that they should be, first and foremost, practical. Do not be fooled into believing you can mimic high fashion models on the catwalk. These shows are put on for inspirational and attention-grabbing purposes only. They usually sell toned-down versions of the latest collections at boutiques anyway.
What do I mean by basic outfits? These are the staples of your wardrobe. The type of staple clothes depends on your lifestyle. They usually consist of blouses, turtle necks, cardigans, jackets, skirts, pants, cardigans, cropped pants in easy-to-match colors such as white, black, beige, khaki and some pastel colors. They may also include scarves, simple dresses, polo T-shirts, sleeveless silk blouses.
If your clothes are not practical, you'll always subconsciously resist putting them on. Think back to the most fashionable item in your wardrobe; it's most likely the one that gets worn the least. That's why we should be careful not to do 'aspiration shopping', which means you buy things that reflect an aspirational lifestyle, rather than the things you need.

Outfits for Different Occasions

A great first step in organizing your wardrobe is to separate your outfits (the best you can) into two categories: daytime and nighttime. Day and nightwear should be distinguished, if only by separation in the wardrobe. This strategy will give you a better understanding of what you have and what you need. Also, one should not neglect house clothes; those being the items you generally wear around the home.

Make an effort and spend some extra money investing in a few nice, comfortable garments to lounge in. Some women tend to neglect themselves after marriage, and even more so after they have children. Yet, making a little effort each day, so that your husband and kids can see you as the beautiful woman you are, not only pleases them, but will make you feel good about yourself too.

Some of my favorite memories as a child are of my mother looking beautiful as she came home from work or while at home making meals for us or doing the laundry.

Also, pay attention to what you wear to bed as well. Why not wear something beautiful? Once again, it not only pleases your partner, but it makes you feel good about YOU too, and that has to be a good investment.

Coats

Try to avoid buying a cheap coat. Invest well – and get a really good one if you can. A cheap coat can spoil the rest of your outfit, irrespective of how expensive your shoes might be. However, a well-made coat that fits you properly (hangs well) will add instant elegance.

I still remember the first good-quality coat that I purchased for $300, which was a lot of money for me when I was young, but I wore that coat for the next ten years. It was like a faithful friend, someone I could depend on. It made me feel comfortable and I gained confidence from knowing that I looked smart and beautiful. **Point to Remember:** Quality not only looks and feels better, but it lasts longer too, and that makes it a much better value in the long term.

Blouses

Blouses are staples of any woman's wardrobe. You may wear them with pants, jeans, skirts, under suits, and any time of the year. They are great for mixing and matching, too. If time is not a luxury you have, then buy blouses that are made from soft materials, like chiffon and silk-like fabrics. They are low-maintenance clothes and often need no ironing, or just a very quick press. If ironing is not an issue, then invest in blouses in lots of wonderfully beautiful, rich materials that are the epitome of elegance.

I'm not sure why, but some sleeveless blouses (and dresses) come with very large armholes that are way too revealing. Avoid them! This is a simple case of being refined.

Belts

Pay particular attention to the ends of a belt after you have fastened it. The ends might irk you! If you're not sure what to do with them, don't buy those types of belts. Some belts can make you look short and fat. These are usually the thick variety. Unless you are tall, stay well away from belts altogether.

Bonings for a Gown Are a Must

Avoid dresses with elastic tube tops because they look cheap and tasteless. Ensure they have proper boning to support your frame and give you a smaller waist. This is especially important if you do not have the 'perfect' figure. Bonings were created to replace corsets; they help with posture too.

Zippers or Buttons?

Personally I prefer buttons. I think they give a prettier look in general, although zippers that are concealed are perfectly fine as well. When buying clothes, it's important to check that zippers are of a high quality and that they don't look cheap. Whenever they are visible, zippers tend to cheapen an outfit.

Elegant Style Notes
Dress Codes

Know your dress code. Check carefully what a dress code means if you're not too sure. For instance, do you know what a dress code of business suit means? Respect your host or business-related occasion by adhering to the dress code. For example, know the difference between cocktail and smart-casual; do not show up at a dinner party ignoring the dress code and wearing whatever you like. Know the differences between black tie and white tie. Call and check if you are not sure or unable to find out by other means. Some people think that following a dress code is not important, and some hosts may even claim as much. However, elegant women set higher standards for themselves and consider it rude to be sloppy.

The Importance of Framing

In terms of a basic elegant appearance, understand that your hairstyle is important because it acts as a frame for your face. Just as the wrong frame for a picture can spoil its appearance, the same can be said for having an unsuitable hairstyle for the shape of your face, which we'll talk more about in detail later.
Your collars are important as well, as they frame your décolletage, or the area between your neck and chest. So, when you shop for tops, check that the collar is a strong one. Why? Weak collars are distracting and unflattering.
In terms of framing your body, think in terms of your belt, neckline (décolleté), and the shape of your dress. You can manipulate your silhouette to a certain extent by the heels you wear. Very high heels are usually unflattering because they alter your posture in a negative way. This will be even more obvious if you can't walk properly in them!

Point to note: The gait of a woman who is wearing very high heels is ungainly.

Women who wear very high heels should only wear them if they feel that they are uncomfortably short. This usually occurs if you're dating or married to someone who looks way too tall for you.

Accessories, such as scarves and necklaces (including chokers) may also be used for framing your outfit. Take some time to find out what is the most flattering for you personally. If you are rather short, long hair and long necklaces give an illusion of height. V-necks help to create shoulder definition for women without broad shoulders. Thinking strategically in these ways will help you formulate a more structured and elegant overall appearance.

Bangles, sleeves, and scarves tied around the wrists, as well as bracelets and watches are all great options to frame wrists and can also look very pretty. Elegance is all about attention to detail.

Dressing Etiquette

Dressing etiquette should be given high priority. It reflects our inner self by the way we communicate with what we wear. Dressing elegant also has a lot to do with dressing appropriately for the occasion. Take time to learn the secrets of clothing etiquette.

Long gone are the days of 'one size fits all'. Before we became bombarded with a wide variety of clothing options, gentlemen wore suits everywhere, and ladies simply wore dresses. Nowadays we are faced with colossal choices in clothing, so just how does one figure out when and where jeans and t-shirts are deemed appropriate garb? And what about dresses; where do they fit in with today's ever changing fashions?

Knowing What to Wear

Fact: Clothes have a secret language of their own.

They communicate more than we realize. That is why big time movie stars pay tens of thousands of dollars for top stylists to dress them and organize their wardrobe. They need to be outfitted in a certain way so as to transmit a precise message to their fans, the media, and perhaps potential movie directors who might send them potential job offers.

Most of us won't suffer the emotional peaks and dips caused by harsh critics expressing their opinions of us and our pictures splashed on the pages of magazines and other publications all over the world. But just because we won't endure being placed on some international 'worst dressed women's list', we still need to care about our personal presentation. Being inappropriately dressed can have a greater effect on our personal lives than we realize. Sending the wrong message about yourself can jeopardize your chances of desired friendships, opportunities, and careers. Making a good impression counts and we don't get a second chance to make a first impression. You may be the most fantastic and inspirational person, but if your appearance does not make a good impression, no one would have a chance to find out.

Have you ever noticed how people who hang out together dress somewhat similarly? If you would like to socialize with a more elegant crowd, then you've got to speak a somewhat similar clothing language (or dress etiquette). Or to put it in more blunt terms, you have to dress in their range of 'acceptability' in order to be accepted into their circle.

The Question to Ask: "What Is the Occasion?"

Knowing what is appropriate to wear requires as much good taste as the wherewithal to dress elegantly. Let's assume your grooming is already immaculate and you have good posture and poise.

Note the difference here. Knowing what is appropriate to wear is NOT THE SAME as knowing how to dress elegantly. You may turn up in a white ball gown at your friend's wedding and look quite elegant, but it is also in bad taste. So, the real mistake in dress etiquette is wearing the wrong outfit for the occasion. Appropriateness and adherence to dress code are the keys to having good clothing etiquette.

Other examples of inappropriate etiquette include wearing the wrong shoes, e.g., heels to go on a hike,, revealing clothing in a conservative country, or at a conservative event, wearing white or black to a wedding, skimpy garments that are too revealing for others to look without blushing, pajamas to the grocery store, and so on. Also, remember that daytime clothes are different from evening wear. Similarly, evening clothes are worn in the evening and never during the day.

Simple Guide to Daytime Dressing

Wear light-colored clothes, such as whites, beige, pastel, or bright colors (if your complexion suits). Dark colors can be too harsh. Also wear only natural looking makeup, with minimal jewelry, unless of course you have a glamorous day event to attend. For shoes, low to medium heels are appropriate.

Simple Guide to Evening Dressing

Come evening time, you can afford to go a little more formal, or not, it is totally your choice. Black, of course, is always accepted, along with darker, richer colors. Those who practice strict dress etiquette only wear diamonds at night. It is definitely more tasteful to wear glitter and high heels in the evening, but scale your amount of glitz to the type of event you're attending.

See my gallery guide to a basic wardrobe for more on this.

Going from Day to Night

Dressing Etiquette Tip: Making an outfit work from day to night.

Since we do not always have the luxury of being able to swap outfits when circumstances warrant a change in dress, we have to learn how to transform an outfit from daywear to nightwear.

If you have a cocktail event after work, you could wear a cocktail dress inside and wear a blouse or cardigan over the top. You could also pair it off with an executive jacket. If your dress code at work is more professional, stick to little back dresses or structured dresses in navy or cream.

After work, you can safety do away with that outer layer and put on some accessories, such as pearls or chandelier earrings. Then dab on some eyeliner and red lipstick that you've tucked away in your purse, and in no time at all, you're good to go.

Common Pitfalls of Dressing Etiquette

In our increasingly casual society, there is a greater need for dress etiquette, especially after all the stories we hear on bad dress protocol, and the shocking things some people wear quite publicly nowadays.

Such fashion blunders include:
- Wearing casual wear to the office.
- Wearing beach wear in the city.
- Not dressing in one's Sunday's best for church.
- Wearing bright and colorful clothes at a funeral.
- Wearing entirely black outfits at weddings.
- Wearing flip-flops everywhere.
- Ignoring the specific dress code of an event.

Stick to the Dress Code

Dressing etiquette also means we honor the dress code, whether it is obviously stated or not. Below is a list of seven events where the dress code is assumed to be commonly understood, even though there is not always a formal protocol stated:

1. Coffee
2. Luncheon / brunches
3. Afternoon tea
4. Dinner parties
5. Cocktail parties
6. Balls & galas

7. Weddings

Remember, aside from specific dress requests written on invites, don't wear all black, and definitely never attempt to upstage the bride.

A Note of Caution for Designers & Logos Lovers

A word of caution for those who love designers and logos; be careful not to become a victim of fashion trends. There are millions of dedicated followers of fashion out there, but the problem with this is that is many women wear items because they're 'in vogue', but that does not guarantee they look good in what they wear!
No matter how important you are, or your friends are, never attempt to dazzle with the overuse of clothes, shoes, and bags emblazed with designer logos.

Many believe that the more expensive and designer their clothes are, the more elegant they appear. This is just not so. In fact, most of what's in fashion is **not** what we consider timeless, elegant styles.

While most big fashion houses must be commended by their elegant designs, they cannot control how their items will be used or how long they will be à la mode. So keep the use of 'logo designer items' minimal or subtle. The object here is to NOT impress.

Timeless Style — Prioritize Quality

With so much cheap 'throwaway fashion' around these days, it can be tempting to put quality on the back seat.
However, quality matters, it really does. Many people think that top quality is unaffordable or not necessary. I'm not asking anyone to ditch buying things that are inexpensive, especially where the quality is acceptable. I'm just suggesting that you explore the notion of treating yourself better. Purchasing the best that you can possibly afford is a means of raising the standards for yourself in a healthy way. I'm definitely not

suggesting anyone should go broke or into debt for the sake of designer goods.

But the rewards of buying quality lead to increased satisfaction, less waste, and a reduction in clutter. More often than not, you'll save money in the long term because you won't have to replace quality made items as often. Robert Kiyosaki, writer of *Rich Dad Poor Dad*, and a well-known self-help author, and motivational speaker, once said:

"You spend less if you buy what you desire. I am very happy with my car, and my wife is happy with hers. We may have spent more by being clear on satisfying our material standards, which includes our house and clothing. But we actually spent less in the long run. These savings come in the form of time, money, and happiness, because we buy what we want."

The Importance of Quality

Quality is essential to elegance. Prioritize quality over quantity in every area of your life, whether it's what you eat, experience, use or buy. Something of good quality is not an extravagance. A well-made item lasts longer and consequently saves you money in the long term because you get more use out of it. It always pays to have the very best that you can afford.

Let's look at food for a moment. Although buying quality may mean eating fresh foods instead of the cheaper, packaged & processed options, the benefits include better skin, improved health, a slimmer waistline, and increased longevity. However, we're only going to be discussing buying and wearing quality clothes for now.

Some women dream of wearing new outfits every day. Imagine that! Something new to put on every single day of the year; it sounds like a dream come true, right? In reality, and contrary to popular belief, more is not always better. Having too much choice in the closet often leaves women feeling dissatisfied. Why? Well, not only do they have to manage an extremely large wardrobe, but they'll have to spend more time and money maintaining their collection. And, surprise, surprise, they still have the same old problem of not knowing what to wear!

My personal experience is that it is easier to choose what I'm going to wear when I stop filling my cupboards and drawers with clothes that I'm only half satisfied with. When you really love an item of clothing, you'll find yourself wearing it over and over. So from now on, make a personal resolution to only buy garments that you genuinely adore.

The rule of thumb for elegant dressing, and shopping, is to think before you buy. Only purchase quality, and make sure you love the items that you're acquiring.

Minimize Quantity
My Personal Wardrobe Story

I discovered the 'less is more' theory on my own, even though I'd heard it more than a thousand times. It's actually a nineteenth-century proverbial phrase that states simplicity and clarity lead to good purpose.

My ideal wardrobe is to have twelve really nice pieces that I can wear several times, mix and match, and dress up or dress down. I know it's natural to think that you don't have enough, and that you need more of this or extra of that, but I've found a small collection of clothes really does work very well.

This personal revelation occurred during one of my long trips. There was a period of time in the past when I had to travel quite frequently, and each trip was quite long, lasting for a few weeks or months at a time. On those trips, I wasn't able to buy too many things because I didn't have the luggage space. This forced me to consider very carefully what to take with me, and to think sensibly about what to buy – if I bought anything at all.

Whatever I packed into my bags had to prove functional. I should be able to wear it with as many other items as possible. It had to survive frequent washing and wearing. It also had to be easily maintained. If I went shopping during those trips, whatever I bought had to be as practical as what I already had packed. Therefore, I found myself picking the most sensible and versatile clothes I could find. After all, my travel-wear would be pretty much what I'd be dressing in for the weeks ahead.

And when I faced the same old gripe of 'having nothing to wear', it didn't take that long before my creative juices started flowing. As the saying goes, necessity is the mother of invention, and needless to say, I soon managed to come up with a few new combinations of accessories for my outfits.

I've since realized that I quite enjoy the simplicity of only having a small wardrobe. I get dressed much more quickly nowadays, and have become more creative in working with what I already have.

If you can create a small, yet very practical wardrobe, there will be less effort required when it comes to dressing elegantly.

An ideal wardrobe is one that works. It helps you get dressed better and more efficiently. In this ideal wardrobe, you'll only have clothes that fit, are in good condition, of colors that compliment you and are flattering to your shape, skin, and body type. It is also well organized. Get this right, and all those what-to-wear frustrations become a distant memory.

In a later section of the book, we look at creating your elegant wardrobe. But first, let's get the buying process right.

5. How to Shop and Make Elegant Choices

Learn to Distinguish Quality (Without Buying Brands or Designers)

First of all, are you able to distinguish quality without relying on brand names? There are some reputable brands that consistently provide quality clothes. However, learning to tell what is good quality is a useful skill. That way, you can shop anywhere and not rely on brand names to buy good things. You'll probably pay a fraction of what you'll normally have to fork out in designer stores. Thus, you are encouraged to be resourceful and learn how to hunt for affordable quality clothing.

If you do not know what quality clothes should feel like, browse through some designer boutiques. Try some of those clothes on. Make a mental note of how you feel. Let your skin and fingers become familiar with the fabrics. Study the garments, look at how they are constructed and formed. Observe the buttons, hems, stitching, zippers, etc.

By doing the above, you are educating yourself on product quality. The more exposed you are to a variety of good quality fabrics and their construction, the more you'll be able to distinguish good quality by looks and feel alone. It'll be easier to shop with authority, knowing you're getting value for your money. If you're in a store that sells overpriced stuff of a lesser quality, you'll be able to tell by your acquired experience. Perhaps you'll notice something about the way the buttons are sewn that is not quite right, or the material looks cheap, and maybe the fit and cut appear shoddy.

You'll soon develop an acute taste for quality. The consequence of this is that you'll learn how to get the same quality clothes at much more affordable places. You also won't have to rely on buying name brands either. You will become a woman that can shop anywhere with confidence.

Timeless Style by Dior

Christian Dior, the legendary designer said, "No elegant woman follows fashion slavishly". He was right. Elegant women are not dedicated followers of fashion.

You have to consider a number of factors. Your age is one. Your body is another, as is lifestyle and personality, among other things. Just because it looks good on a model in a magazine, does not mean it will hang the same on you. And you really don't have to wear it just because everyone else is.

"Individuality will always be one of the conditions of real elegance" ~ *Christian Dior*

If you can, try to have your clothes made-to-measure once in a while. This would be a good way for you to learn about what fits you and why it looks so good. You'll learn about form and fitting from a good shop with a savvy seamstress.

Point to remember: Individuality is not an excuse for eccentricity.

Developing Exquisite Taste

I remember going shopping with a friend who had expensive tastes, and whose father had deep pockets (and was very generous with her). I used to assume girls like this bought shoes from all the expensive brands, shoes I couldn't afford myself.

I didn't like going shopping with her because I thought all girls with money went into those places I couldn't afford. Her family put me up at her place once, while my own apartment was being renovated. One evening we had a party to attend together, and for that I needed a pair of black heels.

She dragged me all over her favorite shops, and I remember trying on the most expensive shoes I've ever put on my feet. They were a $650 pair of Ferragamos, and this was easily more than ten years ago. My feet felt and looked beautiful. But I wasn't prepared to part with $650 so I went on trying other shoes.

At the end of the day, I only wanted to spend around $100, and so I walked into a shoe shop chain and tried on a pair that cost $125. By now I was more conscious of quality, thanks to Rachel, who encouraged me (and out of peer pressure), to try on costly brand name footwear. Suddenly, the $125 ones did not feel good at all. The leather-ish uppers were obviously a cheap PVC material, and they looked so bland on my feet. I just could not bring myself to buy them, even though they were a lot closer to my budget.

We walked around a bit more, and I found a good quality pair for $150. I got to wear those shoes for at least the next five years, but saved them mainly for special occasions.

Since then, I slowly established a habit and knack for finding good quality shoes at reasonable prices. I was so satisfied with my quality purchase, that I felt no need to go out shopping for more 'perfect' things, and certainly had lost all interest in low-quality throwaway fashion wear.

What happened? I had trained my eye and formed a desire for quality. My consciousness for value has increased by leaps and bounds ever since. As a result of this, my senses for filtering out the better quality items meant that design had become more acute. This is how you develop exquisite taste, but without breaking the bank.

What Is Exquisite Taste?

"Exquisite" is defined by the dictionary as having or being of "extreme beauty of delicacy". We can also get a better idea of the meaning of "exquisite" by taking a look at its synonyms. Synonyms of exquisite include: taste, discerning, discriminating, sensitive, selective, refined, cultured, educated, and cultivated.
I always tell my clients that learning to be elegant and developing an exquisite eye or taste, is more important than having money.

I'm of the belief that sometimes when a girl or woman starts out having too much money it may be hard for her to develop good taste. That is why we see the 'vulgar rich' side of some newly well-off folks. They can be flashy and distasteful in their choice of clothes, houses, cars, behaviors, etc. Being elegant and exquisite is about discerning quality, learning how to sift and select, or edit. When you have too many choices, or have the ability to buy absolutely anything you want, when you want it, you tend to be lazy and not think your choices through thoroughly.

When you have too much, it is hard to be elegant. This is why I personally fight against excess in all areas of my life as well. Of course, this is just a generalization, and I'll explain in greater detail below.

How Does One Develop an Exquisite Eye?

Firstly, develop the belief that you want to afford the best for yourself. Treat yourself first-class. Sometimes, the reason why we succumb to buying cheap items for ourselves is not that we want to save money, but we feel we are not worth spending the extra on. We are not good enough! Instead of splurging on a bunch of cheap things, tell yourself you will only allow yourself to buy **one good dress** or pair of shoes, etc.

As you look around for that one pair of good shoes, you'll learn how to discern quality because you are deciding on how best to spend that well-earned dollar.

You'll also start thinking about the type of items that afford you the most use, and naturally, you'll start accumulating the classics, if you haven't already built a classic wardrobe.

Experiencing quality and **being exposed to quality**, inevitably **develops your skill at identifying value**. You'll become a very wise bargain hunter because the things that you buy today, you won't get sick of tomorrow. This means, you won't have to throw stuff away so much, and thus your house will not be filled with clutter. Develop this area and you'll find that you won't have to do a wardrobe edit so often either.

Once you are confident enough in your discernment of quality, and have that knack of finding beautiful things on your own initiative, you won't have to rely on designer labels any longer.

Personally, I find it helpful to learn about good fabric, the maintenance and care for it, and also to have a tailor available whenever needed. It is also helpful to find a few good reliable brands that you can go to in a jiffy, should you need something in a hurry. I have a mental directory of good shops for basics, for dresses, or sports clothes, etc.

Shopping Exquisitely: How to Shop like an Elegant Woman

You can learn how to make elegant choices when shopping by following these classic principles:
If you have been swayed, as I have, to possessing the dream wardrobe of an elegant woman, we must first be ruthless with our current clothes collection. Before shopping for new things, go to your closet and discard all clothing that is not flattering. Wear only those that look good on you. If you don't love it, are not feeling it, or perhaps a little unsure, then let it go!
Tell yourself that from now on – starting today – you'll only invest in terrific outfits! Why do I say invest? Well, it's because you are now only going to buy things with a long-term view in mind.
Although it sounds so cliché, remember, and come to believe, that less really is more.

What to Buy?

Clothes that you will love! Although I've written more specifically about outfits, these principles can be applied to anything we purchase: books, food, things for the house, and so forth. First consider the classics, and then 'personality items'. If you have a tight budget, you may buy a few classics and mix them with cheaper items of reasonable quality.

Think 'Quality'

What to avoid buying? First of all, avoid tight-fitting clothes that show too much flesh, but also consider the following: Steer clear of anything that looks cheap, even though it may be expensive. My friend, who has deep pockets, turned up for my party the other day in a T-shirt imprinted with a photo of Claudia Schiffer naked on the front. I was really taken aback! I always thought he only wore very expensive things. I asked myself, "Why is he wearing this cheap, tacky T-shirt?" Later on, when I went shopping, I realized it was by Dolce and Gabbana, because I saw that exact same garment on display. So the conclusion is, expensive and quality things can still look cheap! Oh, and pass up on anything that is ostentatious.

Ask yourself these questions as you go shopping:

- Does it look cheap?
- Would (insert your elegant role model's name) wear this?
- Does it feel good? Is it a quality material?
- Does it fit me well?
- Will I feel like a million bucks in it?
- Can I pair this with at least 3-5 items in my current wardrobe?
- Where will I wear this to?
- What shoes will I wear with this?
- Does it suit my lifestyle?
- Do you feel a little pinch in the buying this? (If yes, sometimes this is a good sign, which means you really value it.)
- Is it love at first sight? Or are you are buying it only because it is on-trend? (Buy only if it's love).

- How often do I think I will wear this in a month? (This gives you an idea of whether you are shopping on impulse or doing some honest lifestyle shopping.)

Do Elegant Women Avoid Sales?

Elegant women may avoid sales when it looks and feels like a meat market. However, depending on what type of sale it is, more often than not they know about it, and almost never pay retail prices. But the reason why I write this is to caution you about sales. Beware of those that tempt you to spend more than you should. Sales only work well for the savvy shopper!

Shopping at Sales

"You may even get a good deal of satisfaction out of the sales, provided that you are armed with lots of courage and the will power to resist the temptation of some darling little outfit which in the end is terribly expensive when you realize that, while it may have cost you 'nothing', it is worth practically nothing to you." ~ Madame Genevieve Antoine Dariaux

Although sales are great for getting more value for quality items, never let 'sales' influence your decision on whether to purchase or not. Ask yourself, why didn't you buy the item at full price? Did you not love it enough?
Sales are perfect for stocking up on things you love, or for trying out a new style that you've always wanted to but were not sure about. No matter how big the sale, only buy what you absolutely love.

Quote by Shakespeare on shopping:

"Costly thy habit as thy purse can buy but not expressed in fancy; rich but not gaudy, for the apparel oft proclaims the man."

This is to illustrate the essence of good shopping. If you shop badly, you are wasting your money, time, and effort. You also add to the clutter of your home. Your less-than-ideal choice of clothes tells people who you are.

The Issue of Quantity

"One of the most striking differences between a well-dressed American woman and a well-dressed Parisian is the size of their respective wardrobes." ~ Madame Genevieve Antoine Dariaux

I think when Madame Genevieve Antoine Dariaux wrote that the above, she had not met Asians, some of which I know have the most clutter! But that's another story.

I've been to Paris and I've met Parisians. To set the record straight, I don't believe every single Parisian is well-dressed. However, from my experience, I'll admit that Parisians have a propensity towards quality that others don't. And since we are generalizing here, maybe it is more fitting for me to say, the general European.
        While everyone else looks for the cheapest, Europeans look for the best that they can afford, sometimes forgoing necessities in the process. (I'm also aware I'm generalizing.) It is common for them to **go without** until they find the perfect garment. If they want a certain pair of shoes or mink coat, they put money away for months in order to purchase it. **Basically, they take a longer time to buy anything**. They rarely buy on impulse. Thus, you can say that quantity is not a priority.

A Small and Exquisite Wardrobe

In a well-dressed woman's wardrobe, every piece is carefully selected, which means it has passed a high standard of fit and quality, and is perfectly adapted to the lifestyle that she leads.

Once deciding to buy only what she really loves, the clothes are worn over and over and are seldom tired of until they are worn out or out-of-fashion, at which time they are donated. They sometimes go through many states of repair before they are fully done with it. That's how much they are valued.

An Elegant Woman Expects Her Clothes to Last

She owns very few sets of daily wear at one time: items such as socks, lingerie, everyday shoes, gloves, and other expendable items, but replaces them frequently. The classic items, like coats, purses, handbags, luggage, and travel holders are expected to last for years.

For expendable items: Purchase them from a good department store to ensure you are getting reasonable quality. Become familiar with reliable brands and boutiques.

To value quality and to be exquisite is a way of life. Contrary to popular opinion, developing an exquisite eye and taste is the opposite of extravagance. Madame Genevieve Antoine Dariaux writes in her book *A Guide to Elegance*, that the answer (to how a young career girl in Paris can afford its high prices), is that she buys very few garments. Her goal is to possess a single perfect ensemble for each of the different occasions in her life, rather than a wide choice of clothes to suit every passing mood.

Only a few of us can afford to have everything in the wardrobe of the very finest quality, but every budget can be stretched to cover a few basic luxury items, preferably those where quality represents a long-term investment, not forgetting the result of that often means saving money in the long term anyway.

We all know that a classic fine leather handbag can last a lifetime. The quality rule applies to men too. There will be some men that invested in, say, a pair of high quality handmade Italian shoes that they may still be wearing to this day, even though they're probably older than his middle-aged children. Quality pays, it really does!

If you can't always afford the best quality, try going for simple ensembles of medium quality.

Invest in a few quality accessories and these can add prestige to an outfit. For example, a lovely umbrella, a cashmere sweater, a very charming bracelet. These things and more give the appearance of a fine ensemble.

6. Timelessness: The Elegant Dress Code

Elegant women around the world have an unspoken dress code. It may differ from country to country, city or culture, but there is a recognizable quality in them.

I'd like to attribute that to the characteristic of timelessness. Sure, there are many types of elegant dressing that may not be timeless, but stylish and fashionable nonetheless. If you narrow it down to studying the appearance of the most elegant of women, you'll find that they often are timelessly beautiful and their elegance does not go out of style.

Thus, I felt it was important to analyze the timeless qualities of their look, one portion at a time, in order to understand how to bring it altogether to apply the elegant dress code on ourselves.

The following sections are in no particular order, but I would like to start from the crown of our head.

How to Achieve Timeless Hair

The secret here is to let a professional decide the best hairstyle for you. Get a consultation with a good hairstylist to assess your face shape and skin tone. He or she will be able to recommend the kind of hairstyle that best suit your face, along with shades that will best bring out the color of your eyes and cheeks.

Some women suit cool colors, such as ash-toned blonds and browns, whereas others are better suited to warmer tones like reddish golden hues. I am not an expert in this, so try to get color charted professionally. Good make-up artists and hairstylists are far better qualified to do this for you. So why is this important?

The color of your hair either dulls or brightens your complexion. That alone can make a huge difference to your overall appearance! And believe it or not, the hair color you were born with is not necessarily the best one for you! I'm not saying you should all color your hair, all I'm saying is this could be an area to consider.

Your choice of an appropriate classic hairdo also depends on lifestyle. You may already know the type of hairstyle that works best with your face, skin tone, and personality. But none of this helps if you cannot maintain it. You might be too busy, or cannot justify spending the extra cash every six weeks on a high-maintenance coiffure. There are a few classically elegant hairstyles that will suit most of us, if not all of us. They are quite popular by the pedigree class.

These women seem to prefer simple, chin-length bobs, shoulder-length hair, soft curls, wavy or straight. If their hair color is not natural, you won't know it, because they are religious in touching up their roots. They also only dye their hair with colors that look natural for them.

Elegant hairstyles are usually versatile. For instance, a chignon, aka the bun, is elegant whether it's evening or day (especially when paired with smart casual wear). A pony tail can be elegant for those casual days as well. Take some time to explore other elegant cuts. Visit my page on Elegant Hairstyles, or do a search for "elegant hairstyles" on www.elegantwoman.org for some new ideas.

Timeless Makeup for a Classically Beautiful Look
My Tips for Everyday Daytime Makeup:

Wear a light foundation ensuring that it is even (concealing red blotches, etc.). Pair this with a light colored eye-shadow. A blemish balm cream (commonly known as BB cream), is quite popular in Asia. It is similar to a tinted moisturizer.

Wear a natural blusher. If you're unsure what this means, look for the word "natural" when you next go shopping for cosmetics. Classic beauties wear either eye shadow or eye liner, but usually not together, especially during the day.

For Evening Makeup

Wear a heavier foundation and set it with loose powder. The reason for this is because you may look 'washed out' under bright artificial lighting if you don't have enough makeup on. This is why performers look so beautiful on stage, but hideous close-up and personal! Their makeup is probably piled on ten times the normal amount in order to accommodate the strong lighting on stage. You can also emphasize your eyes or lips by adding more color than you would during the day.

Timeless Dressing – Elegance Never Goes out of Style

Clothes with simple styles, neutral colors, or pastel and block colors are usually more soothing to the eyes. Obviously the choice of colors and styles depends on personal preference, lifestyle, personality, and skin tone.

When you make the effort to dress well, remember that your main objective is to simply look like a more refined version of yourself.

If you know which colors suit you best, wear them as block colors. Block colors refer to clothes that are usually only one or two colors and void of any gradations, tints, or shades. Refrain from patterns for now, especially if you have not yet acquired a keen eye for pulling off that elegant aura. Always stick to clean, simple lines and block colors whenever you're in doubt.

Having a trained eye and being confident in dressing elegantly come with practice and persistence. The more exposure you have to elegant styles, the sooner you will become an expert in womanly sophistication. From this point forward, pay close attention to what your elegant role models wear. I'm not asking you to copy their style wholesale, just to notice the details and use their taste as inspiration. Please note that you will probably need to be patient with yourself. Sometimes it takes a while to get a handle on these things.

Unless you are fairly young, be sure to keep your choice of clothes modest. For example, skirts should be at least knee length or slightly above knee, but not any higher.

10 Examples of Classic Elegant Styles:

1. A dress (city or summer depending on season)
2. A blouse and skirt
3. A blouse and tailored pants (preferably in light colors over dark)
4. A blouse and dark jeans (casual Friday or shopping in the city)
5. Lacoste style shirts and long khaki shorts
6. A fitted T-shirt with skirt with sandals
7. A beige coat
8. A classic red coat
9. A dark gray jacket
10. A dress with a cardigan

Timelessly Elegant Shoes | Choosing Elegant Shoes

Though the types of shoes in your wardrobe depend on your lifestyle, your first priority is to ensure that you understand the basics. This means you should have some formal footwear in modest blacks, browns, and beige colors, and of varying heights. For casual wear, go for a Tod's style loafer or ballet flats (a soft ballet slipper style, with no, or very thin, heel).

Even though elegant shoes and stylish heels are the last clothing item to be noticed, they are a very important part of our outfit nonetheless.

If you don't have a big budget to spend on shoes, then all the more reason to select with care. Choose classic styles with basic colors like black, beige, and navy. For everyday footwear, choose a low to medium shoe with a solid heel. Calf-court shoes, also known as pumps, are ideal for the afternoons. Leave the high heels for evening wear, unless of course an occasion warrants them at other times of the day.

The most important thing here is that they have to fit well and be comfortable. Standing and walking around in

poorly fitted and painful shoes will not only ruin your day, and your posture, but potentially damage your feet as well.
Never buy cheap-looking shoes or heels; not even if they are expensive and sport a brand name.

The most elegant heels are the all-closed pumps. They tend go well with most outfits in the classic colors. I think elegance is designed to prevent 'too much fuss'. Another benefit of the closed pump is that you don't have to worry about getting professional pedicures too often.

If you have big feet, stay away from white or chunky shoes. Depending on where you are going, it's always better to opt for a slim heel, as this gives an illusion of smaller feet.

Ankle straps draw attention to your ankles and so give a 'break' in the silhouette. Personally, I avoid shoes that cut-off at the ankle, such as ankle boots, ankle straps, and sandals that have high backs. I've also noticed that they make the ankles look a lot bigger than they really are, so it's better to wear them only if you have very thin legs.
Perhaps the only way to wear an ankle strap successfully is if you are wearing a very short and frilly cocktail dress so that it can be paired up well with silver or shiny black strappies.

It goes without saying, of course, that any shoes showing skin or toenails must be well buffed, and the feet should be perfectly pedicured.

Keep It Simple and 'Categorize Your Shoes

I split my shoes into three categories:
1. Walking shoes
2. Dress shoes
3. Evening or cocktail shoes

Walking Shoes

I wear these everywhere when going about my daily errands. Whether I'm heading to the library, off to get some groceries, or setting out to a cafe for lunch with a friend, walking shoes are the perfect choice. They are also ideal for window shopping, a picnic, or a stroll in Central Park.

I always have these elegant shoes in neutral colors because that way I don't have to think about matching them with what I'm wearing. My current pair is beige and it is currently one of my favorite pairs to wear. I will continue to wear them until they finally perish, then I will unfortunately have to replace them.

I've gone through many pairs of walking shoes over the years, mainly off-whites, beige, black, and navy. Ballerinas, or ballet shoes, and loafers are the perfect choice of footwear for the casual ensemble.

Ballerina flats are very sweet and feminine. These elegant shoes are also slimming for the feet, especially for those who have a wider foot. They've always been a bit too flat for my liking though, but now I see there are ones that offer a firmer heel. It helps to use a shoe-padding insert with ballerina-type pumps too.

Loafers — An Alternative in Elegant Shoes

I usually like to wear loafers with linen pants. They make perfect travel shoes as well. Loafers are easy to slip on and off, comfortable enough to walk in for long periods of time, lightweight, suitable for all seasons, and best of all, they go with almost everything in your travel wardrobe. A good brand to buy is Tod's, although I'm sure you can get similar styles from various other designers.

My other choice for walking footwear is a sport shoe, or athletic shoe, designed specifically for people on the go, whether it's regular strolling or sporting activities. Since walking is currently my main form of exercise, it's important to choose the right shoes so as to lessen the impact on your feet and joints. Because I wear my shoes a lot, I've been advised to change them every half year or so.

A Note about Flip Flops

An increasingly popular choice of footwear is flip-flops. They are called flip-flops presumably because the rubber soles slap against the bottom of your feet as you walk, thus making a flip-flop kind of sound. I personally have a pair of these, but I don't advise you to wear them for walking, unless it's only for short distances or as beach footwear.

It's important to note that flip-flops give no real support for the feet, and the impact from hard surfaces can also cause discomfort to the small of the back if worn for long hours. Furthermore, they provide inadequate protection. I've personally witnessed people tripping and hurting themselves due the sloppy nature of these open-toe sandals. They're also prone to getting caught on stairs and escalators, and offer no defense for when others accidentally step on your feet, as can easily happen in crowed places.

Also, due to the flimsy way they are held under the feet, they can cause your posture to suffer too. If you observe women in flip-flops, you will see that it's hard for them to walk in a proper, dignified way, and they tend to step in a 'sweeping motion'. They may look good in a still photograph, but it is hardly elegant when you witness them in movement. **Points to note:** Do not attempt to walk for long hours or shop in flip-flops. They may hurt your back, affect posture, and when worn regularly, they can be detrimental to physical health.

I'd also suggest staying away from the dressier shoes that are modeled as the 'slipper' or 'flip-flop', no matter how pretty and chic they look with subtle heels. Aside from their impracticality as a walking shoe, your feet will pick up a lot more dirt as well.

I am not saying to stay away from flip-flops altogether, as most of us need one pair of them, if only for the benefit of convenience. They are easy-to-wash, lightweight, and comfortable when used as a shoe for around the home, walking short distances, and as summer footwear for the beach.

I know most beach brands have good quality flip-flops in their range, but right now I only buy Havaianas due to the support they provide the heel on impact. They also don't give me blisters like some others I've had. The downside to Havaianas is that they're rather expensive for a shoe of this type. In fact, a chocolate brown pair I had got stolen, but thankfully, they were miraculously replaced by a freebie pair at a charity fashion show.

The Dress Shoe

This shoe is for those slightly dressier events, such as lunch in the city with a friend, high tea, shopping downtown, a dinner party, going to the movies, or visiting a museum, ad infinitum. In short, this is your 'social & leisure' shoe.
I am in favor of the medium heel, as it helps with posture and therefore reduces the risk of appearing sloppy or slouched. Also, since this is footwear for dressier events, a medium heel is the better choice, as a low heel can sometimes create an impression of negligence.
A very popular city shoe is known as the 'court shoe'. These are basically shoes that have no fastening and a low-cut front. You can usually find a decent selection in most good shoe shops and departments. My current dress shoe is dark chocolate brown, which is an alternative to the usual elegant black color. It goes with all my day dresses and some evening gowns. I also have another cream-colored pair with a slimmer heel.
Remember, the elegant principle for choosing stylish footwear is to always steer towards classic designs and colors. When shoes were first invented, they were made simply with foot protection in mind, but as we evolved, footwear manufacturers began to incorporate more style and sophistication in their creations. Because we're part of a fashion conscious world, most shoes on sale today are made with appearance in mind, first and foremost, and this obsession with fashion has taken priority over support, comfort, and practicality, especially in women's footwear.
I prefer the classic fashion, meaning closed-toe pumps. They are conservative; do not show skin, and give a proper 'balance' to your outfit by not diverting eyes to the feet.
Although they are not as available as they used to be, I'm sure you can find them easily enough in good shoe stores. It is your responsibility to invest in a proper fit, and footwear that is well-made from fine fabric(s).

Other alternatives are those with medium heels, though personally I favor the ones with backing. Without a proper back to secure the whole foot, your walk may become disordered, manifesting in either sweeping movements or a tendency to take long and somewhat exaggerated strides.

The Evening or Cocktail Shoe

This is for the dressiest occasions in your life. Examples may include such times as when you head out for drinks or meals in fine places, a ball, or parties, such as cocktail evenings, wine tasting events, a Christmas party, and basically any time you want to look your absolute best.

How formal a cocktail shoe is will depend on the material, the heel, and its color. If you love high heels, this is the right time to wear them without looking ridiculous or overdressed.

It is really lovely to match the color of your elegant shoes to the dress you are wearing, or your bag (but not both). It's equally exquisite to have matching material for your bag of dress.

Custom shoe makers are becoming somewhat of a rarity in this fast changing world of ours, where mass production and throwaway fashions rule. Industrial manufacturing has also largely done away with those talented folks that that would once make a matching shoe and bag using requested material. You can still find these old and personal services in some countries, but they are becoming harder to locate. But for anyone determined to find such a service, it is still very doable at the time of writing, thanks largely to the internet.

For those with a limited budget, don't worry, you only need to purchase a couple of pairs. But be sure to follow the elegant principles for choosing stylish shoes, as this ensures your footwear will go with just about every garment you own.

Brightly colored footwear can add a little spark to your outfit when matched right. These elegant shoes can be very chic, but make certain your entire outfit is of only one or two colors at most, and that the colors blend well together, meaning there are no harsh contrasting tones. You may add a pair of red heels to your outfit for a chic or smart look.

It's been said that heels that are too high are vulgar. While this is true to some extent, I do feel that wearing higher heels is more accepted these days than it was in the past. Remember though, there is a time and a place for stilettos style shoes, so please confine them to dressy events, and not to ski slopes, mountains, garden parties, or anywhere in the countryside.

Caution: Choose Your Shoes Carefully

The height of your heels affects the way you walk, but you won't see yourself how others see you. Therefore, checking yourself in the mirror when you walk in a particular pair of heels is a good idea. Also, as silly as it might sound, you might want to practice the way you stride in different shoes. It's distracting to see someone bopping up and down or swaying side to side or marching in a kind of runway strut. An elegant walk is measured and even.

Your Comfort and Safety Must Come First

I'm sure most of us have experienced wearing shoes that were ill-fitting, uncomfortable, and painful even, yet we still chose to put them on because we loved the way they looked, despite being left with raw blisters and sore feet long after the event. It is never worth it!

Even if you can tolerate the hurt (I've been told that dedicated followers of fashion have a high pain threshold), a tortured look or inelegant walk is something that just cannot be concealed, no matter how much pain you can endure personally.

It doesn't matter how many fashion magazines have esteemed a designer or brand is, if the shoes don't fit then they're not right for you. What's more is that poorly fitting shoes can damage the health of your feet in the long term. Remember, we are all unique, and that means no two individuals' feet are the same, so we have to choose with the utmost care when buying new shoes; especially if we're expecting them to last a good while.

Learn How to Find the Right Fit

It can sometimes be quite hard to know whether a new pair of shoes simply need to be broken in or are actually ill-fitting. I have wasted probably thousands of dollars over the years trying to get this right. If your new shoes don't seem to have broken in by the tenth wear, then forget it. I always find it a good idea to wear them at home for a couple of hours at a time, for about a week, before I even consider going out in them.

I also like to stick to the smaller boutiques that I've come to trust when buying a new pair of elegant shoes. Such places tend to give more personalized service, and the sales people are likely to know a lot about what a good fitting shoe should include. This means they are able to make better qualified decisions, leaving us to concentrate on the shoes and not worry about the fit.

Timelessly Elegant Jewelry and Accessories

A woman can look elegant by learning how to accessorize in a certain way. She can also increase her elegance by knowing how to use select pieces that do her look justice. Elegant jewelry and fashion accessories are punctuation marks in your style, an accent in your fashion, and therefore something well worth learning about.

While good quality clothes are a must, you can create a more elegant style just by accessorizing, and it doesn't have to be expensive either. You are able to achieve a well-heeled look simply by knowing how to buy and wear the right kind of costume jewelry.

What is the difference between jewelry and fashion accessories? Elegant jewelry refers to precious stones and metals, such as gold, diamonds, rubies etc., and fashion accessories are really just costume ornaments or imitation jewelry.

Of course, there is a big difference in price between the two types of jewelry. Your first piece of quality elegant jewelry might be an engagement ring, for example. However, if you know how to choose well, you should never need to spend those extra dollars on stylish items again. Even imitation jewelry, made with inexpensive materials, can look tasteful once you learn how to choose with confidence.

The Power of Elegant Jewelry and Fashion Accessories

Elegant jewelry and fashion accessories can be used very effectively to create different looks with your existing wardrobe. What this means is that you'll get to discover how you can wear that same little black dress in twenty different ways; all thanks to the artful adornment of accessories.

The ability to transform an outfit makes your clothes work harder for you. You now have more combinations of shoes, bags, and accessories to work with. In other words, when the art of accessorizing is done well, less really can mean more. With a few cleverly placed accessories you can literally dress an outfit up or down, making it go from daywear to an elegant evening dress.

Choosing Elegant Jewelry and Fashion Accessories

Let's say you're saving some money for a holiday and you've got a fabulous party to attend, or maybe you simply don't have time to shop. Having the right jewelry wardrobe can create the impression that you have more outfits than you actually do.

Either get creative with your existing accessories and play around a little by mixing and matching, or get a statement piece of jewelry costing less than twenty dollars. Whenever you're faced with that "I've got nothing to wear!" scenario, just remember to accessorize, accessorize, accessorize!

Express Your Style

Elegant jewelry and fashion accessories are often used to express one's own individual style. Nobody quite wears jewelry the same way, nor should they because jewelry is like clothing, in that what looks good on one, might look awful on another.

Creating your own style requires a little bit of experimentation to find out what you like and what feels right. A few honest opinions from friends and loved ones can also help you make the right choices with your accessories.

Building Your Elegant Jewelry and Fashion Accessories Wardrobe

Just as we do when building a quality clothes wardrobe, we must first stock up on the classic pieces of jewelry and accessory items. Classic pieces of jewelry and accessories are simply those you can wear with any outfit, and that suit almost any occasion under the sun. For instance, you may wear the same pearl stud earrings with an elegant gown or with a casual blouse and skirt.

The Classic Jewelry Wardrobe

- An elegant silver wrist watch (or a silver and gold mix)
- A silver tennis bracelet
- A colorful or bright colored bracelet for a casual look (beads or precious stones)
- A necklace
- Pearl stud earrings
- A single strand of choker length pearls
- A pair of silver hoops
- Solitaire rings (CZ or diamond, pearl)

You can't go wrong with any of the above pieces, so if you're in the process of rebuilding your wardrobe, then copy this list.

Tips for Elegant Accessorizing

- Less is more: The general rule of thumb is not to wear more than one item at a time, with the exception of bangles.
- Take into account color combinations; aim for a cohesive look.
- If in doubt, pick an area to accentuate before making decisions on what jewelry to wear.
- Remember not to get carried away and overdo things. For example, do not wear earrings, a necklace, a watch, and a few rings and bracelets all at the same time. If you do, you'll run the risk of looking like a Christmas tree!
- Keep it simple. When it comes to accessorizing, less really is more.
- Be mindful of the fact that a woman never looks elegant with more than one earring in each ear.
- Aim for balance when accessorizing. You do not want to appear lopsided.
- Accessories can break the shape of a dress or solid colors, which can be a good thing when done well. They can add sparkle to a plain outfit, or create an interesting look by giving color contrast. For example,

wearing a long chain gives you a long neckline, which in turn helps you look taller and slimmer than you are. A lopsided look occurs when you wear, say, a short strand of pearls with a narrow V-neck top. In this case, the 'shape' does not flow. Wearing a short strand of pearls or a necklace brings attention to the neck or the collarbones, which is very desirable.

- Sometimes, wearing dangling earrings can be distracting if your hair is tied back in a ponytail, especially if it swings back and forth as you speak. But when worn well, it can look very chic, emphasizing the ears and neckline.

- If in doubt, only wear one piece of jewelry at any one time.

- To achieve a fail-proof elegant look, go for pearls.

Buying Elegant Fashion Accessories: How to Buy the Right Jewelry

When buying jewelry, consider whether they are classic pieces or statement/accent pieces. You need to invest in good classic pieces first if you don't already possess them.
Have a plan before going on your next shopping trip. Go through the items in your current collection. Take an inventory of what you already have and what you need. Also ask yourself whether you have too much or too many of certain items. Check the list of classic jewelry and fashion accessories above to see if there is anything lacking.

What to Avoid

There are various things you'll want to avoid when shopping for elegant jewelry and fashion accessories. These include:

- Avoid plastic altogether. It always looks cheap and never does your elegance any justice.
- Avoid fake silver or gold, often found in low-end fashion brands. They leave a dirty gray residue on your skin when wearing them. The color also turns after a few uses.
- Avoid costume jewelry that uses cheap beads or fake plastic crystals.
- Check the clasps. Make sure they are not vulnerable or weak. You do not want them falling apart at a dinner party!
- If you are able to, shop for jewelry during the day. If there are any concerns of whether to buy a thing or not, it is clearer and easier to make decisions in daytime. A shopping mall is lit differently in day than it is after dark, probably influenced by natural light flooding in from large windows and sun roofs. At night, everything sparkles and looks better.
- Avoid imitations trying to pass as the real McCoy. It is usually very obvious to others that such items are fakes.
- Avoid pieces that attempt to imitate the style of a high-end designer, as these quickly become trendy items worn by the masses.

Regarding the last point, there was a time when an owl pendant necklace by a certain designer became an overnight sensation. Suddenly all the jewelry shops started selling imitation owl pendants. The point of the story is this: If the item you are buying gives you a feeling that it might be a knock-off from some recent trend, then you might want to check its origins first or simply overlook it altogether, unless of course you don't mind trendiness.

Timelessly Elegant Purses and Bags

In your purse drawer, make sure to have a few simple elegant bags for various occasions. At the very least, you should have one stylish casual bag of medium-size, and one smaller bag. The medium-sized bag is perhaps best used for work. It can also double up as an everyday bag for informal use. The smaller bag should be more formal. This is the one which you can use for those elegant occasions and special evening events.

The work-bag should be no larger than an A4 file size, unless of course you are of a taller, larger build. An evening bag should be no larger than something that has room only for essential items, such as cash, a credit card, mobile phone, lipstick, and keys. The fundamental guideline is to take into account proportion, that is, your bag should be proportionate to your build.

Remember These 'Elegant Bag' Guidelines:

*** The larger the bag, the more casual it is. Therefore, the smaller the bag, the more elegant it becomes. The more constructed (firm), the more graceful, and vice versa. A weekend bag could be slightly larger and more floppy in form.***

My Personal Bag Collection

Personally, I love bags, but I do try to limit excessiveness. I allow myself a separate bag for the various activities and commitments in my life. For example, I am a lecturer and a tutor, so I have one bag that contains my lecture notes and a laptop. I have another bag for all the files and archived notes for the semester. I throw them both away after I'm done with the term.

I am also a ballet student, and I dance daily whenever possible. So, I have a ballet bag that contains all I need for class. I also have an overnight bag that I use for short-trips. My everyday purse is a small tote that contains my essentials. These might include my diary, wallet, car keys, tissues, lip balm, and a few other bits and bobs. I tend to grab that bag if I'm running errands.

Then there's my music bag. As the name implies, this is what I use to store music books and files of score sheets. I also have a library bag that I use solely to transport library books. I have one to two dressy bags as well. These are the bags that match the dressier outfits in my wardrobe.

Don't be one of those women who use one bag for everything. You know the sort I'm talking about. It's usually a big floppy bag that contains their entire lives, even the kitchen sink. Looking like the wife of Santa Claus as you lug your entire life around with you is not a good look. Appearance aside, such a bag affects your posture and will give you a bad back over time.

Elegant Bags – Timeless Style Classics

"The Parisian builds her look around fabulous basics" ~ Ines de la Fressange

If I'm to be totally honest with myself, then I have to admit that I was, and perhaps still am, albeit to a lesser degree, obsessed with bags.

I can remember the gleeful moments when I headed straight to a store to buy my first bag with my very first paycheck. Over the years, I've collected the elegant classic bags and they have been loyal friends and an anchor to my wardrobe. I've also picked up several elegant tips along the way on what bags to buy, and I always purchase the best that I can possibly afford at any given time.

Classic Elegance First

If only our shopping budgets were unlimited! However, I think having unlimited, or very large budgets, are nasty teachers of taste (or rather lack thereof). It is through a small or limited budget that we learn how to develop real style and elegance. Having restrictions ensures we have more thought and consideration prior to making any purchase, especially when it comes to buying a classy bag.

Bags and purses should be seen as an investment. If you are fine-tuning your elegant wardrobe, classic bags are one of the first things to add. But these are not just personal investments, the way most fashion magazines describe them. If you buy correctly and smartly, you can pass your bags down to your daughters and granddaughters in the future. Some can even be re-sold to fetch a tidy sum many years after purchase.

Sometimes, these bags may be hard to come by, depending where you live. They can also be costly or only found in big cities like London, Paris, and New York. However, thanks to the internet, more retailers are selling bags online these days, but it's important to only purchase from reputable stores, and to not be tempted by low prices offered by unknown websites. It's not so unusual for some online market places to sell low-quality knock-offs, so buyer beware!

If a classic bag is out of your financial reach, then your best bet is simply to 'reference' the look (and I do not mean buying fake goods - because such purchases may encourage the exploitation of child labor somewhere, or help to fund terrorist activities). You can get a similar bag of good quality and made of decent leather once you know what you're looking for. Check the linings and the boning of the bag, and see that it has double stitching. Shop smart, select well, and employ exquisite and discrete taste as you go.

Now, before you start shopping for bags, take an inventory of your current collection. You'll become more aware

of what you have and perhaps realize that all you need is a
minor update, and perhaps a little bag purge too.

General Guidelines for Buying an Elegant Bag
Proportion Guidelines for Bags:

- Keep the size of the bag proportionate to your body.
- If you are tall, do not have bags hugged under your arm.
- If you are short, don't carry large bags or bags that hang very low from the shoulder.
- If you are petite, do not carry too large bags, which may cause you to look like a hobo.
- If you are of a larger size, do not carry bags that appear to grab your body tightly. Also carry a bag that has a softer look, as opposed to a boxy style.

For Elegant Bags:

- Keep them clean at all times.
- Get rid of bags that lose their original shape.
- Do not collect clutter in your bag! It is extremely inelegant to have a lady digging around for her phone, keys, or whatever else she might be rummaging for.
- Carry the appropriate bag for appropriate event! Do not use an evening bag for the day. Likewise, do not take an office/work bag to an elegant dinner.
- Do not overstuff your bag. If the things you need can't fit into it, you might be carrying too much. If you do

need the extra item(s) temporarily, for instance, to return a friend's sweater, dig out one of those carrier bags from a designer shop and use that until you have delivered the goods.

- Do not place bags on the floor if at all avoidable. Not only does this soil and potentially damage the underneath, but you might carry dirt and germs back into the home.
- Never empty out the contents of your bag in public. Never ever!

7. How to Build an Elegant Wardrobe

Wardrobe Essentials: A Classic Wardrobe

This is a guide for creating basic wardrobe essentials for the elegant woman. The best dressed women are often those who devote **the most thought** to what they wear, how they wear it, and the process of getting dressed. That does not mean they spent the most money or the longest time getting dressed.

Planning is essential in creating an elegant woman's wardrobe. A wardrobe that works is a wardrobe that has been well thought out. The elegant woman also maintains her wardrobe. She maintains her clothes, and does an edit every three to six months.

How Does She Maintain Her Wardrobe?

She routinely bleaches her clothes to ensure the whitest of whites. She gets buttons and loose zippers repaired, shoes re-soled and polished, and her jewelry cleaned.

What is a Wardrobe Edit?

It is a de-cluttering of her clothing collection. It consists of giving away clothes that do not fit her anymore, items she no longer loves, or has too many of. This will be covered more in a later section.

Shopping Well

An elegant woman knows her boutiques, designers, brands, and fabrics well. Most importantly, she knows herself. She knows what her elegant style is, and what she looks good in.

She will not buy something that isn't 'her'. She does not buy clothes that she thinks will impress others. Despite her love for designers, she knows that the most important person in fashion is herself. She learns to have an eye for picking out good quality and stylish clothing, no matter where she shops. She prioritizes good quality and fit over high fashion trends.

A Well-Dressed and Appropriate Wardrobe

Because an elegant woman seeks understanding first, and then planning, she always has enough good quality clothes to be well dressed.

She is appropriate in her dress sense. You'll not find inappropriate clothes in her wardrobe. She dresses according to the occasion. She is never overdressed or underdressed.

She is a person that does not have too much. She does not have too many shoes, or too many similar items. She understands that she has to keep her collection of clothes in a tight quantity. This is so that she can remain well-dressed, and within a reasonable amount of time. Having a minimal approach to her collection enables her to be organized and punctual.

She understands her lifestyle and the kind of events she is involved in, thus tailoring her wardrobe to fit with her lifestyle. Whenever there is a change in season, or an adjustment in lifestyle (new baby, different job, etc.), she re-evaluates her wardrobe, takes inventory, and modifies it accordingly.

Good Dressing Quotes

"Costly thy habit as thy purse can buy, but not expressed in fancy; rich but not gaudy, for the apparel oft proclaims the man." ~ Shakespeare

"Clothing identifies who you are in your world. If you met someone who was dressed and groomed in such a manner

that you could not relate to them, you would never know if the person had a heart of gold or not." ~ Ginie Sayles

"Change your appearance and change what you do with your time — and your life will change. You are more in control than you think." ~ Unknown.

Wardrobe Refashioning Step One: Wardrobe Edit

To recap, the foundation of an elegant wardrobe that works is based on a few principles: understanding your lifestyle, planning, editing, and maintaining.
We've also established that you do not need a large quantity of clothes to have a good wardrobe. With a good wardrobe and elegant mix-and-match skills, you can be elegantly dressed in a reasonable amount of time.
So how do we build a basic wardrobe? We want the wardrobe of an elegant woman, so where do we start? Let's get some wardrobe refashioning.

"The most important art is to omit." ~ Robert Louis Stevenson

Take everything out from your current wardrobe, including those sitting in boxes and drawers. We will now give your wardrobe the fresh start it needs.

Throw Out:

- Clothes beyond repair
- Clothes that are too big or small, or do not fit properly
- Once trendy clothes that are no longer in fashion
- Clothes that you don't wear anymore because they are too long or short (we all know lengths of blouses and

the waist lines of jeans, skirts, pants change according to fashion trends).

- Clothes with holes
- Clothes that are faded (no matter how trendy you think they are)
- Clothes that have rips in them
- Clothes that clearly have been washed too often
- Clothes with irremovable stains
- Cheap looking clothes (if you think it looks cheap, get rid of it!)
- Scuffed shoes
- Bags that have lost their shape
- Bags that are beyond repair
- Fabric bags where the material looks dirty and beyond a wash
- Hats and accessories that have long gone out of style
- Costume jewelry that looks dull and fake

Repair the Repairable

- Cut all loose threads dangling from clothes
- Replace all missing buttons, studs, etc.
- Bleach any whites that have gotten dull

Tip: Give away anything you haven't worn in the last two years. If you have difficulty giving stuff away, put it in a box marked, 'Salvation Army'. Now, if you don't visit that box in the next six months, just seal it (without looking inside), and drop it off at the nearest resale shop or donation center.

Getting the First Step of Wardrobe Refashioning Done

Do it now, do not procrastinate! Come back here when you have completed this task. Depending on how much stuff you've got, this might take a while, so do it in intervals of 10 minutes if that helps. Believe me, you'll be amazed at what you can achieve.

When you start sorting things out, don't be tempted to try things on! This is the first basic round. If you do not know whether it fits or not, then it's unlikely you love the item anyway.

Once you're all done, it's time to move onto the next step.

Wardrobe Refashioning Step Two: Acquiring Your Basics

"Change your appearance and change what you do with your time - and your life WILL change. You are more in control than you think." ~ Unknown quote

Understanding your lifestyle, planning, editing, and maintaining are keys to building a classic elegant wardrobe. It is not necessary to have a large quantity of clothes to be well dressed, providing you learn how to mix and match tastefully.

Previously, we established Wardrobe Refashioning, and now we'll move on to step two.

After pruning and editing your wardrobe, you'll have to figure out if you have your everyday basics. So just what are everyday basic clothes? Put simply, they are those garments that you wear in your everyday life.

For instance, if you work in an office environment, your everyday basic wear would probably be blouses, black skirts, gray pants, sweaters, etc. If you are a stay-at-home mom, then your clothes might be knit tops and Capri pants, as an example.

Not Enough Everyday Basics Clothes

You can tell the kinds of priorities someone has by what they spend their money on, and this includes the clothes they wear.

If a girl loves stiletto heels because of the way they accentuate her legs, then she will probably think nothing of spending hundreds of dollars on her high heels, but would only part with $20 for a pair of shoes she wears to work every day. If she had put more thought into her everyday basics wardrobe, she would have come to realize that she could enhance her look at work and feel better about herself as a consequence. An elegant woman makes an effort at being impeccable and presenting her elegant best at all times.

There is also another reason why many women have far too many items from one category and not enough of what they really need. Such is 'aspirational shopping'.

I know someone who is crazy about snowboarding, and every time he goes into a shop for snowboarders, he comes out with a new T-shirt. Does he really need so many snowboarding T-shirts? No, or course he doesn't, and what's more is that he'll probably never get to wear half of them. In his day job he's an accountant working in a corporate office, so most of the time he's suited up anyway.

There are girls who buy expensive and glamorous clothes, bags, and shoes, but do not really have too much of a social life and merely aspire to that lifestyle. While there is certainly nothing wrong with that per se, it's often is a waste of good money and closet space. More often than not, they'll end up having more things to sort out, plus they'll have to deal with the guilt of less than optimal use for many of their garments. Everyday basics should be clothes that can be worn throughout the year like a uniform. So, your everyday basics depend on your lifestyle. It's as simple as that!

The short list below should help you to identify whether or not you have enough of the everyday basics in your wardrobe:

- Do you take too long to get dressed?
- Do you have a hard time finding something to go with tops or bottoms

- Do you always feel a slight tinge of embarrassment when you open the door of your house, or when you have chance meeting with your friend?
- Do you feel messy or too casual?

If you work from home, then elegant loungewear are important and should be included in your everyday collection. Take some time to think about your daily basics. Make a little virtual wardrobe or scrapbook of clothes you love to wear each day. Take that shopping with you and be disciplined. Buy only what you have mapped out for yourself. Make some effort, break old habits, and you'll soon be on your way to building an elegant wardrobe that you cherish! Come back to this page when you're done with this step and we'll then proceed to the next stage:

Step Three: Lifestyle and Outfit Analysis

Analyzing Your Lifestyle and Matching Your Clothes to It

"Clothing identifies who you are in your world. If you met someone who was dressed and groomed in such a manner that you could not relate to them, you would never know if the person had a heart of gold or not." ~ Ginie Sayles

The key to having the ideal wardrobe is to have a thorough understanding of your lifestyle, some planning and editing, and then learning how to maintain things. We have also established that it is not necessary to have a large quantity of clothes to be well dressed, as long as you have quality pieces and have acquired the skill of mixing and matching elegantly. Step Three is where you need to find out if your wardrobe works for you personally. If you often feel like you've got nothing to wear, then that's a pretty good indicator that your clothes collection is definitely not working.

The following are further indicators that a wardrobe isn't working for you:

- You take a long time to get dressed (forty-five minutes or more).
- You're constantly telling yourself: "I have nothing to wear!".
- Once dressed and out of the house, you're insecure and don't feel good about yourself.
- You wish you were wearing something else, but it was in the wash.
- You wonder what your friend will think of you because you are wearing the exact same outfit as the last time you met together.
- You find it hard to match your clothes, bags, and accessories.
- You have a random pair of shoes/bags/earrings, none of which ever get worn because they never seem to go with anything you have.
- You find yourself shopping for a new outfit whenever you have to attend an event.
- You don't feel appropriately dressed because you feel you have too little choice.
- You think that what you are wearing is too worn out and should not be seen in public.

Learning how to construct an effective wardrobe for yourself is important, so an analysis of your lifestyle must be done, and done well.

Wardrobe Refashioning Analysis

First make a list of ALL activities and social events that you attend in your life. To get you started, some activities might include the ten listed here:

1. Cooking
2. Cleaning
3. Running errands
4. School
5. Office work
6. Retailing duties
7. Meeting friends for coffee
8. Exercise
9. Church
10. Weekend gatherings, ad infinitum.

Got your list? Okay, let's now proceed to the next part of the Guide to a Basic Wardrobe.

Analyzing Your Wardrobe

As you look at what you have, you may find that you have too many or too much of something, for example, a pair of stilettos that you only wear once a week for cocktails, or maybe you don't have enough linen pants for your elegant casual weekends. You may want to further group your clothes into categories, something like this:

- The Work Wardrobe
- The Weekend Wardrobe
- The Cocktails/Date Wardrobe, etc.

The purpose of this exercise is to know what you have, what you lack, and what you need. To break this down further, your list might looks something like this:

- Career/Work Wardrobe
- Daytime Wardrobe
- Evening Cocktails, Elegant Gowns
- Sportswear
- Housedress/Loungewear (what you wear at home)
- Negligees/Pajamas (those items you wear to bed)

Mapping Out Your Wardrobe

The guide to a basic wardrobe includes mapping it out. If you work five days a week, you could have possibly five to fifteen outfits. (Note that outfits refer to combinations, so actual pieces of clothing could be less, though not necessarily.)

Your weekend wardrobe can range from having eight to twelve outfits. A different outfit for every weekend for about two months!

If your work from home, you can wear a few 'uniform' pieces, white blouses, skirts, Capris, or Crop pants, and sleeveless dresses give you five outfits.

These guidelines are not absolute, and you might want to map out your own guiding principles as you structure your wardrobe. After mapping things out, compare them to your current wardrobe and fill in the blanks. Once that is done it's time for the following:

Organizing Your Basic Wardrobe

Separating your wardrobe into sections for different activities will help you get dressed faster and more effectively. Below are two simple ideas that may help:

1. Have different drawers for different categories of clothes.
2. Buy five pink satin hangers and use them to separate your clothes into sections

Make a Lookbook for Inspiration, Imagination, and Fashion

Some of you will be extremely creative, and as long as you have sufficient options, you can whip out a fabulous new outfit. Others of you may not have the time in the mornings to do trial-and-error in front of the mirror. Whether or not you are creative, a lookbook is an extremely effective tool. It enables you to see an outfit before trying it on, and so minimizes effort. A few different ways to create lookbooks are as follows:

Photograph yourself: Take a snapshot of yourself whenever you are wearing an outfit you feel good in.
Photograph your garments: Take a snapshot of everything you own and put them into categories. When you are mixing and matching, flip through your lookbook, take out those photos, and 'match' items together.

Tip: Always lay out what you are going to wear the night before so you won't be stressed out in the morning! This simple strategy really does help to get any day off to a better start.

Guide to a Basic Wardrobe Gallery

The 'Elegant Woman's Guide to a Basic Wardrobe Gallery' is a visual guide on building an elegant wardrobe that works.

What Is Your 'Daily Uniform'?

Your daily uniform refers to those everyday basics we previously covered. This is the category of clothes you wear in your everyday life, much like a uniform! Keep in mind your everyday routine when building your wardrobe, and remember quality over quantity.

A Basic Elegant Work Wardrobe

Sometimes all you need is a couple of light-colored blouses, a black skirt and pants, beige skirt, and maybe a gray skirt. You can mix and match these with a couple of cardigans and jackets. Add more variety by adding scarves, pins, and by wearing your hair differently from time to time. These simple suggestions will also give you variety with minimal effort. You won't need that many shoes. A good suggestion is to have one pair of black and another pair of beige pumps.

Casually Elegant by Day

As for my 'daily uniform' I'm usually casual, unless I'm meeting someone or have a dinner or cocktail event to attend later in the evening. I love light-colored clothes because they match so easily and have an airy feel to them. As for footwear, ballet flats are my choice to run errands in.

The Elegant Travel Outfit

Again, ballet flats are convenient shoes when you have to go through customs with all that scanning they do these days! And although you have blankets on the plane, I still find it inadequate sometimes, so I make sure to tuck in a pashmina and cardigan into my duffel. If it is a long-haul flight, I bring a pair of sleeping pants to change into once the lights are out.

The Elegant Cocktail Wardrobe

If you can only afford three cocktail dresses, get one in black, one in red or yellow, and one in a silk/satin material. You can easily change the look of these with accessories, belts, scarves, coats, etc.

The Elegant Evening Gown Wardrobe

The classic red or silver numbers are always in vogue, but you will never fade into the background if you turned up in, say, black. Pinks are always feminine and beautiful. Go darker if you would like to be a bit edgier.

Match-Making
Wardrobe Essentials Skill One: How to Mix and Match Your Clothes Elegantly

The better you mix and match, the fewer garments you need to own to achieve an elegant look. And because coordination is essential to elegance, celebrity fashion stylists like Rachel Zoe have emerged simply by facilitating just that.

The job of a good stylist is to provide their clients with a carefully selected collection of clothes, where the dilemma of the right mixing & matching is taken out of the hands of the client. They will even come to your house, dress you, and fit you to perfection before sending you off to your elegant event. Other stylists' services include providing clients with a complete wardrobe makeover, including shoes, bags, and a plethora of accessories.

While I applaud the work of these artists, because their work influences fashion designers and start trends, we do NOT need stylists to learn how to mix and match elegantly. We can obtain   essential wardrobe building skills by following two elegant principles:

1. Practice restraint

2. Moderation is always the best policy

Or as Oscar Wilde once put it: "Everything in moderation, including moderation". Okay, so let us now look into this in a little more depth.

Say you adore Chanel. That doesn't mean you need not adorn yourself from top to bottom with everything from this brand. The most elegant of women, whenever possible, stay well away from clothing and accessories with logos or emblems embossed on them for all to see.

This is good news for the elegant woman who prefers not to spend wads of cash on materials. She learns how to pick out good quality, reasonably-priced items, and to exclude those internationally recognized logos. Yet she can still look very elegant without paying the high costs of designer clothing and accessories!

I'm not saying that you shouldn't wear or carry anything with a designer's mark on it. Certain brands are highly regarded for their dependable quality and well-deserved reputation. But if you do choose to wear designer clothing, be sure to keep the display of the logo sparse. A fashion disaster is when one has her Chanel sunglasses on, her Dior purse (with Dior's logo all over it), a Burberry checkered trench, and Ferragamo shoes adorned with the famous bows. Such a woman is a walking Vogue magazine. Being so logoed-up, one might even perceive her as an egomaniac with an inferiority complex, but that's nothing for this book.

There is a certain sort of refinery to someone who recognizes quality without looking at the label. I admire the woman who does not need brands to have confidence in what she wears, or how she carries herself. There is also great respect for the woman who does not worship labels or talk about them with girlish excitement.

Even if she does love and enjoy catwalk designers (and there's nothing wrong with that), she'll keep her thoughts to herself. That is a private matter and she'll not make others feel 'in want' by talking about designer wear excessively to the point of boring her company, unless of course they share the same passion and mutual interest in the topic. Talking frequently about labels indicates a 'want' and perhaps some dissatisfaction within her life. The elegant woman appreciates her life and values if far more than mere things.

Wardrobe Essentials and Why Colors Matter

If you only could have five new items of clothing for the whole year, then you would be wise to pick garments with solid colors. Solid colors can stand repetition much better than patterned materials. The best basic colors are black, white, ivory, beige, champagne, and navy. When you have these staple colors in your wardrobe, you might consider adding a few pastel-colored pieces to the collection too, as these are excellent for daytime wear.

Why Solid Colors?

You can get the most out of outfit combinations and accessorizing with solid colors. For example, a daytime outfit can be transformed into evening wear by removing a scarf and adding a long strand of pearls.

Point to note: When mixing and matching, avoid being too matchy-matchy. Going too far can mean your outfit loses its elegance and ends up looking too 'costume'. And unless you're actually going to a costume party, this is not how you want to be perceived by others. Gone are the days when shoes were made out of the same fabric as the bag, sash, and the ribbon on the bonnet.

There are certain pairs of things that go very elegantly together though. Here are eight great examples of pairing your wardrobe essentials:

1. Matching your umbrella to your trench coat.
2. Having a full set of matching luggage.
3. Having a full set of matching toiletry bags.
4. Matching your luggage to your outfit.
5. Wearing complete lingerie sets.

6. Matching your outfit to the occasion.

7. Having the same scent in your perfume, body lotion, and body soap.

8. Having a subtle sense of compatibility in outfits between you and your husband.

Refining and employing your own good taste is probably best when it comes to these matters.

Okay, so the third wardrobe essentials skill to acquire is the attention to detail. As they say, God is in the details! If you look at the details, you'll marvel at all the little signatures God leaves behind. Just like artisan designers.

8. How Elegant Women Wear Their Hair and Makeup

Makeup is a kind of clothing for the face and it can make or break a look depending on how well, or how poorly, it's applied.

I pondered for quite for a while whether or not to put a makeup section in this book. First of all, I'm not a makeup guru, so you'll be better off looking for serious makeup advice elsewhere. However, I decided that there are so many styles of makeup in this world that it would be valuable to distinguish 'elegant makeup' from the rest. Secondly, I will cover how elegant women wear their makeup (generally speaking) and lastly, the important things, like achieving good skin, a natural look, and also highlighting the things that an elegant woman would not wear in her makeup repertoire.

I will also discuss very basic makeup techniques. Thus, I would advise those who are beginners to also further their study of the artful way to applying makeup via more credible sources. Tip: Spend some time on YouTube watching makeup tutorials!

Principles of Elegant Makeup

For daytime makeup, try to stick with natural colors. It's important that you wear your makeup and it doesn't wear you! Its sole purpose is to enhance your look, not take it over. My personal favorite is the no-makeup makeup look. Confused? Basically, this means it's not obvious that you're wearing makeup, but you are, and it's doing you justice. With a hint of blusher, you'll look fresh faced, and a natural shade of lipstick will guarantee to brighten your smile.

The eyes should only be 'made up' in the evening. But that does not mean you DON'T wear any eye makeup during the day. It's just that wearing dramatic false eye lashes and blue eye lids do not go very well under the harsh brightness of the sun. The point here is to achieve the 'no-makeup' makeup look. You might play with neutral tones, nude browns, nude pinks, and plenty of blending. These neutral shades can contour and highlight your face beautifully.

Lip gloss is acceptable if you're young. It tends to work well up into your twenties, or if you work in an environment that's more casual in nature. Lipstick is better suited for more formal environments, though the color is what you need to be mindful of. Only wear dark lipstick if you're 35 and above, unless of course, you're a fashion model.

For evening makeup, emphasize more on the eyes. Dark eyes can have a very glamorizing effect when done well.

Also, the general makeup rule (when you do your makeup), as repeated by countless makeup gurus around the world, is that you should only pick one feature to focus on. For example, do not overdo the eyes, then cheeks, then lips, and then draw thick and heavy eyebrows.

The Elegant Makeup Guide

- Age: If you are very young, go for the no-makeup make up look. You probably look better with natural looking lips or simple glossy ones.

- Daytime: In the day, it is in bad taste to wear bright blue or green eye shadow, or sporting too much 'sparkle' such as gold and silver.

- Brows: Don't neglect your brows. If you can, see a brow specialist and get recommendations on what type of brow shape best frames your face and eyes. If in doubt, go for a natural look. Don't make the mistake of going too dark when you line your brows.

- Lipstick match: Your lipstick color should not clash with your outfit. Do a check and ask for a friend's opinion if you're unsure.
- Lipstick color: Elegant lipstick colors include nudes, reds, pinks, and orange pinks, but NOT blues, greens, or whites.
- Lip Gloss: Use a lip gloss only if you're below 40 years of age.

The Color Chart for Lipstick

- Light pink: These lipsticks go well with all blue and violet tones.
- Orange-red: These lipsticks are prettier with beiges and yellows.
- Matching: If you wear a red ensemble, ideally your lipstick should be exactly the same shade of red.
- Tanned skin: If you are tan, you probably don't need too much makeup, except for a clear bright lipstick. You can choose to focus on the eyes by drawing a thin line around them with eyeliner.

When to Throw Away Your Makeup

Having good skin is better than layering the face with makeup. To establish good skin, we need a skin cleansing regime (find one that works for you because we're all different). Equally as important is to make sure your makeup collection is hygienic!

Women are medically proven to carry more bacteria than men, even though we tend to believe we're the cleaner gender. So why do we have more bacteria than men? Because of makeup! We constantly touch our faces whether we realize it or not. Our phones touch our faces too, and then the makeup we get on our hands and phones transports bacteria to the contents of our purse. On and on it goes, we are touching and transferring bacteria and potential viruses, all throughout the day.

Below are a few suggestions on when to throw away your makeup:

- Cover-up/concealer : 2–3 months
- Cover-up/Concealer sponges: Clean every week or get disposable ones
- Lip Gloss/stick: 6–8 months
- Eye Shadows: 4–6 months
- Blusher: 3–6 months
- Mascara: 3 months
- Brushes: Clean every two weeks to make sure you are not applying bacteria on your face.

Essential Elements of Elegant Makeup
Foundation

One of the most important makeup basics is learning how apply a flawless foundation.

Depending on your skin texture, you might get away with just using a concealer. With an even skin tone, sometimes all you need is a BB cream or a tinted moisturizer. The purpose of foundation is to even out your skin tone in order to give you a clear complexion.

There are many types of foundation and many different methods to apply it. However, I'm not here to discuss what types and how, but rather to let you know how elegant women seem to apply them. Here are some foundation makeup notes:

The important thing to note is that foundation must be applied flawlessly and evenly. There shouldn't be hints of foundation brush marks left behind or more product on some areas than others. It shouldn't end at the jaw, but blended in evenly.

It must match your skin tone. To check for this, stand far away from the mirror and see if the color of your face is too many shades different from the rest of your body. Of course, it is natural for most people to be fairer on their faces than the rest of their bodies, but it shouldn't be too stark in comparison.

It also has to be natural looking. Some people apply too much powder and have that 'too much makeup on' look. Ensure that you conceal imperfections with a concealer.

A sloppy or inappropriate application of foundation will vastly reduce the elegant look. Elegant women always look perfectly groomed and one of the first things one notices is that she has a bright and clear (and natural looking) complexion. It may be an irony, but you present yourself well to avoid distractions. When you are sloppy, or have spots on your face, one can't help but notice it. This is very distracting and, believe it or not, it is an act of kindness to present your best face!

Eyebrows

You must present a natural looking, neatly groomed brow. After getting your brows professionally shaped, you should own a set of tweezers to maintain your brows every few days by removing any stray hairs that grow out. When you wear makeup, you should at least comb your brows if they look messy, and use a natural looking eyebrow pencil to fill it in for a more complete look.
If you could only afford two makeup things to do each morning, let it be putting on flawless natural looking foundation and drawing your eyebrows.

Eyeliner

Probably the most distinctive quality that elegant women have in their daily makeup is their reliance on eyeliner (and mascara).

Again, I'm not here to discuss the techniques of applying eyeliner, though it is important to learn to do it well, so do your homework and learn how to wear eyeliner.

The way you draw your eyeliner might be so drastic that it changes the shape of your eyes but in a good way. It also acts as way to highlight your eyes, which I think is probably one of the most attractive features of the body! Most elegant women have their eyeliner on, again, in a natural way. Black eyeliner is popular but drawn in a thin line and very close to the lashes so it is not that obvious. This is unlike the thick eyeliner method, where it looks like a line drawn using a whiteboard marker or a thick felt pen. Some women wear it on the lower lash line as well, though in some cases, it has to be an extremely fine line without the possibilities of smudging, otherwise it can age the makeup and make you look older.

Eyeliners may be used in other colors, such as dark brown, charcoal, graphite, and even a dark olive green and certain shades of dark navy. The lighter colors, such as browns, grays, and greens should be used in the day. Sometimes eye shadow is used in place of eyeliner. Eye shadows and eyeliners are not used together in the daytime unless they are 'fused' together such that you cannot quite see separate applications.

If you've already got pretty dark lashes, you may skip the eyeliner and opt for a natural looking eye shadow instead. Natural eye shadow colors include browns, gold, beige, and dusty pinks.

In this case, the eye shadow application is not quite the smoky look, which is reserved for evenings. It is contoured to define the eyes, but it looks relaxed and fresh.

Remember, applying eyeliner perfectly sometimes takes years of practice. However, don't let that discourage you. You can always start with the basics of finding the right eyeliner that gives you control, will not smudge, and just practice drawing eyeliner close to your eyelashes. When you're more confident with that, you can explore other eyeliner techniques that change the shape of your eyes.

Another note about elegant eyes; it is useful to learn how to wear natural looking false eye lashes, especially when you're attending an elegant evening event. However, avoid using them in the day, unless you're doing a photo shoot or something similar.

Elegant Hairstyles

Learning how to wear your hair tastefully and elegantly is significant. An elegant hairstyle is more than just personal grooming. It shapes your face and actually helps your communication skills.

You might be wondering, 'how this can be?' Well, people look at you when you speak, and they hear your words. However, the impact of your words can be reduced if they are greatly distracted by your hair. It should not take the attention away from your face, your smile, or your expressions. It must be 'a part' of you, and not appear 'apart' from you in much the same way as a hat might.

No matter how well you dress, speak, or carry yourself, if your hair is wild and inappropriate, it has the potential to totally ruin your otherwise classy appearance. Your hairstyle influences people's impression of you more than most women realize, especially in the eyes of those who don't know you personally.

Let's do a little test here. You will soon see how quickly we judge people by their hair, or lack of, as the case may be.

How do you view the following people?

- A rock star
- A gangster
- A queen
- A princess
- A tattoo artist
- A ballerina
- A cheerleader

- A skinhead

Are you surprised by the stereotypes that come to mind? Every now and then people wear their hair to reflect their personality or current mood. Other times it's merely to follow a modern trend. But the point is this; when it comes to hair, we often judge the book by its cover. I'm not saying that's right, it is how it is, whether it's conscious or subconscious.

A while ago, my husband and I found a great deal on rental cars online. When we got to the place, the sales person looked very unprofessional because of his bright orange hair. We thought it was a scam. It wasn't! We just could not associate the hair with a legitimate business man.

So remember, no matter how elegant your dress is, or how well applied your makeup might be, if you've got drastic roots showing or greasy flat hair, it will be challenging to have an overall elegant look.

Picking an Elegant Hairstyle That Suits You

First and foremost, having a clean and tidy hairstyle is mandatory. The next consideration is to determine what suits you best. Again, to find the best hairstyle we need to consider the shape of our face, our lifestyle, and how much time we have for maintenance.

Flattering Hairstyles by Face Shape

Finding an elegant hairstyle that suits you is probably not going to be taken at random from the latest cuts found in fashion magazines, but by defining the shape of your face. Let us now look at the three common forms:

Which face shape are you?
1. **The Oval Face:** Congratulations! You have the most versatile shaped face, as this one suits almost all

hairstyles. So the world really is your oyster when it comes to choosing the mane of your desire.

2. **The Square Face:** Leave some hair around your cheeks to shape your appearance. You might want to consider a shorter cut too, because shorter hair tends to suit the squarer face better.

3. **The Heart-shaped Face:** Do not tie your hair all the way back, play around with soft curls to balance out the lower half.

Other Considerations

Sometimes a person's face shape is not clearly defined, or maybe an individual is not quite sure about the shape of their face. If you can identify with this, then maybe you're more concerned about the features of your face, for example, you may have a high forehead, or your eyes might be a little too far apart or close together? Perhaps they droop a little or are slanted? The appearance of cheekbones can be accentuated by hairstyles too, so consider all of these factors, including your cheeks, when deciding on a coiffure that is going to serve you well.

Do some research on elegant hairstyles and then locate a good, reputable hairdresser. Remember, your hairstyle is important. It is your crowning glory and can make or break your overall appearance.

Your Lifestyle

If you find yourself with ample leisure time, you can afford to have a hairstyle that requires more maintenance, such as a different hair color altogether, with highlights and the works. You may even have a fringe, layers, or perms.

If lots of free time isn't something you have then go for low maintenance. Don't let that dishearten you though, because a low-maintenance hairdo can still give you an elegant look. Preferably, leave your fringe long and learn how to style your hair in elegant up-dos (a hairstyle where the hair is swept up and fastened away from the face and neck), various celebrity styles, and so on.

Etiquette of Elegant Hair

The principles of elegance are also applied to hair. Keep it clean, neat, and definitely free from dandruff. This will prevent you from developing bad habits, such as scratching or picking at your scalp. The hair of an elegant woman is always in place. It should neither be too long nor too short. It must be clear from your face and never cover your eyes. A truly elegant hairstyle never needs to be touched, flipped, or pushed away at any time. Roots ought never to be seen, and tangles are not visible.

When you are speaking, or in conversation, refrain from twirling your hair, looking for split ends or attempting to smooth any tangles. It is also not acceptable to tie your hair in public, or comb it when in the company of others outside the home.

Elegant Hairstyles

Simplicity at its best is the very elegant Chignon. This is a style where the hair is pulled back into a kind of bun. An alternative is a classic French twist. The French twist is shaped by tucking the hair into a kind of vertical roll down the back of your head. It's really very graceful in appearance when done well. Wearing your hair up presents your face elegantly. Not only is not distracting, but it complements all elegant dresses too. This is a style that you can wear to work, a party, or even at home. It is elegant, neat and tidy, and comfortable. The more casual you need your hair to be the 'looser' the chignon can be made.

The Low to Mid-Ponytail

When too high, a ponytail will make you overly fashionable (which is not elegant), or appear too young. The classic ponytail is a chic, casually elegant look that is very wearable for daytime. It can work well with casual, smart-casual, and sports style clothing.

The Half Ponytail

This gives the appearance of a neat and clear face and has a softer, more feminine feel to it. If you have sharp cheekbones, tying your hair way back may give a harsh look. Some hair around the shoulders with a clear forehead is a softer, more elegant alternative.

The Poofy Top

This look can be achieved by using a barrette (a bar-shaped hairclip), with your fringe pulled back. You can also backcomb your hair (with hair spray), and fasten it with pins. Another elegant choice is the use of hairbands. For the rest of your hair, you may wear it up with an elegant chignon or a ponytail.

Using the Classic Hair Band

Hair bands are traditional and are classically elegant by design. However, they are generally for younger woman. Hair bands are convenient for pushing the hair off your face. It only takes a minute to brush your hair and put on a hair band. Add a little chic by wearing it with your ponytail.

Coloring Your Hair the Right Way

When coloring your hair, never lighten or darken it more than two shades at a time. Sorry, I actually can't remember where I read this from, but it makes sense. You see, the idea is to refrain from looking too artificial. I guess if you go from dark to blonde, just remember to schedule in regular trips to your hairstylist to maintain it and fix those roots before they begin to show.

The Elegant No-Brainer Hairdo

The half-up, half-down hairdo is almost good for any day, any dress, and will suit any face shape or hair type!

For Voluminous, Elegant Hair

If your hair has no volume, no matter how hard you try, then it's probably time to visit your hairstylist! It might just be that it's too heavy.

Another alternative is to get some non-permanent hair extensions. That way your tresses won't be stressed carrying all that weight. Personally, I love them! They are so easy to use and you can create effortless volume with your hair in a matter of seconds. This is one of my greatest elegant hair secrets. I sometimes clip in the extensions to make a bigger and more textured bun, and it looks just great.

The Elegant, Loose Bun for Casual Days

A bun is always beautiful when done well, but might be too severe for a casual evenings. Have you thought about a low, loose bun at the side? You could add in some fresh flowers if it's appropriate. Once you've mastered it with your own hair, the loose bun is a simple, quick, and effective way to create an elegant style. Best of all is that it looks like you spent a long time tending your hair, when in fact it only took you a few minutes.

Elegant Up-dos: Invest Some Time in Learning the Basic Up-do

Knowing how to do a basic up-do is an essential skill every elegant woman should try to master. Why? Learning how to do

a basic up-do bea[...]
on casual days.

Learning h[...]
also saves money [...]
salon!

Don't know [...]
YouTube video hai[...]
In terms of hair sup[...]
elastics, bobby pins[...]
pins are the staple t[...]

When you a[...]
can add elegant tou[...]
bejeweled hair pins,[...]

To add volu[...]
teasing comb or use [...]
and added them insi[...]

There are many types of up-dos – something to try
and experiment when you have extra time to get ready!

9. Elegant P[...]
Carriage

Deportment a[...]
Poise, and [...]

While[...]
wa[...]

Poise and

Deportment and Manners: Elegance through Expressions, Poise, and Carriage

While we can achieve elegance through our character and the way we dress, we may not have achieved elegance in the way we move and carry ourselves. Why? Well, we seem to have lost the **art of being graceful** in our modern lifestyles. We're so busy rushing around in today's world, and often overly busy, that we don't take time to consider our movements. Couple the above with the simple fact that many of us have had little or no training in this area; nor are there many examples of graceful women for us to emulate. I believe that in our pursuit of refinement, we should place value on learning how to be graceful. It is important to learn how to move with beauty, style, and sophistication.

Our dictionaries loosely define **deportment** as "a manner of personal conduct; and behavior."

I prefer to describe it as **poise, bearing, walk,** and **carriage**. Of course, deportment is not limited to that, as you will soon see.

Deportment is the way you express yourself through your features and the way you move or hold your body. Your body language says an awful lot about YOU.

A woman who has beautiful deportment is said to be poised, graceful, and elegant. She does everything in the most finished manner. I like to think of deportment as the art of moving gracefully.

How to Be Graceful

Although beautiful deportment may come more naturally to some rather than others, it is still obtainable by training.

If you are a dancer that is schooled in ballet and ballroom, you will likely be better at the art of deportment than others with no dance training. This is because you are mindful of the way your body moves and functions. Additionally, if you happen to have parents that are graceful in their movements, there's a high possibility that you will carry yourself in the same manner. To some extent, education also influences a person's deportment. This relates back to thoughts on how one thinks, which in turn prompts the body to respond based on our thinking.

About 100 or so years ago, children were trained in deportment, but now deportment training is mainly reserved for the acting profession or some unaffordable finishing school for girls. I'm not sure why it was dropped off the educational curriculum. But I happen to believe in its importance, and thus I hope to pass on the essentials of deportment here. After researching posture, acting methods, and physiotherapy sessions, I've found a few ways that we can use to train ourselves in the art of deportment. An overview of this is outlined in the list below. This actually took me a long while to find. The reason why I was so passionate about deportment was because I was one of those girls who struggled with an 'ugly walk', for want of a better expression. I've worked on it over the years, and although it's not perfect, it has improved.

Deportment simplified into seven areas of study:

1. Expression
2. Manners and etiquette
3. Dressing
4. Poise
5. How to walk
6. How to sit
7. Social conduct

Expression

To learn to be graceful, we must first study **expression**. Expression is the result of thought materializing on the face. It is a form of action. This influences the shape of our facial expressions, along with gestures, such as walking, moving the arms, etc.

So, to ensure that we only emit beautiful expressions, we have to control how we think, and control the impressions we make in our head. This means that to obtain beautiful and elegant expressions we have to acquire good **mental poise**.

We also need to utilize the power of analysis and self-correction. Mastering these elements will give you command of yourself and an **appearance of genuine ease**.

Manners and Etiquette

To learn how to be graceful, you must have a decent understanding of basic manners and etiquette because they are what govern behavior. They consist of a general study of how to socialize, how to be introduced, become a perfect guest, when and when NOT to apologize, and so on and so forth. The study of this will give you a measure of confidence. You will intuitively know what to do in any given situation. You will be contributing to your appearance of ease, and thus removing every trace of self-consciousness.

However, don't get caught up in etiquette rules and start judging other people, otherwise, you will have missed the whole point. If I can only leave you with one suggestion in your approach to manners, it's that, "**You should always consider the feelings of others**".

Dress

How much does clothing affect your ability to be graceful? I can tell you with confidence that it affects us more than we think. I've privately interviewed several women who admit that they feel better about themselves when they know they look their best, and they're directly referring to their attire.

Dress as though you might bump into that 'highly-esteemed' someone on the street. Nothing imparts quite the same glow of satisfaction as knowing that we are properly dressed, especially when out in public. This will affect your deportment a lot. When you look your best, you will feel your best, and when you feel your best, you function better.

Poise

Poise is balance, and to obtain it, you have to understand balance in the way you hold yourself and the way you speak.

To obtain poise, a good understanding of posture and the way the body is designed to move (and be still) is required. This is also part of mental poise. By freeing yourself from bungling styles of untrained movement, and bad habits of gestures, your graceful personality will radiate.
Thus, the powers of awareness and observation come into play. This opens your eyes to what you are right now and how you should be carrying yourself.

To be balanced, you will need to know that the right posture incudes having a strong core and a strong base. A strong core is established only by exercise. A strong base is determined by the distance of your feet.
The **right posture is a delicate balance** of a straight back (properly aligned with the head) and a stable chin that isn't too low or too high. Your feet are somewhat apart, your stomach held in, shoulders are back and down, and the arms are neatly to the side. This posture is formed by training,& exercise, and maintained by making these things a habit.

How to Walk

Unfortunately, the majority of women learn how to walk by imitating faulty and ungraceful models. As children who copy their parents, there is no doubt that we have been marred by examples of bad walking from one generation to the next.

So just how we should walk then? We should walk in a manner that is characterized by **grace and freedom**. It should not be hasty or hurried, but legato (not staccato), nor aimless but a deliberate rhythmic movement. All this is in sync with gentle compensating movements of the head and arms, which should move in a slow graceful swing. It might sound like there's a lot going on here, but with practice you'll be walking a graceful walk without giving it a second thought.

When we walk, our **upper torso should remain as strong** as possible. It should definitely not sway back and forth. We should be mindful not to over-arch our back. The head, while relaxed, should not bob. The head needs to be slightly lifted, as though you have an air of confident expectation of life. I suppose that is where the old training method of 'placing a book on your head' comes in. If we have not put ergonomics to use in our work life, we may have developed rounded shoulders and a forward tilting head, a bit like a turtle! If so, work on correcting this right away. We should not waddle, as that suggests obesity, nor strut as fashion models do on the runway, as that suggests arrogance. To learn to walk well, in style and grace, is to attain self-possession and self-mastery.

How to Sit

You should not flop into a chair or throw yourself onto it. Don't sit cautiously on a seat either, as this looks as though you suspect it's dirty, or might break under your weight.

Avoid also sitting squarely on both feet, as that is a bit too mannish. Sit with your legs closed but lean them at an angle to one side.

Avert yourself from jumping up or rising suddenly from your seat in either an abrupt or aggressive motion. Finally, definitely do not lift the feet to 'stomp' as you get up.

Social Conduct

Do not ever rush or be in "time management" mode. Also, while the appearance of "laziness" is worn as a badge of pride in some circles, elegant deportment does not allow for any form of idleness, such as lounging around with your feet up.

The flip side of appearing too comfortable is to appear uncomfortable or self-conscious; you must do your best to mask this until you make it a thing of the past. To appear uncomfortable not only increases your own uneasiness, but it reflects in others too.

Learning how to **overcome self-consciousness** is also part of elegant deportment, and an important one at that. I'm not an expert on overcoming self-consciousness but you can start by building a sort of elegant self-confidence. There are many ways to overcome this, and mastering a beautiful deportment can help. Knowing you are correctly postured and at ease (which prevents further questioning in other people's minds) and armed with the fact that you possess a refined set of skills create a great foundation on which to build elegant self-confidence. Important social skills to master include: good manners, correct diction, decent grammar, elegance in speech, and a progression in the art of conversation while socializing.

"Our words reveal our refinements; they tell the discerning listener of the company we have kept; they are the hallmarks of education and culture." ~ Dale Carnegie

"I recognize but one mental acquisition as a necessary part of the education of a lady or gentleman, namely, an accurate and refined use of the mother tongue." ~ Dr. Charles W. Eliot

List of Gestures That Affect Your Elegance

Similar to how certain clothes, shoes, or bags may ruin a woman's appearance, there are gestures that can also ruin the elegance of even the best-dressed women.

It is true that what a woman wears can affect her elegance greatly. However, that is not the only thing. No woman can convince anyone of her elegance if she is not mindful of her gestures, especially if they aren't exactly graceful. For example, inelegant gestures include such things as fidgeting, talking loudly, slapping thighs when consumed with laughter, leaning, etc.

Self-analysis of your own gestures is important in attaining an elegant deportment. Remember, we aim for progress, not perfection.

List of Gestures That Demolish Elegance:
- Picking scabs or squeezing pimples.
- Slapping someone's back when they laugh or clapping hands together loudly.
- Sluggish walking, e.g., dragging one's feet.
- Swinging arms like a marching soldier.
- Wiping teeth with the tongue.
- Bending to the food as opposed to bringing it to the mouth.
- Folding the arms.
- Resting the head or chin on hands and elbows.
- Leaning on the walls of elevators, counters, etc.
- Putting a finger in the mouth to remove bits of food.
- Scratching or fidgeting.
- Tugging on jeans or tops.
- Pulling up bra straps.
- Examining complexion or teeth with compact mirrors in public places (restrooms are exempt).
- Putting makeup on in public (other than a quick dash of lipstick after meals).
- Staring vacantly into space.
- Keeping the mouth slightly ajar.
- Biting fingernails.
- Sitting with legs apart.

- Exposed underwear, or the top of a bottom.
- Bowing over and locking knees instead of bending them to pick something up.
- Combing hair or fiddling with it in public places.
- Talking loudly.
- Stirring drinks noisily with a teaspoon.

There are others, but the list above includes the most common.

As superficial as it sounds, these gestures alone hinder a good impression. Studies have shown that it can harm your chances for love, meeting people, forming new friendships, or getting the job you want, no matter how lovely a person you might be.

We may blame everyone and everything else for the superficiality of it all, and curse a person for not making the effort to get to know us better, but such is life! We sometimes only get a few seconds to help the other party form an opinion about us. Or as the saying goes, "You never get a second chance to make a first impression".

Gestures are non-verbal communication, also referred to as our body language. What are your gestures saying about you?

From *Guide to Elegance by Genevieve Dariaux*:
"The charm and grace that are the foundations of elegance are made up of graceful gestures and self-controlled movements which are developed and acquired hopefully from earliest childhood.

With that said, a complete lack of spontaneity in a woman is extremely irritating and, in the end, it is just as destructive to her elegance as the undisciplined behavior of a tomboy."

A large part of elegant gestures is the way in which we hold ourselves in all manners. An elegant woman has a certain chic poise.

The Importance of Posture

Years ago, attending a finishing school was the mark of a well-bred girl. She would undergo cooking lessons and etiquette lessons, as well as classes on posture. Today, we enroll ourselves in dance lessons to hopefully gain the beauty, grace, poise, and posture of an established dancer. We send our daughters to ballet school in hopes of developing graceful posture and acquiring poise and body confidence.

Though I choose to use positive quotes, the citation below has been etched into my memory and it has served me well. Sometimes we need a slight kick up the backside in order to move forward.

"A rounded back, sagging shoulders, and a drooping chin create an image of extreme lassitude of discouragement with life, and giving an unfair reflection of a certain sloppiness, and lack pride in a lady".

Elegant Posture: For Health, Poise, and Elegance

Fact: One looks more elegant when one has good posture.

Good posture contributes to an elegant poise. Years ago, women invested in posture lessons and learned how to walk properly. It was as important as learning to put on makeup. View some posture photographs and learn about your own posture and the body language it signals to others.

What is Posture Exactly?

It is the position in which you hold your body upright against gravity. It relates to standing, sitting, or lying down.
A perfect stance has also been referred to as a 'proper form' or 'carriage'. It is important to have a proper form no matter what you are doing.

A proper form means the best position for your body to be in at any given time. This way, we function at our most efficient. The correct form means there's the least amount of strain on supporting muscles and ligaments during movements.

What Does Stance in Good Posture Mean?

A correct stance ensures that the bones and joints are in precise alignment, thus enabling your muscles to be used at their most efficient. It is one of the many secrets of developing poise.

Learning Good Posture

First and foremost, good posture has to be learned. It's more natural in some than others, but everyone can improve on their stance. We have to train our body to stand, walk, sit, and lie in the most efficient positions if we're to achieve the posture we so desire.

Assess Yourself

Before you can work on your posture, you must first assess yourself. Like I've recommended earlier, having someone videotape your walk and general movements is the best method of self-assessment. You can begin by examining your most recent photos. Study carefully how you sit (we often have pictures of us at a dinner table), how you stand next to your friends, or carry yourself on a beach, etc.

Do You Have Rounded Shoulders?

Study your photos or movements in a full-length mirror. This way, you'll be able to get a good idea of how much work is required to improve your posture. I always assumed I was aware of my bearing. Now I think that one can never be too 'aware'. I look forward to the day when I no longer think about it, when my muscle memory takes over and it becomes a natural part of how I carry myself.

Gain Self Awareness of Your Posture

Awareness of your stance is the first step. Once you identify your weaknesses, you can begin working on them, 'they' being standing, sitting, and walking.

Meanwhile, I'll recommend ballet classes; for you and your children, if you have any. Remember, too, that good posture comes from having a strong core as well. Search **"core strengthening"** exercises. They help you develop a stronger torso and back, which in turn will help to hold you up effortlessly. Think of elegant posture and work towards achieving that.

Although a strong core means stronger muscles, don't overdo things here. You don't want to get too muscular and end up looking stiff and bulky.

Correcting Bad Posture

This section is all about correcting poor posture, maintaining stance, and posture improvement techniques.
I've said it before, and I'll probably keep on saying it: Correct posture is essential to poise, elegance, and complements elegant dressing. It is also part of good personal grooming.

How to Correct Your Posture

Do a self-check. See if you can 'draw' an imaginary straight line from your ears, shoulders, hips, knees, and ankles.

The old fashioned tip is to balance a book on your head. Even if you can balance well, be sure that a straight line can be drawn. I know women who can model, strut, and slouch while keeping a book balanced on their heads, though it doesn't mean they have good posture.

At the moment, my posture correcting journey is to wear a back brace for my upper back, and I use a LumbarWear to suck in my tummy. I also do some ballet movements and take brisk walks regularly. These help to strengthen my core.

What Are Your Bad Posture Habits?

How do you know what good posture habits to develop if you don't know what bad habits you have now?
My back is slightly too curved in, which makes me look a little too slouched. My shoulders tend to be slightly rounded. These two problems affect my walk. To figure out if you have good posture, take the following posture test.

The Good Posture Wall Check

Stand with the back of your head and your bottom touching the wall. While doing so, do not push your heels back, let them position naturally.

Then, place your hand between your lower back and the wall, and also between your neck and the wall. If you can get within an inch or two at the low back, and two inches at the neck, you are close to having an excellent posture.

The Mirror Test

You can gauge the elegance of your posture using the mirror test. Stand facing a full length mirror. Imagine that a rope is attached to your chest and tied firmly to the ceiling. This will ensure that your back is not fully arched. Make sure to keep your eyes looking straight ahead. This will cause your head to be straight.

Now check the following:

- Your shoulders are relaxed and level.
- Your hips are level.
- Your kneecaps face the front.
- Your feet are facing front so that the ankles are straight.

Turn to the side and assess the following:

- Your head is not slumped forwards or backwards (very evident in photos).
- Your shoulders are in line with ears.
- There is only a slight forward curve to your lower back.

Fixing Bad Posture Habits

Do you have any of these bad posture habits? Common posture mistakes include:

- A forward head
- Rounded shoulders
- Arched lower back
- Excessive anterior pelvic tilt (protruding backside)
- Excessive posterior pelvic tilt (protruding abdomen/pelvis)

The Proper Stance

Do you know how a beautiful woman stands? I really do love studying the stance of elegant women. When standing correctly, a proper posture involves aligning the body so that the pull of gravity is evenly distributed.

Good posture includes:
- A straight line from your ears, shoulders, hips, knees, and ankles
- Head is centered
- Shoulders, hips, and knees are of equal height
- Sleeping Posture

Sleeping Posture

The best positions for sleeping and lying down include:
- A bed pillow should be under your head, but not your shoulders. There should be a thickness that allows your head to be in a line that is straight to your body.
- Try to sleep in a position that helps you maintain the curve in your back (hence the need for a lumbar roll because our backs are not straight).
- Avoid sleeping on your stomach. This position can, and does, produce back and neck strain among certain folks.
- Find a good mattress with back support. A decent mattress should provide support for the natural curves and alignment of the spine.

Your Next Mattress

There are certain mattresses that are recommended by your county's chiropractic association. These usually have a mark/brand on them. Look for them when shopping for your next mattress.

Try to get some help from additional products if you need them. These might include such items as a special posture chair for your office, or a posture correction brace (if you suffer from terrible posture or back pain). There are pillows you can buy that are curved at the neck position. You may also want to use a back support (aka, lumbar-support) at night, as this is for the curved part of your back and improves the back's posture. A rolled sheet or towel tied around your waist may be helpful as well.

The Correct Sitting Position

Sit up with your back straight and your shoulders held back, but not too rigid though. Your buttocks should touch the very back of your chair. Imagine the string from your chest pulling you up. Now check that your back is not too arched and that you bring your chest out.

Note: You might want to invest in ergonomic chairs and seating, especially if you spend lots of time in the office and in front of your computer desk. Try not to sit for too long either. Get up and move around periodically if you can. Your good posture deserves it!

The Training Posture

Schools used to have posture lessons, but unfortunately today they are rare. However, posture training is still needed. It is our own responsibility to work on this. Here's an extract from a website called Daylife on how China prepared their service staff for the Beijing Olympics in 2008.

> *Chinese young women holding plates walk as they receive etiquette training at a vocational school for the upcoming Beijing 2008 Olympic Games medal ceremonies' hostesses in Beijing, China, Wednesday, Jan. 9, 2008. The polished young women practice proper stance by balancing books on their heads while squeezing a sheet of paper between the knees. A*

perfect smi
teeth, a skil
carefully cla

It is importan
have good posture. C
for it. Sitting at a desk
toll on our body. We n
order to have good po
and neck pain. Of cour
posture and increase c
standing and sitting.
Some of the wa
help with our posture is   ...ask him
or her to assess your po   ...e may give you some
feedback and exercises to do. Make it a point to see him or her
regularly for a while, for instance, once a fortnight/month. In
between sessions, you'll have to do your homework – the
exercises that he or she may give you so that you'll see
improvements made on your posture.
Of course, attaining the perfect posture is not achieved
in one day. It is a gradual process, depending on how far you
were from good posture at the beginning. Other ways to
maintain or improve posture is by taking Yoga or Pilates
classes, or dance classes such as ballroom and ballet.
I would recommend ballet classes because it has
helped me improved my posture by leaps and bounds from
decades of bad posture! Friends and their daughters who
suffered bad posture due to habit or scoliosis were
recommended by their doctors to take up ballet.

Ballet for Developing Elegance, Good Posture, and Gracefulness

Ballet is an art form but it's also an excellent sport or method
of exercise. I would encourage anyone who is not particularly
fond of the gym (or exercise in general) to try a ballet class.
Most of the ballet exercises are stretching workouts with slow,
purposeful movements of the body. It is typically accompanied

by a live pianist (though these
or classical music from a s
definitely be acquired fro
Benefits from reg
1. Grace
2. v

are becoming rarer these days), ound system. Better posture can m taking ballet classes.

lar ballet practice include:
ulness (ballet exercises are all purposeful and ry mentally engaging).

Good posture.

3. Poise.

4. A lean feminine body (without looking like a muscular athlete).

5. Flexibility.

6. A taste for classical music.

7. Exposure to the beautiful art of ballet.

8. Body awareness.

9. A useful exercise routine without exposing oneself to harmful UV rays.

A Short History on Ballet

Ballet started in the fifteenth century and was developed to perfection in the French courts. It is rated on a measure of physical endurance, skill, physical demands, stamina, flexibility, and a number of other scales. It's considered to be the second most difficult and challenging sport in the world (soccer takes the number one slot).

Until you have taken ballet classes yourself, it's impossible to know just how much work goes into creating the gracefulness within these ballerinas.

Ballet dancers move with incredibly refinement, elegance, beauty, and softness. Yet there is so much strength, control, and discipline of character that goes on behind it all, but to the audience, it appears to be conducted with such precision and ease.

Audrey Hepburn attributes much of her stance and poise to her absolute devotion to ballet during her younger years. She wanted to be a ballet dancer but was deemed too tall. She turned to acting to supplement her income and, voila, the rest, as you know, is history.

> "When we relax we never get sloppy...Dancers learn to feel when their posture is not graceful." –Audrey Hepburn (*abridged quote*)

Ballet for Elegance Training

It is not surprising that many mothers sign up their tiny tots for baby ballet. Rather than wishing their daughters become prima ballerinas, they merely want their offspring to attain good posture, grace, and poise.

Ballet students need discipline and relentless ambition. They have to adhere religiously to the following:

- Stretching every day for twenty minutes to one hour.
- Maintaining a very strict diet.
- Attending a class three times a week, minimum.
- Forming a regular sleep pattern and maintaining it at all times.
- Focusing on getting accepted into a good ballet school.
- Learning how to audition and handle rejection.
- Aim to get a job with a prestigious ballet company.
- Spending a fair amount of money on classes, ballet gear, etc.

It's not just another activity. Ballet is pure devotion to the art, period.

As you can imagine, there was a lot of work and research that went into developing the art of ballet. In ballet class, the exercises that are used are extremely different from your usual jogging, aerobics, cycling, step classes, etc.

Many of these exercises develop the inner thighs which slim the thigh instead of bulking the muscles. We don't really get to use the inner thigh too much in our everyday lives, so it is important to focus on it. Ballet exercises also strengthen your ankles, back, and even your upper and lower abdomen, without all those nasty stomach crunches. That doesn't mean these exercises are easy, not at all, but they are effective and they are different.

I remember my ballet teacher telling us to jump in five sets of 16. And we had to point our toes upwards as hard as we could, while maintaining a very still, lifted body posture. We were also required to keep a calm face (and not pant).The arms had to be held gracefully (including the fingers), and each landing had to be soft, and definitely not with a "thump".

It was incredibly hard to do, but the idea was to make it look easy and effortless. That is why in ballet, professional dancers always make their moves looks so easy, perhaps to the point where you yourself might even dare to think, 'Hey, I could do that!'

Recently, when Pilates and yoga became popular, I noticed a few exercises that resembled those used in ballet. The probable difference is that ballet is always performed upright at the barre, and in the center of the studio without support.

I first started ballet lessons when I was about five years old, but quit after a few years because all my friends had left the class.

Without my friends I lost interest and stopped going, much to my regret later. I picked up ballet again in my late teens, and at this time I came to understand and appreciate its value for developing elegance. I vowed never to leave it again and became somewhat obsessed with the art. I was dancing

3-4 times a week at a ballet school and university at the same time. Even though I ached perpetually, I was determined that nothing and nobody was going to get in the way of my renewed appreciation of this dance.

I am not practicing to be a professional ballet dancer, I'm merely exploiting it for the great benefits it provides, such as, exercise, maintaining flexibility, strengthening posture, and so on. I have a couple of friends who had back problems in the past, and their doctors recommend ballet classes as a way of healing.

Personally, I've always been a dancer, so embracing it is an effortless activity for me. I love dance and I especially love the art of this type of dance. None other is as graceful or as beautiful as ballet, which, by the way, is one of the oldest forms of dance in the world. Think of ballet as dancing for elegance!

Your First Adult Ballet Class

Things you'll need for class:

You'll need a pair of ballet shoes, obviously, regular 'gym' clothes, preferably with a pair of tights that taper to your ankles so that the teacher can see your movements clearer.

This attire is more acceptable now than in the past when a leotard, ballet tights, and hair neatly tied up in a bun was required. I still try to make an effort to dress this way so that my mind is 'in the zone', if you know what I mean.

Call to check if the ballet class you are taking is for absolute beginners. If you are not too concerned, just go for it, monkey-see-monkey-do style! If you feel intimidated, you can watch a few videos that introduce you to a few ballet terms and offer insight into what goes on in a class.

Check out adult-ballet.org if you are interested in taking up ballet for all its benefits in terms of developing elegance.

What Is Poise and How to Be a Woman of Poise

There's something quite delicate about how women once stood. A few generations ago, every well-bred young girl was given lessons on posture.

Today we send our young daughters for dance lessons and enter them into beauty pageants, in hopes that they will grow up to be graceful young women.

Have you ever wondered why so few women today are poised? Maybe it's because we do not place value on posture, manners, and behavior as much as we did in the past? I decided to research the subject further.

To begin, I found examples of elegant women who were also very poised:

- Audrey Hepburn
- Coco Chanel .
- Bree Van de Kamp (character in *Desperate Housewives*)
- Ashley Judd in *De-lovely*.
- Melinda Clarke (as Julie Cooper in the televisions show, *The O.C.*)
- Blair Waldorf & Lily Van der Woodsen (in the television show *Gossip Girl*).
- Wing Cheng, wife of Ip Man in the movie *Ip Man*.

I'm inspired by the way these women maintained their poise when insulted or when caught in an embarrassing situation.

The Definition of Poise

Poise is composure and dignity of manners. It is a graceful and elegant bearing in a person. I believe elegance and poise come together, though poise is perhaps best defined as a fruit of elegance. In other words, you have to learn to be elegant first.

There are occasions where you can be poised without necessarily being elegant, just as you can be composed even though you've walked into an important meeting late and looking disheveled.

In my opinion, I feel that being poised is not just about having composure, but dignity as well. A poised person has elegant mannerisms. The movements of her body have a lot of style. It's the manner in which she walks, talks, and the way she carries herself. She is fluid and gentle, yet strong and purposeful.

You can't take your eyes off a woman with genuine poise. You watch as she gets out of the car, smiles at the doorman, and says "thank you". She walks to the front door, which is already opened for her. She pauses for a moment, and her eyes smile as she walks towards the person waiting for her. She is quite unaware of the impact her presence has on the atmosphere in the room.

My Favorite Quote on Poise

I came across this passage in an article once. I liked it so much that I saved it, though I can't remember where it was from. For me, it embodies the essence of poise.

> *I almost ran straight into her in the lobby of a French hotel. I turned a corner, and she was coming the other way, walking quickly, surrounded by a pack of photographers and journalists. She seemed oblivious to the frenzy, to the babble and camera flash: the expression on her face was remote and introspective. This became an abiding image for me of celebrity containment, of self-protected glamour wrapped in a bubble of poise.*

Have you figured out what the opposite of poise is? You can spot it a mile away! Just think clumsy, awkward, and clunky.

So How Do You Acquire Poise?

Study the lessons of elegance so that you maintain an attitude of grace and composure. Also improve your posture if necessary. Posture plays a big part in the visual element of poise.

Remember the definition of poise:

Poise is **composure** and **dignity of manner** and the **graceful** and **elegant bearing** in a person.

Develop Poise for Beauty and Grace

How can we develop poise? Poise in a lady is a beautiful thing. It is one of the signatures of an elegant woman. Poise is the beauty of being in the moment, of being unrushed, and the exquisiteness of sitting still.

Wouldn't it be just fantastic to look graceful from every angle, and to be free from awkwardness, stumbling, and gruff gestures. But developing poise takes time. If only we could acquire it all today!

To develop poise, one must study herself and increase self-awareness of how she communicates through her movements. If she stirs her coffee, she does so quietly. If someone is standing across from her talking, she listens politely and attentively, without fidgeting, looking at her watch or phone, or letting her eyes wander.

As we develop poise, sometimes we can feel very self-conscious. The only way to combat this is to practice and proceed with certitude. Don't worry about making mistakes because mistakes often lead to our most valuable lessons.

Developing poise is a process that involves ridding our bad habits by developing new, much improved ones. It is also a matter of retraining our body's behaviors, and we have to relearn to walk, sit, and move in a different way. It is known as muscle memory.

The old rule of the book: Balance one on your head!

History of Poise Development

All princesses have a deportment trainer who guides them in all areas of social grace. Just like in the movie *The Princess Diaries*. Did you ever watch that film? This type of trainer has existed since a long time ago, even during Biblical times. We can see its existence from the book of Esther in the Bible.

The Story of the Common Girl Who Became Queen

The king organized a big feast and had many important guests. He ordered his wife Vashti to display her beauty before the guests. She refused to come. He got mad and removed her as queen. He then orders all "beautiful young girls to be presented to him", so he can choose a new queen.

Quoting from the Bible (Esther, Chapter 2):

(The following numbers are verses or sentence numbers)

8. When the king's order and edict had been proclaimed, many girls were brought to the citadel of Susa and put under the care of Hegai. Esther also was taken to the king's palace and entrusted to Hegai, who had charge of the harem. (Hegai was the royal trainer.)
9. The girl pleased him and won his favor. Immediately he provided her with her beauty treatments and special food. He assigned to her seven maids selected from the king's palace and moved her and her maids into the best place in the harem. (Why did he do that? See how Esther won his favor in verse 15.)

10. Esther had not revealed her nationality and family background, because Mordecai had forbidden her to do so.

11. Every day he walked back and forth near the courtyard of the harem to find out how Esther was and what was happening to her.

12. Before a girl's turn came to go in to King Xerxes, she had to complete twelve months of beauty treatments prescribed for the women, six months with oil of myrrh and six with perfumes and cosmetics.

13. And this is how she would go to the king: Anything she wanted was given her to take with her from the harem to the king's palace.

14. In the evening she would go there and in the morning return to another part of the harem to the care of Shaashgaz, the king's eunuch who was in charge of the concubines. She would not return to the king unless he was pleased with her and summoned her by name.

15. When the turn came for Esther (the girl Mordecai had adopted, the daughter of his uncle Abihail), to go to the king, she asked for nothing other than what Hegai, the king's eunuch who was in charge of the harem, suggested.

Imagine Being Singled out for Royal Treatment?

(Other girls turned into divas, but Esther remained humble. And she won the favor of everyone who saw her.)

16. She was taken to King Xerxes in the royal residence in the tenth month, the month of Tebeth, in the seventh year of his reign.

17. Now the king was attracted to Esther more than to any of the other women, and she won his favor and approval more than any of the other virgins. So he set a royal crown on her head and made her queen instead of Vashti.

18. And the king gave a great banquet, Esther's banquet, for all his nobles and officials. He proclaimed a holiday throughout the provinces and distributed gifts with royal liberality.

The moral of this section is that Esther won the king with her poise!

Definition of Poise: Graceful elegant bearing in a person, composure, and dignity of manner.

Imagine Training for One Year in Beauty and Poise?

Grace Kelly begged for a voice recorder at the age of 18 from her father, and she worked terribly hard to remove her 'country' accent because she wanted to elevate herself. She is now an icon of eternal elegance and poise.

Both the book and film versions of *Memoirs of a Geisha*, allowed us to peek into the fascinating world of women who devoted their lives to beauty and mastering the art of a woman's form.

In the movie, *Memoirs of a Geisha*, little geishas-in-training are shown learning how to develop poise. They practice siting and then getting up from a seated position. "Not like a horse!" Michelle Yeoh, acting as the trainer, would say.

Learning how to develop poise is like learning to put on makeup, but for the body! While you apply makeup to present your best possible face, poise is putting your best presentation out into the world.

Obviously we don't have to train ourselves to please and entertain men. Rather, the take-away message here for developing poise is that it is something we do for ourselves, which is more than enough.

More on How to Develop Poise

So far, I haven't found anything or anyone that gives in-depth training on poise. No books, no classes, not even personal trainers. But I would love to see a society made up of poised confident women (us!). Our goals to communicate composure, dignity, respect, and graceful movements can all be achieved through poise.

Here are some basic steps on how to develop these attributes:

Dress Your Best

Dress your best because dressing well gives you the confidence of knowing that you look great. There is a positive psychological impact to feeling confident. Your body, in turn, responds to your thoughts and projects how you feel.

Videotape Yourself

Most of our digital cameras and cell phones have a handy little recording function these days. Have someone film you as you walk; video the way you sit, stand, talk, laugh, eat, drink, etc. It is through awareness that we get a better understanding of our actions. That understanding will help us to better edit ourselves, both consciously and subconsciously.

Study Your Walk

There is a misconception that girls think they have to strut like a model for a beautiful walk. Get rid of the supermodel walk. It is reserved for the catwalk and is definitely not an everyday walk.

My dance teacher once told me that to develop a graceful posture I should imagine a string in the middle of my chest gently pulling upwards, but without overarching the back.

To be honest with you, even after many years of practice, I'm still working on my walk! I have made some good progress in correcting a number of bad habits, but there's still some way to go. Be patient with yourself and persistent in your efforts.

Fifty years ago, it was very common for girls to be taught how to walk. These lessons existed in schools, not specialty or finishing schools, but all schools. I wonder why it's no longer a requirement to learn how to walk properly? Learning to walk the 'right' way is important. It helps us to breathe better, plus it helps us learn how to sit and use our bodies ergonomically. Walking correctly is also good for health, helps with self-confidence, and self-esteem. It definitely projects elegance.

Part of Audrey Hepburn's charm, I believe, was attributed to her very beautiful walk.
It is certainly no easy task correcting a walk and learning how to move more beautifully with dignity and grace. If you watch movies from the Victorian times, actresses had to portray a perfect carriage and posture.
I'm sure you already know and have seen firsthand how ridiculous it looks to be perfectly dressed but unable to walk gracefully. Stylists can dress you well, but no one can be poised for you.

Elegant Posture with Extra Help

While the 'string in the middle of your chest' trick can help, I also wear a back brace from time to time that helps to shape my shoulders. It helps to keep them relaxed, down, and not rolled forward.
I use a LumbarWear as well, which is a kind of girdle that works on my lower back. I don't use corsets, but Victorian women did. It's no wonder they always had such great posture and poise, though corsets are not recommended.

Exercise for Poise and Posture

I've noticed that people who exercise regularly do not seem to have problems attaining good posture. With good carriage, half the battle is won in achieving an elegant poise. Dancing helps too, especially ballet and ballroom.

Keep Your Arms to Your Sides

Another tip to develop poise is to keep your arms close to your sides as much as you can, though in a relaxed way. When I took posture lessons, my instructor told me to constrict movements from the elbows as much as possible. Obviously, don't stick your arms to your slides as if they're glued there. If your shoulders are hunched upwards, it means your arms are held too tightly to the sides.

Don't Rush

To be poised is to never appear as though you're in a hurry, no matter what! Never walk too quickly or strut, making loud tapping sounds with your heels. Do not eat in a hurry, regardless of how hungry you happen to be. Take your time when unzipping or zipping up your purse. Be as quiet and as unhurried as possible in your actions. Be mindful not to slam car doors, house doors, fridge doors, or any other deeds that portray a hectic lifestyle.

Obviously, measured movements are harder in practice than in theory. Living in a fast-paced society doesn't make things any easier. If you find yourself scurrying around, it is either due to poor time management or you could be simply be taking on too much. Slow down and select (root word of elegance is *select*). Elegance is, after all, a way of life, and not an act to be put on when the time suites.

Be Gentle

There is a certain kind of chic gentleness in being poised. Gentle and elegant gestures increase our overall beauty. Clothes are not the only 'covering' we wear.

It is much easier to be gentle when you are kind and tender. Gentle is an all-encompassing word. If you're gentle towards little animals, you'll be gentle towards someone's feelings. You'll also probably not bang doors or slam things around if you have a gentle nature.

Smile Often and Laugh Softly

Being poised means having a gentle smile (ready and often) as well as soft harmonious laughter. Knee-slapping, hand-clapping, back slapping, or laughter with the mouth wide open and head tipped back do not contribute to poise. Laughing very loudly, especially in restaurants and other public places, is not acceptable behavior for an elegant lady.

Watch Your Hands — Do Not Touch or Fidget

Some of us have difficulty keeping our hands under control. The problem with fidgety hands, and wanting to touch everything, is that it signals an inability to relax. If you want to develop poise, work on relaxation techniques.

Other no-no's include rummaging around in your purse, looking at your phone every few seconds, touching your face, fiddling with your hair, and so on. It is good to practice restraint.

Have a Deep Respect for Others and Things around You

I've observed that women with poise seem to have a deep respect for other people and things around them. For instance, they leave a place the way they found it. They are not ones to touch things that don't belong to them, unless invited of course. If they borrow something, it is returned in the exact same condition (or sometimes better) they received it.

They'll never leave a hotel room in a complete mess just because they don't have to clean it up. They won't drive a rental a car in a way they wouldn't drive their own. You'll never catch them saying, "Who cares? It's only rented". They'll also never steal blankets from airplanes, etc.

Conclusion on How to Develop Poise

Tips on how to develop poise:

- Dress your best at all times.
- Videotape yourself (observe and improve).
- Study the way you walk.
- Work on developing an elegant posture (with aids if need be).
- Exercise for poise and posture.
- Keep your arms loosely at your sides.
- Never rush or do things in a hurry.
- Be gentle.
- Smile often, laugh softly.
- Watch your hands; do not fidget.
- Have a deep respect for others and things around you.

A Beautiful and Elegant Countenance

"The thought-life behind a beautiful and elegant countenance is an elegant spirit. These are the very first steps to Elegance – Eunice Leong"

What do you wear on your face? What kind of face do you deserve? What does your face really say about you?
Some of those questions might sound a little startling, but they are meant to drive home a point, and that point is you can

grow into beauty and elegance — it is not something you have to be born with. So don't lose hope!

Not everyone is born with great looks, but everyone can become a gentle and elegant spirit, to look at others with kind eyes and literally grow lovely and radiate their inner beauty. So how can you achieve this? Well, it is done by influencing your countenance.

Countenance is defined as, "a person's face or facial expression". I think it is best described as the face you wear when you're 'in limbo'. It is the face and expression you have when you are walking by yourself to the mall, or when you're driving or waiting for a bus. You might just be standing around at a party, not knowing anyone and waiting for your friend(s) to arrive. This is what I mean by 'in limbo'.

A facial expression has influence. It's why some people simply look approachable and nice, whereas others do not. A face that is pleasing to the eye can say a lot about a woman's character. They do not have to wear or carry designer labels to have a refined look. They appear naturally pleasant, intelligent, classy, and confident. There is no doubt in your mind that such a person is elegant. Thailand, for example, is a very popular destination for tourists because the people always appear welcoming and happy. This is why it's called the 'Land of Smiles'.

Countenance Is a Form of Communication

Facial expressions and countenances give off different vibes. For starters, try people-watching. Observe the expressions of individuals walking down the street, dining at a restaurant, or waiting for a train.

Make a subtle observation of people at a party or event. You can tell almost immediately who is confident or shy, awkward, warm and friendly, cold and distant, uninterested, or too eager.

Even if you don't openly observe, your subconscious mind takes in the 'countenance' of the person in your company. Sometimes you feel warm and welcomed. Other times, you feel as though there is an invisible barrier. Their tight smiles, icy stares, or insecurity are subconscious visual and nonverbal cues.

Try putting yourself in those shoes and ask these questions:
- What signals and visual cues are you giving to others?
- What does your face say about you?
- What expression are you wearing on your face?

Most people aren't aware that their thoughts, feelings, moods, and emotions show up visibly on their face. These are their facial expressions during 'limbo' mode, and are what make up their countenance.
 While we cannot control other people's countenance, we can influence our own. We subconsciously wear a facial expression that is similar to the screen saver of a computer screen. If you're now reading in a public place, just take a moment to look up and around and observe the following:

1. What kinds of facial expressions do you see on others?

2. What kinds of impressions are they forming on you?

Think about what the person is like and try to fathom their story if you can.

Does the lady to the right look like a stay-at-home-mother doing grocery shopping? Maybe the man in a hurry is a corporate executive who has just finished lunch and is now on his way to a meeting. What about the young man walking towards you, is he a university student heading off to the library perhaps?
 You can almost guess what each person is like and imagine their story. You may be able to estimate their social status accurately too. (Please don't take this as a judgment or exercise of prejudice — this is to simply illustrate the natural behavior of human assessment. You are not to treat anyone differently based on social status or anything else.)

Now, think about your own facial expression. If you can, have someone take a photo of you while you're doing something. It's best if you are not aware that your photo is being taken. You could be working on the computer, watching television, walking to school, or any typical action. Ask a family member or friend to take spontaneous snaps of you over the coming days, but without your awareness.

I had a few unintentional pictures taken of me a couple of years back. To be perfectly honest with you, I was totally shocked at my own facial expressions! I came over in the images as someone with the weight of the world resting heavily on their shoulders. I looked both worried and grumpy.

So just how do these facial expressions form? There are two explanations; one is by your thoughts alone, and the other is contingent on the current state of your life at a particular time.

Your facial expression and peace of mind are also affected by your lifestyle. Are you, like so many others in modern society, exhausted, stressed, or always in a mad rush?

I'm sure we all have some sort of chaos in our lives, obviously some more than others. For instance, you might have three very young children or you're a working single mom. If you're younger, then your pandemonium likely derives from a very busy school life, where you have to juggle jobs and education as you pay your way through college.

The reasons are endless, and in many cases, we have no idea why it's such hard work being who we are. One thing is certain though, and that is there can be no peace or serenity when we're having a tough time with daily living. However, there are some ways that may help solve the problem(s). One of the techniques is to minimize commitments, reduce clutter, and try to keep things better organized. Cutting out what's not necessary, be that people, events, and stuff in general is a surefire way to introduce a little more peace into your everyday life.

I'm sure we all try to be neat and tidy in more ways than one, but we don't all achieve it. If you are not born organized (like me), don't worry, there is help out there for you. For example, I love the site, Flylady.net for helping me get the housework done and clutter cleared. I lapse from time to time and have to go back to Flylady for that extra help and motivation. I'm just grateful that the site is there for people just like me.

There are several great cookbooks for the messy food planner too. I especially love the simple and healthy ones. It is possible to make nutritious meals that take very little time to prepare.

Thoughts also affect your facial expressions. In fact, most of our facial appearances originate from thought. Think of happy and peaceful things. Avoid pondering work or the next task at hand. Get a journal to offload your thoughts and worries. You'll be surprised at the clarity you might obtain. Write down all your chores, then prioritize them into a checklist and tick them off as you work through them. There's a great deal of satisfaction that comes from visible accomplishments (as in the priority check list).

Oh, and please don't forget humor. Thinking about things that make you chuckle is not only great for lifting spirits, but a good laugh has actually been proven to be beneficial for health and wellbeing (both physical and mental).

Another personal recommendation I would make is to join a church. Not just attend church, but participate in the church community. The best choice would be to some sort of ministry that requires you to serve others. Be an usher, the church booklet designer, the pianist, or coffee maker. Sing in the choir, take care of the little ones, and dance in church performances.

If you're not a Christian, you can volunteer for a non-profit organization that serves a cause that you believe in. Serving others reduces negative self-absorbed thoughts that we have of ourselves as we gain a larger perspective of others around us. Sometimes, all we need is to hear of others in help, and that really puts things into perspective. We realize how blessed we are and how small our problems may be. The act of reaching out to others and helping them offers joy and fulfillment like no other activity.

We Can Grow Beautiful

Our desires to grow beautiful can manifest when we have an elegant countenance because that comes from within us. Inner beauty influences outer beauty, and inner beauty is more enduring. It goes way beyond powerful makeup.

We've all had those moments when the atmosphere of a room changes because a very elegant lady walks in. She has a sort of majestic air about her that commands respect, although she is very gracious. You don't know who she is, but in your mind's eye you think she's probably someone very important. You almost gawk as you admire her from a distance.

Then, there are some who are very pretty, but they give off a sour vibe. Pretty is not the same as beautiful. You'll feel as though you've got a hunch that tells you she's not a very nice person. Then you'll discover you are right the moment she starts to speak, or when you see her in action. Suddenly, she is not pretty anymore.

That is probably why some faces (pretty or not), look elegant whereas others don't. Even 'plain' faces can look elegant, smarter, classier, and wealthier than the pretty ones. Why? Well, it's a number of factors. Things such as the language they speak, the makeup they wear, their clothes, their education, and so on, do help. But alone, none of the above is enough. These things do matter to a certain degree, but it is their countenance, the non-verbal cues, that leave the right impressions on those around them.

Ines de la Fressange says: *"You can go out and hate everybody, hate your age, and hate all the things you don't have, but it will show; you have the face you deserve."*

I've also said before that whatever is in your heart turns up on your face, irrespective of our regular beauty treatments. None of it matters much if we don't **look after our heart**.

Proverbs 4:23 states:
"Above all else, guard your heart, for it is the wellspring of life."

What Does It Mean to Guard Our Heart?

There are many things you can do to guard your heart. Honestly, in my opinion, this is the very FIRST step to elegance.

Henry Fielding must have had a moment of revelation when he wrote: *"A truly elegant taste is generally accompanied with excellency of heart."*

Personally, for me, this means to exercise restraint, edit, andfeed myself with good quality thoughts and actions. I find that praying, meditating, and reading daily reading in my Devotional and other good books to be really helpful. Listening to a good message or sermon CD is something else that encourages and uplifts me.

Going to church weekly keeps my internal life in check, as does being involved in a charity or ministry that allows me to serve others. These things help me keep the focus away from myself. Wallowing in one's own problems and thinking too much about I, I, I, me, me, me can be a toxic way to live.

I edit my life constantly, just like a graceful woman edits her elegant wardrobe. Editing is a form of refining and refinement. I try my very best to refrain from thinking negatively or complaining about things. I also hold back from watching, owning, or reading any bad material or buying low-quality items. I try to exercise discipline by limiting the number of possessions I have, and from having too much of anything in particular.

But to be perfectly honest, I feel that all of above are much easier to implement when I live a spiritual life.

How to Be Gentle

Lessons on how to be gentle are derived from elegant women who possess poise and grace that are inspiring to all of us. It all began when I asked my friend the following, "How is it that you're so gentle?" He told me that he was gentle as a child. He attributes that to his calm personality. But being gentle does not mean a lack of passion or strength. He went on to be a competitive tennis player and a well-known tennis coach.

Gentleness can be seen as passion and strength directed inward, instead of outwards. This sparked my curiosity on how to achieve the same effect if we are not born with gentle-inclined personalities.

There are many misconceptions of being gentle. It is often associated with weakness and fragility. But I'm not here to dispute the concept of what 'being gentle' means to others.

Maybe you grew up with parents who yelled often, and so you learned to yell. You tend to stumble, drop things, spill coffee. You can't seem to speak softly on the phone but have the tendency to say too much, too fast, and a tad too loud. We all have these struggles to various degrees. So do we refine ourselves and betray our roots to mimic the **beautiful refined gentleness of graceful women**? Thus, I want to focus on the gentle movements and deportment of an elegant woman.

Elegant Women Are Gentle

Elegant women are gentle. There is no disputing that. We notice their gentle nature. They are gentle in all ways; with their words, even in the manner in which they pour tea or tie a ribbon on a present. The way they touch, brush, make sweeping movements, cuddle children or pat little dogs is altogether lovely. So how do we become gentle and where does one start?

Slow Down, Declutter, Obtain Peace

In my book, Secrets of Elegance, I talked a little bit about achieving authenticity (being who you are), the importance of having a devotional to read, editing both yourself and your wardrobe, and **obtaining peace**.

One of the concepts of that book is how **peace is important to elegance**, and how we should remove anything that does not give us peace (i.e., anything that causes stress). Similarly, it is a lot easier to be gentle if you are peaceful from within.

Editing is very much a process of achieving elegance and **we must get rid of "too much"**. This includes too much stuff, too much on our schedules, too much commitment, expectations, and demands.

Slow down. Meditate. Engage in peaceful, slow-moving activities that require patience, such as reading novels, painting, yoga, ballet, Tai Chi, sewing, knitting, etc. With a slowed-down and simpler life, we have a greater propensity to learn how to be gentle. We need not be in a hurry and we will never have to rush again.

Have Corresponding Values for Gentleness
Value People

If you value others, you will be more patient with their shortcomings and learn how to be gentle. You will be kind and considerate and punctual because you won't want to keep valuable people waiting.

Value What You Have

I have this theory of telling whether a person values her things by how much she has of that particular item. If she has too much of something, it shows that, contrary to what she thinks, she doesn't value her things as much. If she understands she truly values for instance, her sunglasses, she'll know that one or a few is more than enough. She will not be out looking for yet another 'perfect' pair. Also, my point is, if you value something, would you abuse it and throw it around, or leave it lying in some random place in the house? More likely you will take care of it, treat it with respect, and use it regularly but carefully.

The act of using something preciously shows that you value your things. Unfortunately in our era of wealth, we acquire things easily, and therefore take no pains to treasure them. Likewise, manufacturers realize this so we are bombarded with inferior goods with shiny promises. This reminds me of what many of our grandmothers say, "They don't make them like they used to!"

I recently watched a cute video on how to teach your child to be gentle. The video emphasized the **"One Finger Touch",** which I thought could apply very well to ourselves. When we teach our children how to be gentle, we show them to use **one finger to touch** something first, instead of grabbing.

Similarly, we can **pretend that everything is made of glass or gold** and we carefully pick up or put down when using it. Now, would you rashly grab something that costs $100,000? This is another reason why we should buy good quality things for ourselves, instead of spending the same amount on a whole bunch of non-lasting stuff. By valuing our things and practicing this habit of being gentle and light, we will learn how to be **gentle and graceful women.**

Elegant Japan

Side note: While visiting Japan, I was able to learn a little bit of the elegant culture in a traditional Japanese tea house, where my host taught me how to sit properly, hold a Japanese tea cup, position it properly to drink, and the way to eat Japanese mochi (flour snack). I was as graceless as one can be. While in the tea house, we were instructed to take off our shoes and move as quietly as possible in within hollow-ish rooms. Once seated, we ordered our tea and snack. The tea was mysterious tasting and did not taste like the 1,000 cups of green tea I'd had before this experience.

I had a good time learning Japanese tea etiquette but I struggled when it came to the flour sweet cake. I couldn't put the whole thing in my mouth, and so I resorted to using my chopstick (yes, just one) to "slice and chop" it into pieces suitable for placing in my mouth. I forgot my posture in my intense intent to cut the cake into pieces. My gracious host showed me the way. Who knew that by gentle tugging or pretending your chopsticks were a pencil and "drawing a line" through them you could make less of a scene of eating your mochi cake?

I admired the elegance of the whole process and realized that I had a lot to learn! Now, if I can remember this lesson every time I'm eating…

Be Gentle with Ourselves

In my research on how to be gentle, I stumbled upon a powerful life lesson derived from a *Time* magazine article about one woman's struggle against Alzheimer's disease. ("Alzheimer's Unlocked," from the October 25, 2010 issue) In the article, Mary Ann Becklenberg states, "Teach me to be gentle with myself". She keenly observed that **we are short on others because we are frustrated with ourselves**.

In order to be gentle, we have to not punish ourselves or beat ourselves up over a mistake. We have to learn to let things go, be easy-going, be chill. Strive for improvement but not perfection.

Have an Abundant Mindset

If you read works like the Bible and positive thinking books, they will show you how your thinking shapes your behavior. Having an abundant mindset aids you in learning how to be gentle.

"I learned that it is the weak who are cruel, and that gentleness is to be expected only from the strong." ~ Leo Rosten

To obtain a gentle spirit like Audrey Hepburn, focus on thinking well. Be aware of abundance, not what is lacking. That will cause you to be gentle...to take sufficient helpings instead of piling your food high on your plate for fear of not having enough.

Focusing on abundance will also allow you to be generous. You will be the one to let others walk out the elevator first (if you are not in their way) instead of rushing to be first out the door. It's okay to let the kind elderly woman use the restroom first, as you can wait for another three minutes. You have abundance!

You don't have to fight for your 'rights' because so what if you 'lost' the argument? Though it's not fair, you see it as a small matter, not worth you getting upset over. You have plenty of other blessings in your life to rejoice over. If it is worthy of your attention, you approach it in a gentle and firm manner. You don't have to react with drama to every issue that you face. The opposing party sees your poise in the matter, and often they will calm down, and now both parties can logically work the problem out.

How to be gentle requires a quiet strength that results from intelligence. Gentleness is more a **thinking** way of life rather than a way to make things happen by brute force.

Eat Well For Gentleness

Last but not least on the issue of gentleness, if you are the high energy, excitable sort, and you find it hard to control your 'hyperactivity', **you need to find a way to calm down**. Some find it helpful to wake up to peaceful melodious tunes in the morning, instead of a heart-stopping shrill ring of the alarm clock. Others practice yoga and meditation or quiet time in prayer.

Practice 'letting go' in your speech, for instance, if you are telling a story and get interrupted or intercepted by someone else, as you might feel a little angst that you can't finish your story. Chant in your head, "let it go", take a deep breath and continue listening to the conversation. If your story gets brought back into the conversation by an interested friend, you may continue. Otherwise, just let it go.

Eat well. If you tend to be too hyper, I suggest cutting down on carbohydrates (carbs) and sugar. Do not eat pasta, bread, or take sugar in your coffee/tea or drink soft drinks for breakfast. That is surely to send you off to a hyped-up start. Take in limited amounts throughout the day or avoid them altogether (refined carbs). Of course, you will need some carbohydrates in your diet, so eat those with slow burning capabilities like oats, wholegrain, Weetabix, etc.

10. Manners, Etiquette, and Acquiring Social Ease

Manners and Etiquette: How to Be Exquisite

Do you know that etiquette and manners is not the same thing? Most people usually agree that there is always room for improvement when it comes to their manners and etiquette.

I think the desire to improve and be a well-mannered person is a beautiful thing. By doing so, we are acting with love. Love is kind and patient, because with it, we are thinking about others before ourselves.

Why You Should Pay Attention to Your Manners

I loved the manners of Linda and Cole Porter in the movie *De-Lovely*. Have you ever met someone you really liked? She most probably had the most beautiful manners and made you feel at ease. She was a true lady, and just by her presence, she was able to bring out the best in you.

Without a doubt, the greatest test of elegance and refinement is a person's **manners**. Manners are wonderful to have. It makes a person beautiful. Manners are love, they are kindness, and they are refinement. I enjoy being in a family where everyone speaks kindly to each other. It is something you must cultivate in your kinfolk. It has to become the family culture. Having harmony in the home is a truly wonderful thing.

What Are Your Manners Saying About You?

- They tell other people who you are.
- How you were brought up

- The kind of family you have
- Your socio-economic status (or class)
- Your level of education
- The extent of your reading, travel, and other worldly experiences
- Your thoughts (self-absorbed narcissist, or a wonderful, inspirational person?)
- Your self-control, i.e. the way you handle conflict, what it is like to live with you, among other things.

A Little Secret about Manners

Here is a little secret to acquiring unusually refined manners. Despite any insecurities you might have, you can rise above all that and communicate a better sense of yourself (as opposed to reality or history), with fine, elegant manners. I love this quote:

"It is our choices that show what we truly are, far more than our abilities." ~ J. K. Rowling

In other words, when you have fine manners, you can be whoever you want to be. You can choose who you want to become. People won't even have a clue about your supposed lack of education, wealth, connections, and so on. They might even think way off the mark! That is, they may think much better of you than expected.

There will always be those times where you'll think you're just not good enough. You might feel that you aren't educated enough, sophisticated enough, or feel shamefaced because of your family's lack of resources. Perhaps you felt that you ruined any chance of successful living by not attending the right schools, or hanging out with the right people, etc.

Despite any of these insecurities, you can rise above by embracing the best, most beautiful, exquisite manners a person can possess. That is the little secret of having great manners. Let this little gem of wisdom empower you!

If you have impeccable manners, people will probably assume that you were educated at top schools. They'll like to be around you because of the way you make them feel. They'll feel impressed and inspired by who you are, and maybe even admire you in the privacy of their own heads.

If one day, you get 'found out', by that I mean it becomes known that you aren't from a wealthy family, or that you didn't get into Ivy League schools, you will realize that it no longer matters because you have assimilated. You've become one of them. You're now friends with people you like and choose to be friends with. And let's not forget, you haven't said to anyone you're wealthy, or highly educated; they may have formed this impression because of your grace and radiance.

At the end of the day, we are not interested in people who do not like us. We want to find friends of similar tastes and goals, people we can connect with naturally and relate to easily.

Whatever your social circle is, everyone likes those who are well-mannered. People who know how to conduct themselves appropriately are comfortable to be around. If that's you, don't worry about your supposed shortcomings. Just know that people like you. They want to be around you. They warm up to you. They think you're great. Nothing else matters. Manners are kindness, and people respond to kindness positively.

Speaking kindly to someone regardless of who they are or what their social standing happens to be is a show of respect. You are not one of those women going around leveling people, judging them on whether they are higher or lower than you, and treating them according to their place in society. That is rather crass, though it happens a lot. Being well dressed is pleasant and inspiring. Otherwise, it is distracting and negative. When you communicate with manners, you've considered the other person's thoughts and feelings. That is sincere kindness.

However, it needs to be clarified that manners are NOT etiquette. Here we look at why manners are not the same as etiquette. Manners are the result of a kind heart. Etiquette is an orderly way of doing things and a customary code of conduct and good behavior. Etiquette is like the law but **it is not the law**. If you have ever read books on etiquette, you may already know this.

In general, etiquette is a list of (almost boring) rules. While some are helpful, others can get quite nonsensical. I'm not saying we should shun reading etiquette books from time to time, because we shouldn't, but trying to memorize etiquette rules is rather an insane and somewhat overwhelming task. It's simply impossible to remember them all.

Manners, on the other hand, are a result of graciousness. Having manners is a telltale sign that one possesses grace.

An elegant person, despite wearing a pretty dress, poised, and looking gorgeous can still be far from possessing true elegance when her face turns sour as she complains bitterly about something or someone.

How to Have Both Manners and Etiquette

If you have manners first, etiquette will follow. Etiquette is a list of well thought out rules that present themselves as an orderly way of doing things; a way that materializes in the most considerate, conflict-avoiding manner. Having good manners is also about **putting up with the bad manners of others**.

I t's easy to get offended, especially when you've put considerable effort into refining your manners, yet someone else has done nothing to improve theirs. How tempting it is to say, "She's so rude!" and get on the verbal complaints wagon.

Firstly, the harsh expression that will appear on your face is not exactly becoming. Secondly, you can still be gracious in spite of the behavior of others. In reality, most people have good intentions, but do not realize their offence.

Always try to be patient and see others in the best light. There is good in us all, even though it might not always be obvious.

An Elegant Woman's Etiquette
Why Is Etiquette so Important?

Elegantwoman.org focuses on *Elegant Living* and *How to Be a Lady*, and is not so much an 'etiquette site', though I still recommend you study the topic loosely, and here's why.

It is a subject associated with elegance. It is the fruit of good manners, kindness, and the consideration of others. Etiquette presents an orderly way of doing and saying things.

However, I don't believe in memorizing the rules of etiquette. I'd much rather see them used as guidelines. I do not enjoy rules and I've never believed in 'governing' through rules. I've always believed refinement comes from within.

If you're looking for specific etiquette topics then simply do a search on elegantwoman.org. You can also visit the index of *Etiquette Articles*.

Etiquette Basics

So here I am, tackling just the very basics of etiquette, only pausing to refer to Miss Manners or Emily Post, just to grab a second opinion on what I've researched from personal experience, observation, interviews, film history, and lessons indirectly taken from history. Then there's the traditional training of a princess, finishing and charm schools, and old books from noble authors like Jane Austen.

The Definition of Etiquette

Wikipedia defines etiquette as follows: Etiquette is a code of behavior that influences expectations for social behavior according to contemporary conventional norms within a society, social class, or group. Rules of etiquette are usually unwritten, but aspects of etiquette have been codified from time to time.

Rules of etiquette encompass most aspects of social interaction in any society, though the term itself is not commonly used. A rule of etiquette may reflect an underlying ethical code, or it may reflect a person's fashion or status.

The Differences between Manners and Etiquette

Manners are not the same as etiquette. What is the difference?

To be honest, I'm not a huge fan of etiquette even though I believe it has its place. The reason I'm not a dedicated devotee to etiquette is because it seems as though etiquette is just a bunch of rules that are to be followed in order to attain it.

Those that take great pride in knowing a lot about etiquette can sometimes get offended by those who do not. That's just plain silly in my book. It would seem that there is some sort of grace within those rules, but there's not. Nobody should take offense at 'wrong etiquette'. If you can justify that the offending party has kind intentions, then their lack of etiquette, or mistake of sorts, is perfectly excusable. Etiquette, I believe, is a byproduct at the height of your refinement. Even if you don't read etiquette books, you will figure out what's right and proper, and what's not, sooner or later.

For those that do love rules though, I'll be writing three principles to help get you started. Use them as a framework to govern your polite behavior. While rules of etiquette change over time, along with the evolution of social norms and mores, these kindness principles never alter. Follow these values, and you'll *almost* never have to read another etiquette book again.

Etiquette Rules 101

1. Put others before yourself.
2. Make others feel at ease.
3. Always be kind and considerate.

Etiquette Tips

- Always ask yourself, "What is the kindest way possible of doing this thing?"
- Etiquette is not putting others first in a way where you completely abandon yourself.
- Etiquette rules should not be memorized because that is a miserable task. It should be born out of a kind and gracious spirit.
- Etiquette rules should be 'realized' and 'caught'.
- Etiquette differs from country to country depending on culture, language, and social norms. Never take offence at the differences in etiquette. Respect, learn, and accept those variances.
- When in Rome, do as the Romans do. Don't compare, don't criticize, just accept.
- Social etiquette is the most important because to master it's directly about being considerate towards others' feelings.

Being Elegant at Work

If you would like to be **elegant at work**, or if you need to travel around the world as part of your job, then I'm sure you would like to be internationally savvy. To accomplish this, you will need a combination of **professional and job etiquette skills**, as well as **knowledge of local cultures and traditions**.

Do Not Try to Memorize All the Etiquette Rules!

If nothing else, try to remember this one principle: To improve your awareness of etiquette, or to achieve excellent manners, **expose yourself to elegance and elegant women** as much as possible.

Read about them, find someone who is adept at these things and start to hang out with her. Remember, every decision you have ever made, or will ever make, has consequences, and the consequences of exposing yourself to elegance and elegant women are all good.

You can also watch and study movies with elegant actresses shot in elegant settings, in elegant time periods, etc. Watch how they move, speak, conduct themselves in general. See how they decorate their homes, entertain guests, dress, do their hair, and so on and so forth.

It is far better to be inspired and to have elegance and have etiquette rub off on you in the 'real world', than it is to spend a lovely afternoon engrossed in some stuffy old etiquette book that cannot update itself as quickly as the world evolves.

Start with visual inspirations, a memory, or a role model, as examples. Begin your journey with an earnest desire to be elegant. You can do it! Have courage, turn your thoughts into actions, and great things will come to pass.

The Art of Conversation

Seek "conversation topics" in a Miss Manners advice style-article, and learn about the importance of manners in conversation. Such advice is based on a book of manners by Emily Post.

The Good Conversationalist:

"Ideal conversation is an exchange of thought, not an eloquent exhibition of wit or oratory" ~ Emily Post's Etiquette

Contrary to popular belief, it is not essential to have a wide vocabulary or lots of experiences in order to master the art of effective conversation. A good conversationalist does not mean one has to be a naturally chatty person either.

Conversation is a two-way street. It's all about give and take. But how often are conversations all 'take' or all 'give'?

Self-Check Time

We've all seen the WORST types of conversationalists. These include:

- The one who never stops talking. Your turn to speak never comes.
- The one who interrupts.
- The one who gives monosyllabic answers.
- The one who always argues.
- The one who has no opinion.
- The one who sounds rude (and probably is rude).
- The one who asks too many prompting questions.

Now, don't fret if you identify yourself in the above.

ALL of us have been one of these bad conversationalists at some point or another. The aim of this section is to learn how to be a better conversationalist, so you're already on your way.

Don't Be Afraid to Pause

Emily Post Manners states there is a simple guideline that one can live by to keep from becoming a pest or a bore (which I think is pretty funny, by the way).

The golden rule to refrain from being a pest or a bore:
Stop and think!

Audrey Hepburn said her mother told her "I" in conversations is boring.

Don't Panic!

Not all of us are extroverts and born-naturals in the social scene, but that's no excuse to avoid social events. Remember, progress is within us all. *Emily Post Manners* says that if you dread meeting strangers because you might feel awkward, or fear not having anything to say, or perhaps just can't relate to the conversation, then don't panic.

"Most conversational errors are committed not by those who talk too little, but by those who talk too much."

If you can't think of anything to say, remember to ask general questions, and don't be afraid of pausing or saying something simple like, "Hmmm, that's an interesting point". Such tricks buy time.

Don't worry about the rest of the conversation; just one response at a time is all that's required of anyone. In fact it's all anyone can manage anyway.

Not from *Emily Post's Manners*, but my own personal experience of striking up conversations with strangers is to ask a few general questions. A bit of small talk is a great way to break the ice. I find this to be the best and easiest approach. After that, you can develop, or branch off naturally to a more interesting topic, especially if you discover some common interests. Otherwise, you can 'give' something of yourself and offer information to try and generate more topics of conversation.

For example, try describing something you have been doing lately, such as planning a trip, vacation, new hobby, cooking, food etc., but be mindful not to come across as boastful, but rather conversational.

Throw the ball in their court; ask for suggestions (keep it light-hearted and general), invite an opinion, some ideas, and show interest. Practice and you'll eventually be able to talk to anyone about most things, whether they're topics you're familiar with or not.

One tip to remember is this: try and avoid getting into a deep conversation with someone new for more than five minutes or so. At a party or other social settings, the idea is to move around and mingle. Don't linger or try to make a friendship out of a new person.

Less Talk, More Listening

Listening Is the Art of Conversation
- Really listen. The best conversationalists are those that say little and listen a lot.
- Look at the person when he/she is talking and pay attention, show interest.
- Don't interrupt.
- Don't give advice unless asked.
- Rely on sincerity, clarity, and an intelligent choice of subject.

Are You Giving a Speech?

Here's a funny passage that I just had to include. It goes something like this:
"If there are three participants in a conversation, and there's one who talks for more than one- third of the time, then that one isn't having a conversation, but giving a speech."

Thinking before Speaking

Emily Post is correct when she says that nearly all the faults in conversation are caused by a lack of consideration.
Think about whether the person you are talking to is interested in your topic, at least pointedly. Would a person who does not know anything about classical music be interested in the latest schedule of the San Francisco Orchestra?
The same can be said for newly engaged brides who talk incessantly about their wedding in the presence of their single

friends, or new parents who talk of their child as if no one else had ever had children.

Also, don't speak in another language in the presence of others who do not understand that tongue. Don't speak in your professional lingo either because if I'm not a doctor, I wouldn't appreciate anything you have to say in a conversation filled with medical terms that only other health professionals would understand.

Do employ tact. Use phrases like, "It seems to me..." or "Maybe I've misread..." (especially when someone insists on a piece of information). When disagreeing, do so gently with lots of polite disclaimers, otherwise the opponent will think you are calling him or her a liar.

Try to change the subject the minute you feel it might escalate into an argument or heated debate of sorts.

"I" is the smallest letter in the alphabet. Don't make it the largest word in your vocabulary." ~ Dorothy Sarnoff.

Good: *"What do you think?"*
Bad: *"I think..."*

Emily Post Etiquette Tips:

Pay compliments!
Responding to compliments:

For example, *"That's a beautiful dress!"*
Respond: *"Thank you very much! I'm so glad you like it."*

Don't belittle yourself and say, *"Oh, this isn't an inexpensive dress"* or, *"Oh it's an old dress"*, or *"Oh really? I don't think it's that nice"*. If you want to return the compliment, say "Oh yes, it's so hard to find a pretty dress these days, where did you get yours? I was admiring that too" (but only if you mean it).

How to Tell a Secret

Never tell anyone about a bra strap sticking out or a run in her stocking unless you are a close friend. But if you see an unzipped skirt, a popped out button, a smudge of makeup on her nose, or greens in her teeth, please tell her discretely. However, if you see a man's fly unzipped, do not tell him unless you are a dear friend. Better still, ask another male to tell him.

Converse with Class and How Not to Converse

This section is a continuation of *Emily Post Manners* on the art of conversation. Remember to see the message beyond the blunder. Sometimes all we need is to employ a bit of grace towards the blunderer, just as we would like grace extended to us in awkward moments.

"The secret of success in conversation is to be able to disagree without being disagreeable." ~ Unknown.
Now let's take a look at some tactless blunders.

Tactless Blunders

Guilty as charged. I'm sure all of us have made these mistakes at one time or another. I also wrote this list from personal experience, as someone from the receiving end. *Shudder!* I hope I'll never have to answer these questions again!

Some common blunders include:
- "What happened to your complexion?"
- "Are you really getting a divorce?"
- "Why aren't you married?" or, "Why don't you have a boyfriend?"
- "Are you seeing anyone special?" (Unless you're a close friend, never ask.)
- "What's the matter with your baby?"

- "Are you tired? You look tired." (Sigh, don't we all hate to get this comment.)
- "Have you had cosmetic surgery? Work done?"
- "I can't believe you dated her!"
- "How old are you?" (Which we can respond to with, "Old enough!")
- "What is your profit margin?"
- "How much do you make? Earn?"
- "Where do you source your products from?"
- "What is your secret recipe?" (Especially if he/she owns a restaurant.)

Common Blunderers

I'm sure we are all familiar with these conversational blunderers:
- The bragger
- The one who uses, "Oh, it is trés chic!"
- Conversational monopolies, story snatchers, and bores
- Correctors, patronizers, and condescenders
- Argumentative types
- The one who insults
- The one who uses slang
- The one who interrupts
- The name droppers
- The unfair conversational exchanger

- The snoop
- The one with wandering eyes
- The one who asks too many questions

The Bragger

A good conversationalist does not go on about how expensive her handbag is, what a wonderful job she did, or how talented her daughter is. Nor does she use big words that no one understands in order to try and sound sophisticated.

The Subtle Ways of Bragging:

I've seen it happen ever since social media, such as Facebook, Twitter, and blogs came about.

"Thank you to Singapore Airlines for bumping me up to first class!"
"I'm in an upscale restaurant in X, thanks to X."
"I'm such a foodie; I dine there at least once a month."

Well, it is their social medium after all, so all you can do is laugh at their bragging. When held captive of a braggart though, comment politely and redirect the conversation. If she has a fabulous story to tell you about herself, yet again, simply excuse yourself unless you are thoroughly enjoying listening to her (or him).

"Oh It Is Très Chic!"

Ahh, so you're in the midst of a pretentious girl who wants you to believe she is sophisticated. Sprinkling conversation with phrases from another language is also pretentious, unless it's a language you speak all the time, or there is no parallel. Whenever you're in the company of such a person, simply ignore it.

Example: "Oh, this definitely happened to me!"

Conversational Monopolies, Story Snatchers & Bores

It's good to self-check and listen to yourself talk.

How to Spot One:

Monopolizing a conversation, never giving anyone else the chance to agree or disagree, insisting they are right, the story-snatcher changes the topic from you to them, sometimes because they have a similar story or feel the need to outdo your story with a fabrication of their own. These types are insecure, ego driven, and poor company. Sometimes, they themselves have no idea of their behavior or as the quote below so aptly puts it:

"If only I could see myself the way others see me." ~ Unknown

Definition of a Bore: The one who talks about himself when you want to talk about yourself. (*Emily Post Etiquette*). When someone repeats a story, a kind way to let them know is by saying, *"Oh yes, I remember you telling me before."*

The Correctors, Patronizers, and Condescenders

My mother told me a story once of a woman who attempted to correct the pronunciation of someone in front of a group of ladies at church. She said, *"Now repeat after me..."*
       She had no business doing that. Never correct someone unless she or he is your spouse or child, or it is your name that they mispronounced. Just use the right word in your sentence and hope they notice.
       Some people just want to feel better than everybody else or they have a secret agenda of being jealous of you, which can also explain patronizing behavior.
       Try not to give advice if not solicited. It's hard not to be patronizing when giving advice and does take some

practice. There is not much you can do when being patronized or appearing defensive and angry, but you can say, *"Well I appreciate you trying to educate and simplify this for me, but I'm very familiar with ___ "*, and then move the conversation on calmly.

The Argumentative Type

These are the ones who are set on an opposing view and insist on being right no matter what! There is no point in arguing with people who have little EQ. Simply say: "You may be right, even though I see things differently, but who knows - really?"

Coping with Insults

I once told someone that I can't stand horror movies, and she made a derogatory remark in the form of a joke, and in front of others, *"Oh you'd better stick to the Legally Blonde types then!"* Grrr! What should I have done? I stared at her for a while, then managed a grim smile and changed the topic.

      Unless you are extremely close friends with someone, it's poor manners to insult them, even if it's in the form of a joke. If the joke went on, or becomes too much to 'let it go', tell the speaker frankly that you find her remarks objectionable, then either walk away or change the subject.

Point to note: Laughing with someone is quite different than laughing at them!

Slang

Make an effort to speak properly and avoid slang because they can become distracting. The excessive use of, *"Hmmm"*, *"Like..."*, *"You know"*, *"You know what I mean?"*, *"Really?"* and many others are not generally appreciated.

      I once had an American lecturer teach me at university. He punctuated with "you know" during each and every lesson. It was highly annoying so we decided to amuse ourselves by it. We decided to count the number of "you knows" in a single class. Once we counted up 51 in a single hour. That's almost one for every minute!

The Interrupters

Only interrupt someone if it's an emergency. That's it! If you're interrupted, listen politely for a few seconds and then finish your sentence. Don't finish someone's sentence unless they appear to be struggling.

The Name Droppers

Most name droppers try too hard to impress others and want people to feel they are important and well connected. It's all too obvious, actually. It's best to act unimpressed, though it will probably do little to change their habits with others, but they may refrain from name-dropping to you in the future.

After listening to a name-dropper talk and realizing how insecure she sounds by bragging about her association with various well-known and respected acquaintances, you might end up feeling disgust. If you do, remind yourself that you will never take advantage of famous or important people you know, by dropping their names in conversation as an attempt to influence your company.

The Unfair Conversational Exchanger

If you want to exchange information, you'd better be willing to spill the beans on your end of the deal.

The Secret

Never whisper in the presence of others or cup your hand over the ear on an individual to tell them information (gossip) about someone else. Again, refrain from speaking in a foreign language when others within the group don't understand it. That is extremely disrespectful.

The Snoop

How do you answer personal questions about the cost of a gift, renovations, a dress, etc.? We are under no obligation to disclose that information and there is no polite way of saying, "It's none of your business". As flimsy an excuse as it sounds, *"I don't know", or "I honestly don't remember what it costs"* are better responses. Inquiring about money matters is usually in poor taste, no matter how politely the question is asked.

Another famously snoopy question that seems to be 'accepted' everywhere is, *"What do you do?"* A good response is: *"Oh I'd rather not talk about that if you don't mind? It's the weekend, and I promise myself never to talk about work in leisure time!"*

The Wandering Eye

Never let your eyes wander around the room when someone is talking to you. It indicates a lack of interest and its distracting, not to mention extremely rude.

The One Who Asks Too Many Questions

You get an idea that you are asking too many questions when you are given replies in short simple answers that lack details.

Other styles of questions are direct questions, such as *"Is his family rich?"* or, *"Is she from a wealthy family?" "How much did you pay for your wedding dinner?" "How much does that cost?"* (It's akin to being socially interrogated.) Questions like these are highly inappropriate.

Gosh! I've experienced these sorts of questions too many times to count. I feel absolutely uncomfortable in these situations. You get to know it's not a real conversation when it starts to sound like a Question and Answer session.

My Favorite Conversational Reminders

"There are seldom regrets for what you have left unsaid." ~ Peggy Post
"Better to keep your mouth closed and be thought a fool than open it and remove all doubt." ~ Bible

I like to read this page over again because none of us are perfect. These examples serve as a good reminder, something worth reflecting on periodically, especially before going to a party or other social gathering!

Social Ease: Grace Your Way through Parties

How to Be an Elegant Social Butterfly

Grace your way through any party with elegant communication. As you increase in elegance, you will more than likely get invited to more parties and events. Being elegant socially is always about other people, isn't it? The greater your confidence grows, you might want to start to reciprocate all those social invitations and host some parties of your own. But let's first start with the basics!

Social Confidence

The most important aspect to gaining social confidence is to believe that we are all human. Of course, we may well be different from one another, but being different does NOT mean we're any better or worse than the next person, regardless of outward appearances.

At any social event, your 'goal' is to make someone else comfortable in your company. You can do so with respectful, non-intrusive, light-hearted friendliness when speaking with them.

Start with warm greetings. Talk about light-hearted yet positive topics, such as the food, the weather, how lovely the decor is, and other similar subjects. Stay away from heavy conversational topics, such as work, what others do for a job, money, politics, and religion. Don't hog someone's time unless both parties are obviously enjoying one another's company. The basic rule of thumb is to move on and mingle. Find a new person to talk to after about five minutes.

Point of note: Don't underestimate the power of small talk. It's a great ice breaker and brings people closer together. It also helps them find common ground, reduces social anxiety, and acts as a great foundation on which to build more interesting topics of conversation.

Read more about *learn how to make introductions properly* (search the words in italic on www.elegantwoman.org).

By the way, we women can bond too quickly sometimes, and thus reveal too much about some person, place, or thing when speaking with a new person for more than ten minutes.

Social Tips: When Invited to a Party

RSVP Quickly!

This means you notify your host as soon as possible whether or not you can attend. We often make the mistake to decide on whether to go at the very last minute. Rsvp'ing early is an act of kindness because we give more time for our host to prepare.

Don't Cancel on a Whim

Having thrown several parties myself, I find this very distasteful. Last minute cancellations are disrespectful, unless of course, there are mitigating circumstances.

I've toiled, prepared, and spent money to throw this party. That's why I can't help but feel disappointed when those last minute cancellations occur; sometimes hours before the party. This especially peeves me when they are really lousy excuses.

Those who don't even bother to cancel at the last minute and simply don't turn up may think the party is too big and that their absence won't make a difference, or perhaps that the host won't even know they aren't there, but when it's a carefully planned party, this just isn't the case. Most hosts know exactly who they've invited, not matter how big the event may be.

I find this casual approach of not rsvp'ing and last minute cancellations to be more common nowadays, thanks, or not, to social media and texting, which make it so easy to contact someone at a moment's notice. It really is quite appalling.

Bring a Gift

It is an elegant touch to bring a gift as a token of your appreciation for the invite. Use your own discretion concerning whether to bring a gift or not. You may sometimes ask, *"Can I bring anything?"* And if the host says something like, *"Oh, some ice cream would be nice,"* then please remember to honor that request. Personally I'd always try to bring something, whether asked or not. It might be chocolates, flowers, a scented candle, or another small token of my appreciation.

Adhere to the Dress Code

Check what is appropriate to wear for the party you're invited to. Is it a fine dining event? If so, then dress up in your favorite classic gown. If it's a cocktail party, then pull out that little black dress. Sometimes there may not be a dress code, but think carefully about what the occasion is: Is it a dinner party? Is it a beach picnic? Is it a get together to watch the finale of the Olympics?

I do find it insulting when people ignore the dress code, or just don't make an effort to dress up appropriately for a party.

When You Arrive at the Party

Adhering to etiquette:

- Greet everyone with your biggest smile at a dinner party. Try to find the host first to greet her.
- Introduce yourself if the host is too busy to introduce you.
- Keep conversations light-hearted and cheerful.
- Be discrete when exchanging contacts.
- Do not ask intrusive or potentially intrusive questions!
- Praise the host in conversations.
- Mingle. Do not linger too long in one person's company.
- Do not talk about work, your problems, dreams or aspirations, unless it's not intense like, "I would love to go to Greece!" or, "It's my dream to one day ski in Whistler".
- Be mindful about making business or business contacts at a party. Click the link to know how to do so discretely.
- Do not arrive late. Additionally, do not leave too early or too late.
- Find the host before you leave and thank her once again for a pleasant time.

Social Greetings — What If We Don't Know Anyone?

We are often nervous when invited to a party, especially if we do not know anyone. It helps if we arrive smiling, well-dressed, and with a small gift in hand. Also remember to ask light-hearted questions and listen (a lot!). Float around and do not linger in conversations. You'll get better at this the more you practice and the more events you attend. Below are some pointers on how to become comfortable at parties.

Social Tip: What to Do When You Feel Intimidated or When you Meet Snobs

Sometimes we may meet people at a party that we find intimidating. Here is an example and what to do if this happens to you:

> *"Did you watch the movie, Slumdog Millionaire?"*
> *"Did you hear about the new shopping mall?"*

If the person is not very responsive and has a bored look, say something like, *"It was nice meeting you"*, and promptly move on.

Don't Take It Personally!

Just as we will not like everyone we meet (for whatever reason(s)), some people will not like us either. Again, just move on and mingle with those you *do* like!

When Someone Intentionally Intimidates You

When somebody intentionally intimidates, or snubs you, the best response is to hold your head high and ignore them. Don't even bother being rude because that is giving her/him attention! If she tries talking to you, simply answer politely, excuse yourself and move on to have a great time with the other, more compatible people at the party.
Remember it's not about you. Show a genuine interest in others. Pursue your interests and passions. Become fascinated with the world outside of yourself.

Party Etiquette: Intrinsic Details of Elegant Socializing

Learn party etiquette for making friends of your choice the elegant and confident way. Social events are an integral part of your life. Parties are a good way to extend your network and deepen friendships. Good things happen to good people when they make the effort to socialize correctly. They will find that opportunities expand as they grow in confidence, and they get to travel more in areas of their personal, professional or business lives.

Oftentimes, many of us feel nervous going to a party for all kinds of personal reasons, and that is what party etiquette is all about. This next section is about what to expect so that you'll be prepared when, and if, situations arise.

So let's start from the very beginning: when you first arrive at a party.

Party Etiquette: When You First Arrive

Greet the Host First

When you enter a room full of people, find the host first and greet them with your gift. It could be a bottle of wine, flowers, a box of chocolates, or anything else you deem as appropriate for the occasion.

A good sense of party etiquette is to never arrive empty-handed, especially if it's a party at a home. Call your host a couple of days before the event and ask what you can bring. If she says something along the lines of *"Nothing, just bring yourself"*, then arrive with something small as a token of kindness. Some examples might be wine, champagne, and chocolates.

Never arrive late to a dinner party. Don't arrive too early, either! The host might be wearing curlers and stressing over her menu.

Party Etiquette: Breaking the Ice

Realize that not everyone is an extrovert and feels completely at ease talking to strangers. Once you realize that, it takes the pressure off yourself and others to be the perfect conversationalists. Nevertheless, the first part of any party is to break the ice, and you can do so by **gently asking questions and offering information about yourself**. Try and remember to keep your conversations light and cheerful!

Party Etiquette: How to Socialize

Ask Light-hearted Questions

Find something about the other person that you genuinely find interesting. Do this, and your eyes will inevitably glow with sincerity when speaking with them. The other person will also feel flattered by your interest and attention.

After you ask a question, pause and wait for the person to finish her answer and then contribute your own thoughts. Speak in a relaxed manner, allowing the other person to return a question and ask about you.

Focus on Similarities

When speaking with another person, focus on similarities, but try not to shift the conversation topics back to you; let them talk about themselves.

Party Etiquette Caution: Sometimes when we are excited, we tend to ask a stream of pointed questions. The person whom you're getting to know is at risk of exhaustion answering all the questions. He or she will feel interrogated. If you don't allow them to ask questions about you, there will be frustration! Remember, conversation is a two-way street. When asking questions, be sensitive about what is appropriate to ask.

Party Etiquette: Taboo Topics

Some taboo topics and inappropriate questions you should NOT venture into include:

- How much do you earn?
- How much do you make in your business?
- How much did you pay for your car?
- How expensive was [fill in the blank]?
- Are you married? Why aren't you married?

People Fall Off the Party Etiquette Ladder Fast When...

- They let you and everyone else know they are richer than anyone at the table. For example, they brag about the fine dining restaurants they often go to, their connoisseur knowledge of food and wine, and basically talk about everything that is out of reach for everyone else.
- They hijack the conversation with statements like, "Oh, we went there too! The pasta at _____ restaurant was the best in the world!"
- They namedrop and speak about their privileges from knowing the other person who's an impressive type: "Oh we didn't have to make a booking at such and such a restaurant! This guy is an exclusive luxury ___ owner, and a very good friend of ours."
- They brag, boast, and attempt to impress. Don't try this technique, as people always know when you are trying to impress.

- They're highly competitive at any friendly social function, yet poor losers.
- They talk about themselves incessantly, especially about their excellent skills or achievements: cooking, skiing, playing golf, etc. They have no clue that people are rolling their eyes at their self-centered, egotistical waffling.
- They are not sensitive and speak about how, "Although we can both not work and travel around the world, if we want to, we choose to...instead", when they know there are others listening who might be struggling to pay their mortgage.

How to Be a Seasoned and Savvy Conversationalist

Follow the French Style of Indirectness

The French are known for their sarcastic conversations mixed with humor, especially if they adore you. The thing to take away from French culture is their awareness of being non-intrusive.

For instance, if they would like to know if you had offspring, instead of saying, *"Do you have any kids?"* they would probably say something like, *"What a beautiful garden! It's perfect for kids to be running around in"*.

With this conversational approach, you get choose to **either offer the information**, *"Oh yeah, my kids go crazy with their dog out there"* or, *"Yes, it'll be perfect when we have children of our own"*. Or they might just smile and agree if they don't want to reveal any information on the topic.

Other French party etiquette examples include the use of correct titles. Let's say you look fairly young to be married, others might address you as "mademoiselle". However, if you

ARE married, you politely correct them by asking to be addressed as 'Madame'.

Other indirect questions used to probe into one's marital status might include, *"Does your husband like to cook?"* And you can laughingly say, *"Oh I'm not married, but it would be wonderful to have a husband who does cook!"*

Offer Your Information First As 'Bait'

You can also politely, discreetly, and elegantly offer information that you are single, especially if you have an interest in the other party, or would like them to recommend you to their friends. Say things like, *"I do enjoy the opera but it's hard to find someone to go with these days; everyone is just so busy!"* or, *"Oh, on the weekends I usually go with my mother to church, etc."*

You try to invite questions with your statements, and responses such as, *"Oh, so your boyfriend doesn't like opera?"* or, *"Why do you go to church with your mother, does your husband oversleep?"*

Bridging the Gap of Social Class

You may be aware of the differences in social classes, especially if you are from a more **privileged background**. You will surely know about the hierarchy in social standing, financial status, education, and intelligence. Never ever make a person feel less-so, and **always attempt to make the other 'lesser' party at 'home' with you, simply** by being down to earth using everyday conversation.

Examples might be:

- *"I also have a difficulty getting up early!"*
- *"The weather was so cold this weekend; I wanted to stay in bed too".*
- *"That was one of my favorite movies".*

- *"I look forward to my afternoon tea every day."*

Treating everyone as equal, no matter what their social standing happens to be, is one of the strongest traits of a classy person.

It's natural human instinct for anyone to want to feel better, to impress, to feel important, and wanted. Perhaps the root cause of this behavior is insecurity, and a lack of attention and love. Well, it's time to take the focus off ourselves and let us remember that it's a kind act to not make someone feel less than you, or poor, uneducated, stupid, small, or with resigned envy. Ridding ourselves of 'self' is gracious, kind, and elegant. After all, it's nice to be nice; it's not nice to be nasty!

How an Elegant Person Socializes

Let's now look at the party etiquette of an elegant woman.

If she is aware of her privilege in wealth, education, and travel experiences, she would be sensitive about it, and not speak about anything that others can't relate to.

During the dinner conversation, if asked, and in an admiring way, keep a straight face (showing no evidence of reveling in all the attention), and speak graciously, but without putting yourself down, and respond something like this: *"Oh yes, I had the chance to travel to Italy. It was very nice. I'm glad you enjoyed it too. Tell me, what is your favorite Italian city?"*

Tactfully move the conversation back to her. Let her be the star tonight, since it is she that has just got back from the country. You can always share your experiences another time or privately with friends.

Party Etiquette: Making Friends at a Party

We all make friends with a motive. It may be because you have lots in common, or maybe you have a future business agenda. So let's now divulge into the normal conversation pattern.

The very common conversation patterns are as follows:

James: *"Hi, my name is James."*

Kate: *"Hi James, very nice to meet you, I'm Kate."*

James: *"So Kate, what do you do?"*

Kate: *"I am the marketing director for the BBC. What about you?"*

James: *"I am the executive director for Macquarie Bank."*

And then the conversation falls flat. Why not avoid that dreaded questioning pattern altogether?

"What Do You Do?" the Dreaded Question

Honestly, let me just say, **this is not the most elegant way to start a conversation**. It can feel intrusive and is rather aggressive. If you really want to know, ask the friend who brought you.

Some people are proud of their titles and what they do, but others are not. Some people do not feel comfortable discussing their work and may even be embarrassed by their occupation. Or perhaps they just don't tie their identity with their jobs. Also, it's important not confuse **what you do** with **who you are**.

Steer Away From "What Do You Do?"

Rather than asking very pointed questions, such as "What do you do?" steer away from that common pattern and open up conversation with general interest topics. For instance, I like to talk about travel, weekends, hobbies, ergonomics, sports, and so on. Such broader topics can spin off in many different directions. People are more passionate and interested in talking about what they love to do, and if it happens to fall into the category of what they do for a living, that's even better because they will be speaking with heart-swelling pride.

So, when someone says to me, "Eunice, what do you do?" I will obviously give a reply. Even though I'm passionate about what I do, I respond with a general answer, *"I work in content management"* or, *"I work in retail and distribution", "in education"* and so forth.

By being general and downplaying the importance of your work, sends out a **more elegant message**. You're not out to impress, you're relaxed, elegant, and perfectly content and at peace with who you are, which can be quite different than what you do for a living!

Giving off titles can either impress or intimidate others. If the other party really needs, or wants, to know more they will definitely ask pointedly, and you can reply with something like, "Oh, I'm a (title here), and I work **with** (company name here)". 'With' is more elegant than 'for'.

Seriously, it's more elegant to talk about everything generally and in a light-hearted fashion, such as the weather, hobbies, movies, recent news and events, than it is to get into heavy topics that may have deeply conflicting opinions.

I'd Rather Talk about the Beautiful Weather

Talking about the weather is safe small talk, at least for the first few minutes and as an ice-breaker. This and a few other conversation starters might include:

- ✓ *Gosh, the weather is so beautiful today.*
- ✓ *Did you watch that movie last night?*
- ✓ *What do you get up to on the weekends?*
- ✓ *How is your evening?*

Party Etiquette

Generally, in a party atmosphere, we want to move on to meet new people and stick to brief conversations, and remember to keep your conversations light and happy.

Some 'Don'ts' in Party Etiquette

- Do not linger for too long.
- Do not ask for phone numbers right away.
- Avoid talking about work and your career aspirations (unless asked).
- Avoid girlish bonding right away and talking about 'men problems' or other personal matters.
- Do not talk to any one person for more than ten minutes at the start of a party.
- Flit around like a butterfly; meet everyone by introducing yourself and asking if they are having a good time at the party.

The following are tips if you meet someone new and you would like to establish a friendship:

To Establish a New Friend or Potential Business Contact

If you feel a connection with someone, either for friendship, business, or a potential love interest, quickly get their business/personal cards, an email or cell phone number, or jot down their details.

You could also remember their name so that you can look them up on Facebook or another social media platform, but you might want to first casually ask them if that's okay by saying something along the lines of, *"Oh, by the way, are you on Facebook?"* Or you could discreetly exchange phone numbers and take your friendship up a level by scheduling a lunch over the next few days. If it's a business contact, feel free to talk business, but remember your party etiquette!

Taboo Conversation Topics

Emily Post Etiquette on Taboo Conversation Topics:

Conversations should not be about someone else, especially in a group, even in a group of close friends. I know it is impossible sometimes, but limit the conversation about another person to 30 seconds. If they talked the way they did about someone when they were not around, imagine what they would say about you when you're not there!

How to Stop a Person from Talking Badly about Someone You Know

Peggy Post states: "One of the kindest people I know, when faced with this situation, immediately halts the speaker by saying, 'Goodness Barbara, Adriane always says such nice things about you!', and then immediately changes the topic."
    No matter how strongly tempted you are to pass along a nasty comment, or to join in a group talking unkindly about another, don't do it. It doesn't just defame the character of the other; it makes you look bad, too.

11. The Importance of Refinement

Refinement: Qualities of manners, courtesy, and gentility.
There are some people who feel that these qualities are not
terribly important. Why is refinement important? Day after day,
I tirelessly pursue a refined elegance. So why is it important to
establish how to be elegant, how to be classy, and what
exactly is refinement?

The following article is adapted from Chapter 11 in, *All about
Raising Children.*

Helen Andelin writes:

*"Refinement is that polishing down of the human being,
casting out the coarse and vulgar and retaining that which is
fine and elegant."*

This act of refinement is the same process that is used on
diamonds; as they are polished down to gain their tremendous
brilliance. In their raw form, they are not shiny at
all. Refinement consists of subduing the tendencies of
slovenliness, crudeness, bluntness, nerviness, and gaudiness.
It encourages good manners, kindness, courteousness,
considerateness, propriety, and gentility.

The act of pursuing refinement is synonymous with
learning how to be elegant and classy. A refined lady is an
elegant and classy woman.

Why Is Refinement Important?

There are some people who feel elegance, refinement, and
having classy traits are not that important. I'll admit that
sometimes I, too, question its significance. It does appear
superficial at times.

We all agree that what's inside your heart and brain are what really count. To my great surprise, I've discovered and concluded that one cannot be truly elegant unless her insides (heart and mind) are refined and elegant **first**! You cannot be truly elegant without an elegant spirit and mind. That marks the pursuit of elegance.

Thus, by pursuing refinement and elegance, you are developing your character, both your heart and mind. You'll also end up with a bunch of high-quality skills. Your God-given talents will be honed. Therefore, the pursuit of personal refinement is not superficial at all.

Refinement also helps a person of worth to be more fully recognized and appreciated. It **elevates their social standing and confidence**. A refined person gains considerable influence much more easily than a person with slovenly habits, despite the fact that the less refined person might be a wonderful person.

When a woman pursues and values her refinement, not only will she earn the approval of people around her, she will respect and appreciate herself. **She increases her feelings of self-worth**. She may also increase her opportunities, both personally and professionally.

When a person is refined, she also **increases her own chance of succeeding socially**. Unfortunately, all too often in life, we are given about 30 seconds to make a good impression. If we fail to make a favorable impression within that short timeframe, most people won't stick around to find out if you have a heart of gold or not. If you would like to walk with dignity, mingle with the elite, and be accepted in the finest circles of mankind, we have to invest into the training and education of the refinement process. By doing so, we'll begin to attain self-respect. We'll also acquire an elegant personal confidence.

Refinement Builds Morale

When you encounter a person who is slovenly, careless, blunt or rude, it may seem that he or she is confident, and therefore cares little about what others think. In actuality, he or she may be experiencing low morale and feelings of inferiority. As elegant mothers, we can teach our children, and ourselves, the values of refinement. We make efforts to learn how to speak correctly, how to think of others and be courteous, and to engage in personal grooming so as to maintain a proper appearance at all times.

This type of training, as rigid as it may be, will **produce fine ladies and gentlemen**. If you find yourself wallowing in insecurity, know that the pursuit of elegance and refinement WILL help you feel equal to everyone else. According to Mrs. Andelin, this is why the armed services insist upon rooms being spick and span, and why military personnel need to stand in line with clean uniforms and highly polished shoes. They know that this type of refined living keeps confidence and discipline high.

The Pursuit of Refinement

Refinement is a work in process. It is not an inherently human quality. It has to be learned and practiced constantly. I like to say that learning to be refined is simply a habit of **getting better at being you**.

Ladies and gentlemen are not born. They are created. If they are fortunate, they are accomplished by persistent parents.

Mrs. Andelin also says that once a person becomes refined, it requires a constant effort to preserve this refinement, and if we do not constantly strive towards propriety, we will slip back into the direction of the uncivilized.

The pursuit of refinement makes you a better person; it equips you for a higher quality life, a life that you deserve. You gain favor in the eyes of people that you meet. You'll be better equipped as an elegant mother and as a good wife who makes her husband proud.

I've always admired elegant women and wish to be like them. Working on my own refinement is a way of becoming the dream woman I hope to become.

Qualities Needed for Refinement

By embracing the following qualities, refinement becomes automatic, as they are the basis of good manners, courtesy, and gentility. This page is adapted from Chapter 11 from Helen Andelin's book, *All about Raising Children*.

Traits of a Refined Character:

- **Sensitivity:** Acutely aware of the feelings and needs of others
- **Consideration:** To be considerate of the feelings and needs of others, and adapting our behavior accordingly. This is a fundamental quality necessary for tact and courtesy.
- **Practice Restraint:** This means to control our thoughts, feelings, and expressions. To curb what may be offensive.

Andelin covers the practice of restraint in her book, and I would agree that this is a necessary quality in all elements of refinement. Not only is it vital to manners and courtesy, but to good taste, music, and all forms of art. The truly beautiful is restrained. It is never overdone.

Tact and Diplomacy

One must be careful in discerning the right thing to say to another person so as not to offend them. Tact is the opposite of bluntness. There is a lack of regard for the feelings of others in a blunt person.
A refined person understands the difference between bluntness and frankness. She will only speak frankly if she is convinced that it is necessary and appropriate.

Speaking Correctly

The first step to refined speech is to speak correctly.
What is speaking correctly?

- Correct pronunciation of words: distinct and correct.
- Avoid the tendency to slur words together.
- You are encouraged to move your lips while speaking and to use your facial muscles; this is a part of correct speech.
- The proper use of words and the avoidance of slang (unless in extremely familiar and casual circumstances, and usually only then if you lack a better expression).
- Refrain from vulgar language, profanity, swearing, and telling unrefined stories.
- Expansion of vocabulary (perfect for when writing and used as discretion in speech).
- Keep away from using big words deliberately to people who may not have your language skills. This is both pretentious and rude.
- A refined accent.

"From the general characteristics of a person's accent, we can usually tell where that person is from, and very often what social class he or she belongs to." ~ Robert Blumenfeld

Good Personal Habits

- Establish good habits of standing, sitting, and walking posture
- A love of reading and learning

- Not interrupting when someone is speaking
- Not fidgeting, looking at cell phones constantly, scratching, belching, etc.
- Not opening the mouth too wide when surprised or when laughing

"Any unusual contortion of the body is considered unrefined. ~ Helen Andelin

Awareness of Etiquette

A refined person is aware of social etiquette, be it promptly responding to all RSVP for social invitations, or being a gracious conversationalist.

She respects the privacy of others. She will never intrude into someone's home. She conducts herself properly at all times. She will not ask for cheeky favors, such as borrowing things, or attempt to get a free service or consultation from a lawyer, accountant, doctor, or friend.

Good Taste

The mark of a refined person is good taste. This is a term that refers to one's ability to appreciate or judge what is beautiful, appropriate, or excellent, whether it's art, dress, consumer goods, and so forth.

A person with good taste employs a lot of thought and discretion in selecting her clothes, hairstyle, jewelry, home furnishings, and art. She is also prudent in spending, mindful of her manners, and conscious of her speech.

How Does One Develop Good Taste?

I believe it develops from a good heart and mind, exposure to the finer things in life, and creativity, such as in the areas of art, music, and dance.

Two principles of design that contribute to good taste are simplicity and restraint. Good taste is never loud, gaudy, or overbearing. Good design is often limited to simple lines, color, and texture.

Mrs. Andeline writes that music and art help to refine us, subduing our rough nature and awakening finer characteristics. She also says that refinement can be cultivated by frequent exposure to excellent music and great art.

She continues to say, *"Children who have little or no exposure to the fine arts are found to be lacking in refinement, and those who are limited to only crude music or cheap, gaudy art tend to develop coarse and vulgar tendencies."*

Table Manners

How you dress and dine at the table is another way to establish refinement. The table should always be set beautifully, with proper placement of cutlery and preferably ironed linen, along with china and silverware. When it is dinner time, everyone should arrive appropriately dressed, and most certainly not garbed in pajamas.

The dining area should have a visually pleasant setting. Everyone should be sitting up straight and bring the food to their mouths. No one should be fidgeting, chewing with their mouth open, sticking their fingers into the food or mouth, licking knives or plates, or playing with their dinner.

There is good conversation, which is polite and relaxed. "Please" and "Thank you" are used without thought. There is no cutting-in or interrupting others. There is no name-calling or slamming down opinions. No one leaves the table unless he or she asks to be excused, or until everyone is finished eating.

No one reaches across the table to grab an item; they'll politely ask for something to be passed. When your family is done, they wipe their hands and mouths on the napkin provided, not on the tablecloth or the sleeves of their clothes.

To sum up, refinement has got nothing to do with money or social status. Good manners and courtesy are based on a sensitive consideration for others and good taste.

Art Appreciation

This section will focus on how I've found my passion and my little niche in the art world. It's also about how I've discovered the interconnectedness of all art forms. Learning to appreciate the arts is a pleasure and a joy; it is fulfilling and much more accessible than some may think.

Why Are the Arts so Important and Why Should You Support Them?

I've always been a lover of '**the Arts**'. From an early age I enjoyed literature, history, musicals, ballet, and vocals. I also loved to sing, dance, write, paint, and decorate. I appreciated elegant design. I enjoyed discovering art history, painting, drawing, and so on. However, it was only recently that I discovered they are all somewhat related to each other, i.e., ballet and opera, ballet and literature, music and musical theater, dance and music, design and the stage, art history and architecture, to name a few connections.

I don't know about you, but I always felt that art appreciation had a bit of a snobby reputation. There are pretentious people out there who seem to go on and on about some painting, or artists, or opera. They don't speak an everyday language, and if you're ever caught in one of those conversations that seem to fly over your head, all you wish for is the ground to open up and swallow you in.

I didn't get a chance to study art history in school, though I did my fair share of visiting museums and tried to read and understand more by self- educating.

To me, I wasn't trying to be sophisticated, nor was I really motivated by hoping to speak the 'arts' lingo. I was genuinely trying to understand why the great artists were so great. I tried all sorts of things. I looked online; I read various books in the library, and considered signing up for several expensive art appreciation courses. While all these things are good, I didn't feel totally gripped with passion, and at the end of the day, **I just didn't get it!**

So the outcome was that I gave up trying and went on with my life. However, I later discovered my little niche in the arts world and it propelled my art appreciation forward naturally. I've since realized that there's a place in the art world for everybody; art is for everyone, it is just a matter of finding an entry or a small component of the art world that means something to you, something that captivates your imagination without effort.

What Exactly Is Art Appreciation?

The website Arty Factory (http://www.artyfactory.com) defines it this way: **Art appreciation is the recognition of those timeless qualities that characterize all great art.**

Learning to recognize the timeless qualities of art simply means that you start exhibiting these timeless qualities, and in a way grow more beautiful as a consequence (though not just for that reason, so please read on).

Art Appreciation: A Sign of Richness

Should we ignore the arts then, if we don't seem to understand them? Definitely not and here's the reasons why:
One of the indicators that a nation is doing well economically is a flourishing art scene. For the arts scene to flourish, people in these nations have to have a sense of art appreciation, which is indicated by their support. Similarly, among refined, cultured groups of people (not necessarily those who have a lot of money) there is often heavy involvement in local arts programs through participation, attendance, or financial support.

Admittedly, some people get involved in the arts because of tax, networking, and socializing benefits. However, this article is focusing on personal benefits, such as **love, joy, and fulfillment.**

The arts can include anything from music, fine art, dance, vocals, opera, plays, theater, musicals, literature, and much more. Now, this is a general definition, but I'm not here to discuss what constitutes 'real art' (as the art connoisseurs do), I'm just for writing for people like me. Also, I'm not saying that you need to know everything there is to know either, because you don't. I'm just going to show you how you can start your art appreciation journey by finding out what you enjoy, and then hopefully you will discover how they are somewhat linked to each other in your own life.

Art Appreciation: How to Make Art Personal

Firstly, loving some aspects of music, dance, or literature gives you an emotional high. You will likely have this feeling of seeing life through new glasses. Before your world was in black and white, and now it's more colorful than all the colors of a rainbow! It glitters and shines. Through the arts, you'll find some ways to express yourself (just as an enthusiastic photographer might). It is as though there are so many more ways to 'nail those feelings' that we have.

I feel that way when I discover a great old classic, a particular song in a musical or opera, or my absolute favorite *pas de deux* (dance between a man and a woman) in a ballet. Don't laugh at me, but there are moments when I feel tears well up in my eyes, and sometimes my heart feels as though it's going to burst with emotion when watching a beautiful dance.

If you are passionate about something, even if it is not the arts, say bird watching or gardening, then you'll know exactly what I mean.

I see my life through the arts sometimes. I chose to live it that way. When I learn a new song, such as "Caro mio ben" by Giuseppe Giordani, I can hear the passion through a certain quality of sadness, and maybe I'll identify it with something like, say, losing a dear friend, and the experience can be very cathartic.

When I see great dancing, such as a *pas de deux* in a ballet, I admire its beauty with all my soul. I aspire to the ballerina's gracefulness, softness, and elegance. I take pleasure in the strength and masculinity of the male ballet dancer, because I know how long and hard it took him to get there.

I love identifying myself and the people around me in the characters of great books. I take my favorite songs in musicals and apply them to my life, which is another great benefit of learning about the arts!

Forming emotional connections to the arts is one of the ways anyone can begin to enjoy the arts. When you find your place in the world of the arts, you'll become familiar with many different types of art, and that is how you begin to rise and become more sophisticated in art appreciation. While art appreciation courses are good, I believe they merely acquaint you with the arts world. You've got to make your own journey and make them personal to you.

Without cultivating genuine art appreciation, I somehow feel that there is much to miss out on! It may sound silly, but I feel that life is more beautiful with knowledge of the arts. **After all, ART is devoted to beauty.**

Art Appreciation – A Method of Refinement

Secondly, spending time pursuing the arts brings about a refining quality. I'm sure there are exceptions, but after some time, those who get involved in any aspects of the arts, no matter how rich or poor they may be, tend to develop a **polished and relaxed ease**, with the right tone and pace of voice. Their posture seems to resemble nobility, and their eyes widen with delight and grace when they find someone who shares a love for, say, symphonies as much as they do.

Art also awakens creativity. We all need to be creative in our everyday lives, to solve problems, to bring fresh approaches into our relationships, to decorate our homes, pick out elegant presents, etc., and knowledge of the arts can help us approach our lives with more creative input.

Lastly, and most importantly, art is a form of inspiration. I believe we need inspiration to live our life colorfully!

Anna Morgan says it best. She writes:

> ***Art is man's effort to produce the ideal***. *It divides itself into as many branches as there are vehicles*

*used. A beautiful house, a magnificent temple, a jewel finely cut and uniquely set, the mind and character of a man suggested by the sculptor's hand in plaster or marble of by the painter's brush on canvas, a rug rare in design and coloring, a chair or table the form and color of which provoke our admiration, a song which is repeated by **poet** and **peasant, each and all are works of art, vehicles used for the conveyance of the thought and emotion of man**.*

Find Your Place in Art

Finding your niche in art is what art appreciation is all about. Pick something in any area that interests you and go from there:

- Pick up a great classic book, like *War and Peace*.
- Read basic art history books, like *Art History for Dummies* .
- Buy tickets to the theater (and read about the show before you go).
- Take singing or ballet lessons.
- Take a literature class.
- Join a book club.
- Study acting.
- Pick up the cello or the piano (as two examples).
- Take an oil painting class and create a masterpiece for your home.
- Rent a musical or classic movie.
- Admire great artists, whether it's their work, dedication, or passion.

- Appreciate great works of art. Learn about the process of how much time and effort it took to create them.
- There are more ways to get started in the arts than I can list here. Can you think of any that might be of interest to you?
- Not only will art awaken your finer qualities, it will also bring you pleasure and joy, perhaps like nothing else you may have experienced.

There are more ways to get started in the arts than I can list here.

Can you think of any that might be of interest to you? Not only will art awaken your finer qualities, it will also bring you pleasure and joy, perhaps like nothing else you may have experienced.

12. Classical Education for Elegance — A Path to an Elegant Mind

Why Classical Education? Well, it is beneficial to be classically educated as a woman, especially if you desire to obtain a sophisticated sort of elegance. In my research on the study of elegance, I've discovered how certain types of education produced elegant and sophisticated women. I then began to realize the importance of classical education.

What Is Classical Education?

In *The Well-Trained Mind: A Guide to Classical Education at Home*, Susan and Jessie Bauer define **classical education.** To begin, a classical education is language-intensive and not image focused. It demands that students use and understand words, not video images. It is also history intensive and aims to help students understand important human endeavors throughout history. It trains the mind to analyze and draw conclusions. It cultivates and enforces self-discipline.

To quote from the book:
"It [classical education] produces literate, curious, intelligent students who have a wide range of interests and the ability to follow up on them."

In short, it trains students to be self-reliant and to learn how to learn. That would essentially give them confidence and skills for life.

How Does a Classical Education Relate to Elegance?

Though *The Well-Trained Mind* was written as a guide for parents to homeschool their children, it serves as an invaluable reference for obtaining a sophisticated sort of elegance. It works wonders for your mind and your self-confidence.

In some of the pages on my website, I discuss the need to further educate yourself; there are many reasons for this and I hope you find your own.

By pursuing knowledge, I hope you'll find more fulfillment, understanding, and satisfaction in life. An education helps in all areas of life, not least is confidence and the development of character. An interesting person is an interested person.

You can cherry-pick things you want to learn about and discard those you don't. It's not necessary to follow the strict classical education school curriculum.

You can gather and customize your classical education by exploring whatever most piques your interests and curiosity. You can also choose subjects or areas of interest, where you do not feel sufficiently confident, but would like to be. For example, if you feel ill at ease in certain restaurants or luxury boutiques, go to them, read about them, etc., until you feel some familiarity. It is by understanding that confidence grows.

Points to note: Remember, going to these places does not mean shelling out your life savings. Window shopping is free, as is trying things on. Having a cup of coffee or afternoon tea is also inexpensive.

Similarly, I've noticed that elegant folks prefer a liberal arts education, which I was fortunate enough to have; though it was not as 'liberal' as I had hoped! Regardless of that, I am convinced that a classical education shapes your mind for elegance. It helps you become an accomplished individual with wide-ranging knowledge.

Value of Liberal Arts Education

What is the value of a Liberal Arts Education? Why is it important in learning to be elegant?

"The quickest way to cut across 'Class lines' is through education." ~ Ginie Sayles

Better yet, combine your education with an overseas liberal arts education (if affordability is an issue, there are many scholarships available for study abroad programs). There is great respect for education among the high achievers, or the upper classes, as one might say. What type of education is best to pursue? Not all fields of study are considered equal. Those possessing finer feathers stress that to be a worldly woman a liberal arts education from a private college is preferable. But why, you may ask? Why study the liberal arts when it is not a profession or skill as such? What is the value of studies that do not offer a professional skill?

A liberal arts education does more than prepare you for work. It is education that focuses on transferable skills. It is a well-rounded education that centers on more than just facts. You learn to make sound judgments and think independently. Your horizons will be expanded, your perspectives challenged, and you'll acquire ways to defend your point of view.

A liberal arts education is said to help establish a moral and historic compass. No matter how advanced our society, there is still a need to reflect and ponder, from justice and injustice, the right from wrong, and to identify between the good, the bad, and the ugly. We can learn from history and not make repeated mistakes. Such an education can inspire us for the future. Liberal arts are the skills derived from the classical education curriculum. Wikipedia describes it like this:

> *The term liberal arts denotes a curriculum that imparts general knowledge and develops the student's rational thought and intellectual capabilities, unlike the professional, vocational, technical curricula emphasizing specialization. The contemporary liberal arts comprise studying literature, languages, philosophy, history, mathematics, and science. In classical antiquity, the liberal arts denoted the*

education proper to a free man, unlike the education proper to a slave.

What Is the Goal of a Liberal Arts Education?

The value of a liberal arts education is best summed up in the following quotes.
"The value of an education in a liberal arts college is not the learning of many facts but the training of the mind to think something that cannot be learned from textbooks." ~ Albert Einstein

Chapter One of Howard and Matthew Greene's, *Hidden Ivies: Thirty Colleges of Excellence*, defines the goals of a liberal arts education in the following manner:

> *In a complex, shifting world, it is essential to develop a high degree of intellectual literacy and critical-thinking skills, a sense of moral and ethical responsibility to one's community, the ability to reason clearly, to think rationally, to analyze information intelligently, to respond to people in a compassionate and fair way, to continue learning new information and concepts over a lifetime, to appreciate and gain pleasure from the beauty of the arts and literature and to use these as an inspiration and a solace when needed, to revert to our historical past for lessons that will help shape the future intelligently and avoid unnecessary mistakes, to create a sense of self-esteem that comes from personal accomplishments and challenges met with success.*

The Benefits of Being Educated in Liberal Arts

1. A liberal arts education teaches you how to think:

The mind is like a muscle. Exercise makes it stronger. It becomes easier to learn and grasps concepts when it is exercised and enlarged by varied study. It helps us develop an 'ordered' mind. Good thinking habits help you in all areas of your life. You will be able to think for yourself, enabling you to develop your own opinions, attitudes, values and beliefs. It helps you employ independent judgment.

2. A liberal arts education teaches you how to learn:

It will not be simply acquiring a 'giant file of facts' but focusing on the learning skill itself. The strategies and habits you develop also help you learn more easily.

"People are best taught by using something they are familiar with, something they already understand, to explain something new and unfamiliar." ~ George Herbert

Liberal arts education creates an improvement of perception and understanding.

3. A liberal arts education allows you to see things whole:

Its goal is to provide a well-rounded education.

4. A liberal arts education makes you a better teacher:

While you may not be a teacher, you may one day be a mother, a confidant, someone's wife, and definitely someone's friend. Being able to explain things in a clear and rational way enhances your communication skills.

5. A liberal arts education will contribute to your happiness:

A cultivated mind enjoys itself and the arts. With an increased knowledge, you will have more abilities to tackle and solve the problems in your life (loosely adapted from the website Virtual Salt).

Elements of Liberal Arts Education

Currently, this varies from school to school. If you pursue a liberal arts education, you'll be able to pick your subjects, with a focus on humanities. These subjects range from literature, languages, philosophy, history, mathematics, and science. The foundation for a liberal arts education is a **classical education**.

How to Get This Education Trait of Class

First of all, believe you can. It does not matter what age you are or what you are currently studying.
Secondly, take an interest. Do it slowly, in small parts. You do not have to do it all today! Explore the universities in your area and look for a part-time class or two (a community college is also a great place to begin taking liberal arts classes). Sometimes all it takes is a trip to the library to read your first classic book, say, *Pride and Prejudice* (it really is a great book).
        You may not have many possessions, but you can always acquire more knowledge. It does wonders to your self-esteem and confidence, as part of the benefits.

The Classically-Educated Woman

By learning and undertaking a useful skill, such as Japanese cooking, as an example, the classically-educated woman is able to gain greater self-confidence. She realizes enough knowledge to be an interesting person, and to be a great host and friend. She defines herself (without losing her identity, dreams, and ideas) by her mass of responsibilities, i.e., her job, children, housework, and other commitments. She becomes an avid reader, growing in both inner and outer beauty. She is a better and more confident mother, thus gaining respect from her children and husband.
I also believe, as silly as it might sound, that our thoughts, heart, and values shape the beauty of our face and influence our body language and expressions. An interesting person has

an interested face. An interested face is more beautiful than just a pretty face, which you can sometimes tell is the result of superficial thoughts.

You Can Be Classically Educated

Susan and Jessie Bauer have made a classical education possible as something that can be undertaken at home. Though it was written specifically for homeschooling, Jessie (who is the mother of Susan), said she learned more by homeschooling her children than she ever did at college. It's often said that the best way to learn something is to teach it!

While I would love to go back to school and pursue a liberal arts education full-time, I, like so many others, usually have too many other commitments going on in my adult life, thus making this dream unfeasible.
Please understand that I don't think one needs a classical education to be elegant. It is, however, heavily beneficial in more ways than one. With a classical education, you'll most certainly acquire self-confidence and the said traits of class. It is one of the easiest ways to cut across the 'class lines' of society.

SO...

Personally, I've majored in science, math, and grammar, but feel a strong void in my education of literature, history, and languages. I've, therefore, tailored my own studies towards those areas, using the resources and references mentioned in The Well-Trained Mind.

Elegant Motherhood Stories

The following quotes highlight the impact mothers have on raising elegant minds.
The first quote is taken from Helen Andelin's book, *All about Raisin Children*:

"A generation of excellent children would have a profound effect upon society. We would eliminate vice, corruption,

violence and most of our social problems. Instead, our youth would begin to build our country in a positive way. Our children would be our country's greatest wealth."

And to quote David Oman McKay:
"Our country's most precious possession is not our vast acres of range land supporting flocks and herds; nor our mines and oil wells producing fabulous wealth. Our country's greatest resource is our children."

Elegant Motherhood Story: The Importance of Education

I've always had an interest in education, even though I didn't fully grasp the importance of Classical Education until more recently. It was when I read the book *The Well-Trained Mind*, and reflected on my own education and upbringing, that I thought more about classical education.

My favorite motherhood story in the book comes from Chapter One, written by Jessie about how she 'stumbled' upon homeschooling. It was more meaningful to me than the many other pages, which are focused strictly on curriculum.

As great as her classical education school curriculum is, we all know that any attempt at homeschooling will never be perfect. Most of us will try and feel confident teaching in some areas, and struggle in others.

Nevertheless, some of her motherhood stories, especially her thoughts and experiences, really encouraged me. For example, she writes about how she first taught phonics to her eldest son at the age of four, and how her three-year-old daughter wanted in on the lesson, too. I remember my phonics lessons, yet my brother didn't have those classes. And to be honest, I'm the more confident reader out of the two of us.

In kindergarten, Jessie's daughter Susan preferred to read instead of play during recreation time.

Jessie filled her children's heads with facts when they were small, and she taught them to read at an early age. She kept books everywhere in the house; even used books as presents and rewards. And she took her children to the library every week!

She would make each of them borrow the following books:

- One science book
- One history book
- One art or music appreciation book
- One practical book (craft, hobby, or how- to)
- A biography or autobiography
- A classic novel
- A fiction book
- A book of poetry

She taught her daughter to follow a custom-made schedule, balancing academics and personal interests, like music and creative writing. Susan continued to read at every available opportunity.

By the time Susan was in high school, she wrote papers, book reports, stories, and even wrote two novels, even though it wasn't part of her classical education curriculum.

I thought making a classical education a priority was a very elegant and inspiring way to bring up her child. That doesn't mean that experiential learning such as taking them to the aquarium is not important, but I believe Jessie is trying to bring the focus back to a proper education, which **focuses on words and the alphabets** rather than visual learning.

I personally believe in this method. I reason it this way: when the child first learns the words, before pictures, his brain is forced to work harder. He looks at the words and then brings up the pictures/images in his mind that are associated with those words. If he is accustomed to looking at images, his brain doesn't have to work hard to bring up images because it has been already fed to him. Images do not force the brain to recall words thus it does not help to improve his reading.

When the brain works harder, it makes more connections and he develops more intellectually. That is why I believe Susan was such an educated child. She was confident and calm in her approach to her studies. This is certainly a more pleasant way to live through school and life!

13. Classical Elegance

How to Be Classy and Classically Elegant

This is a write up about how to be classy, classically elegant, and simply sophisticated for sophisticated women.
Important disclaimer about the words "Class" and "Classy": I only use these words to describe a certain quality, one that communicates what I'm trying to say the best. Other than that, these words are not part of my conversations or speech. I do not use those words at all. However, learning about them brings about a certain confidence, and that is my goal for this page, so please take these terms with a grain of salt.
Learning to 'be classy' is about changing your feather to a finer quality. Contrary to popular belief, money and class are not the same things.

What is "class" then?
"Class refers to a group of people according to the things they have in common, including money." ~ Ginie Sayles

Unfortunately, many think that once they have money they acquire class. See 'How to Be a Lady'. It is possible to have loads of money and no class. On the flip of that, it's also possible to have high class and no money. We'll talk about what it means to be classy in specifics.

Classy, Classically Elegant, and the Word 'Classy'

If you Google the number of websites that have the word "classy" somewhere on their pages, you will find something like 111,000,000 results (at the time of updating this page).
It is one of the most misrepresented words around. People use it to describe elegance, sophistication, and style. They also use it to describe art, a hotel, restaurant, etc. While this is not 'wrong' per se, it is very subjective. What appears to be 'classy' to you may not be deemed classy to someone else.

Even dictionaries have very little to say on the subject. Dictionary.com simply classifies it as an informal word that represents the traits stylish and sophisticated.

As defined earlier, class refers to a group of people according to the things they have in common, including money. The key then is to acquire as many of these traits as possible.

Be Classy — Classify Yourself

The root words of "class" are "classification" and "to classify." That is true in our everyday lives. We categorize people and things, whether consciously or unconsciously.

When we look at others, meet up with someone, eat something, or go somewhere, we automatically classify (meaning to pigeon-hole). For example, you may have these thoughts:

- *"Oh wow, he's a doctor. He must be smart."*
- *"This is the kind of place that teenagers go to."*
- *"How can she afford such things? Her dad/husband must be rich."*

Though we are all different, the stages of refinement are similar wherever you go in the world. The characteristics of a 'classy person' are identified by people of different backgrounds, though they may use another word.

This explains why every royal princess from a different culture has similar traits. These include being well-groomed, educated, having good posture, being gracious, and various other qualities. In other words, in order to be classy, we continue to grow towards refinement in every sense of the word.

Refinement

Is refinement important or is it superficial and silly?

Many scoff at the term "self-improvement". They believe their high salaries are enough to buy themselves into the world of luxury and an elaborate lifestyle. They think they are classy, but it doesn't work that way! There is some value in wealth, as it means you are able to afford luxuries that can help you learn how to be classy. But affording luxuries is not what makes a woman refined.

Stop Feeling Guilty!

Sometimes, you may feel that the desire for refinement is a silly pursuit. The dream for the finer things in life, the hope for an exceptional way of living; perhaps it is all just pie in the sky thinking.

There is a sense of guilt when we indulge in some form of luxury. We think it's bad. It's wrong to spend money in this way, immoral to want nicer things. Isn't this just greed, pure and simple?

You need to put a stop to this line of thought right now! Don't confuse a healthy desire to improve yourself with extravagance.

When we feel guilty and confuse our dreams with extravagance, we have (unknowingly), placed a low value on ourselves. We are telling ourselves that we are not worthy. Refinement is an act of improvement.

If the most accomplished men and women on Earth did not invest their lives, time, and money into improving medicine, furniture, electrical appliances, etc., etc., then we wouldn't be where we are today. We wouldn't have the things we have now. We wouldn't be enjoying gourmet food, typing emails to our friends, talking on mobile phones, or taking digital photographs. We are far wealthier than at any time period in the past. Being classy is simply a way of life. It is being all that you can be and living as best you can.

Is Classiness Important?

Firstly, let me just say that embodying classiness leads to a more beautiful way of doing things and experiencing life. It improves the quality of your life.

Maybe you'd like to socialize with people you admire. People who are refined will identify you as 'one of them'. Perhaps you want to do business with high net-worth clients?

Because **you've acquired the common traits of these classy folks**, they'll identify you as one of their own. They will want to socialize with you, do business with you, befriend or perhaps marry you. They also will welcome the association of your children!

Having these connections can help you access opportunities that were not available to you before.

Characteristics of a Classy Person

This is a modified version of Ginie Sayle's theory that I've refined and added to the list below. As long as you develop these areas, you can be classy, regardless of how much money you have.

Note: These are merely intrinsic values.

Characteristics Used to Develop Classiness

- Wealth
- Lineage
- Clubs and memberships
- Education
- Appreciating and getting involved in the arts
- Social savvy
- Political clout or influence and connections
- Travel sophistication
- Appreciation of certain sports

- Values
- Achievements
- Hobbies
- Philanthropy (volunteering, sitting on a board, and fundraising)
- Manners
- Personal grooming (and the language of clothes)
- A good command of your native language and an appreciation of at least one other language
- Refined speech and accent
- Aristocratic titles
- Deportment

More information about these class distinctions are elaborated in my book (May 2011), *Becoming a Woman of the Finest Class*.

Be Classy by Developing These Characteristics

Each layer adds quality to your life. Developing these layers gives each of us a personalized roadmap on how to be classy. In doing so, we increase our self-confidence and knowledge. We expand our minds, widen our horizons, and begin to believe in ourselves more. That is how, in general, we become classically elegant.

How to Be Classy — Mastering the Art of Being Classy

This page does not encompass the entire subject of classiness but is rather my observations on how to develop one's character to become classy. I also use the terms "classy woman" and "pedigree woman" synonymously, simply because I am not fond of the words "class" or "classy", and use them only to illustrate the concept.

For starters, being classy is a mark of refinement. You can be classy without the full measure of elegance or beauty. A classy woman appears to come from a long line of class, and is more definitive in society.

Some women are naturally classy. They are the way they are because of how they were brought up, both by example and circumstance. Because of how they were raised, they enjoy the benefits of that culture, and consequently assimilate easily into a community of like-minded folks.

Others, who do not know how to elevate themselves, and do not carry the **mark of refinement**, find themselves frustrated at the unspoken code.

So, maybe you want to identify yourself with the character of being classy, or perhaps you want to learn how to be classy because you want to be identified that way. To work towards these goals, I have summarized the five most important basics of achieving classiness. Being mindful of these fundamentals at all times, you will be able to springboard your way to becoming the woman you want to be.

How a Classy Person Is Identified

Here are the main five qualities of a classy person.

1. She Treats Everyone as an Equal

Henry Higgins from *My Fair Lady* states in this awesome quote:
"You see, the great secret, Eliza, is not a question of good manners or bad manners, or any particular sort of manners, but having the same manner for all human souls. The question is not whether I treat you rudely, but whether you've ever heard me treat anyone else better."

Of course, he wasn't very sympathetic to Eliza Doolittle, but the point is that the pedigree woman has the **same manners towards every person**, no matter what their status or level of social hierarchy happens to be.

Such a woman would speak to the janitor, waiter, or hotel receptionist just as she would to her friends; she is polite, unhurried, and undemanding. She does not gush or laugh a little louder to try to impress or please. She neither elevates nor humbles herself. She has one manner for all.

This is a must for anyone learning how to be classy. Only average and very common people save their best manners for someone more important than them.

2. She Is Kind, Thoughtful, and Considerate

Most people think they are kind, thoughtful, and considerate of others, and I'm sure many of them are, but how does this guideline set the pedigree woman apart from the rest? What is it that makes her so classy? Well, knowing how to be classy is all in the details.

She is always extremely **punctual** because she does not want anyone to wait. If you are late, she will tell you to take your time. While she doesn't mind her guests being a little late, she hates to be unpunctual herself.

She is **properly dressed** at all times. Why? She does not want to convey sloppiness, which translates to: *"I don't think you are important enough for me to make an effort."*

If you spill coffee on her rug, she will make light of it because she thinks **your feelings are more important than her rug**.

Her **speech** is always **gracious** because complaining and being negative ruins someone's mood. In other words, negativity is infectious, and someone with class doesn't spread pessimism.

3. She Is a Quality over Quantity Type of Woman

She develops an acute taste and eye for quality. This requires discipline, be it shopping for books or for food. **To prefer**

quality is a form of respect. She respects herself, the workmanship, and the cost it takes to create some of quality.

She **does not take shortcuts** in any aspect of her lifestyle, and takes great pride to be the best that she can be — always. She also treats herself well. There is a misconception that you need to be able to afford a lot in order to enjoy quality. However, if you forgo quantity and buy less, you'll soon come to realize that you, too, can enjoy quality. An example of how to be classy in an everyday situation might be to avoid the convenience of picking up a low-quality micro-meal at a supermarket, and taking the time and effort to select the freshest ingredients and prepare a wholesome meal. This way, you know that you are consuming high-quality nutritious foods.

If one lacks the time to do so, a little ruthless discipline is required, omitting those non-productive, yet time-consuming activities from one's schedule. This will free up time so that you can devote more of yourself to quality pursuits.

4. She Values Education and Self-Improvement

She who is classy seeks an understanding of herself, of others, and the world as a whole. How else is she going to be a useful and contributing member of society if she is riddled with personal problems?

She makes an effort to be interested in matters outside of herself. Therefore, reading is a mainstay hobby for intellectual pursuits. Sports, or sporting activities, are also beneficial because these things contribute to developing character. Travel is valued because it expands horizons and helps her gain perspective. It increases her understanding of culture. Ignorance has no place in the classy female!

However, education and self-improvement are not seen by her as chores. They are enjoyed and pursued relentlessly to further develop mind and character. Great personal satisfaction is derived from it. She doesn't **have** to do these things, she **gets** to do them, and for that she is extremely grateful.

5. She Contributes to Society

She often thinks about how she can give and serve as a useful and contributing member of society. She realizes the secret of giving and living a fuller life as a source of great happiness and fulfillment. Remember, you can't keep anything unless you give it away.

Thus, she is generous. She wants, in her own way, to make the world a better place. Being a **useful and contributing member of society** is important to her.

How does she do it? She contributes using whatever resources she has at her disposal, be it time, money, or connections. She might volunteer for a charity, or the church. She may sit on the boards of events that have noble causes. It is those people that have deep pockets who donate, build schools, or help raise funds.

The Conclusion:

While the pedigreed woman can show us many more ways to be classy, I believe these five qualities are the principles of being refined. They are the starting points, or foundation if you like, and everything else is in the details, which are built on naturally as you go along.

Elegant Woman Case Study

Kate Middleton — a brief biography

In her brief time in the spotlight, Kate Middleton has shown the world grace, elegance, and poise. Here's a little bit about her. You will also see why she is a role model for elegance.

After one of the highest profile weddings in the world, Kate married Britain's Prince William, and is now officially known as Catherine, Duchess of Cambridge.

Kate Middleton was born as Catherine Elizabeth Middleton on January 9, 1982. From the ages 2–4, her family moved to Jordan for work. She later returned Berkshire, England in September 1986.

Kate Middleton's Education

In September 1986, Kate attended St. Andrew's prep school in Pangbourne, Berkshire. She later attended the Downe House School for girls in Newbury until July 1995. She then went on to Marlbourough College in Wiltshire, where she studied A-levels in chemistry, biology, and art. She also played tennis, hockey, and netball for the school, and was known to be good at athletics, especially the high jump.

According to the Official Royal Wedding Site…

Kate took a gap year after leaving Marlborough College in July 2000. She spent her gap in classic British fashion; she studied at the British Institute in Florence, undertook a Raleigh International program in Chile, and crewed on Round the World Challenge boats in the Solent, which is a strait off the English Channel, located between the coast of Hampshire and the Isle of Wight.

The royal bride followed Sloane convention by going on a volunteering trip to Chile in 2001, working on environmental projects and a community program with underprivileged children, which was organized by Raleigh International, the educational development charity. (Information quoted from *The Telegraph*).

The British Institute

The British Institute was the first British cultural organization to operate abroad. Its original aim was to promote understanding between Italy, Britain, and the Commonwealth through the study of art history, and English and Italian languages.

University of St. Andrews

After her gap year, Kate enrolled in the University of St. Andrews In 2001, from where she graduated in 2005 with a 2:1

in History of Art. She continued playing hockey for the university. It was during this time that she met Prince William. In March 2002, he noticed her when she modeled at a charity fashion show. He told a friend he thought she was beautiful. (See their relationship timeline.)

Kate Middleton's Career and Hobbies

Career

After completing her degree, Kate worked as an accessory buyer at Jigsaw, a clothing chain. She also worked in her family's business, Party Pieces, as a catalog photographer, webpage designer, and in their marketing department. In 2008, she was said to have launched 'First Birthdays', a junior brand to Party Pieces.

The Hobbies

In several of the Kate Middleton biographies, it is unclear whether she has specifically stated any hobbies as such. However, she certainly seems quite active and sporty. Her reported activities and interests included: athletics, hockey, crew, photography, fashion and accessories, tennis, sailing, painting, and a love of the arts.

Newly Crowned Duchess of Cambridge Is a Role Model of Elegance for Women

There will always be those who disagree, but I think that Kate Middleton makes a good role model as an elegant woman to us all. Now, when I say role model, I don't mean that Kate Middleton is perfect, because none of us are, not even royalty.

She is indeed a breath of fresh air when it comes to grace. She is tasteful, appropriate, beautiful, and has an impeccable sense of taste from what I've seen so far.

Inevitably, there are some people who are jealous that a 'commoner' like Kate was lucky enough to catch the eye of one of world's most eligible bachelors (now ex-bachelor).

While luck is one factor, women like her don't usually marry out of their class and social circle, especially if they are not exposed to other worlds. In other words, their paths must cross and the two parties must be able to cope or assimilate without too much ado. Kate fulfilled those two conditions admirably. So what do I mean by that exactly? It basically means that she leveled up to the occasion.

Attending Countless Events

People from the elite classes (network, community, society, socialites, or whichever term you prefer to use), such as royals often feel uncomfortable if they feel unmatched in terms of dress, manners, and outlook on life. If someone else from another culture is constantly gasping and amazed at everything you wear, do, or say, it will conjure uncomfortable feelings and occasional guilt. This is human nature, regardless of social status.

If they do choose to marry out of their social circle, it's either because they want to leave their society, or the person they marry can comfortably absorb and integrate into their own.

Prince William knew that his life was not normal by usual standards, and that his new wife would have to cope with the relentless demands of being a royal; things like the immense media attention, and a never-ending list of royal duties to perform. William knew only too well that to marry him would mean Kate would have to sacrifice a lot, and many of life's choices and decisions would be made for her by the royal establishment.

No more would she be able to do regular jobs, set up a business, or walk around freely as most of us take for granted. In many ways she would become 'property of the State'. William said he gave her enough time to see if she really wanted to take on all that comes with marrying a royal prince, one who is second in line to the British throne (which I thought was really sweet).

I believe Kate Middleton is not free of faults, having grown up out of the limelight and away from any association with royalty. She got to have a long courtship period with the Prince, thus allowing her to get attuned with royal etiquette and culture. She showed us that it was not effortless. Like all things, acquiring elegance takes a bit of work.

"Kate Middleton not only undertook intense etiquette training in the lead-up to her marriage to Prince William, but also has an army of royal minders whose job it is to make sure she doesn't put a McQueen-clad foot wrong." ~ Sydney Morning Herald

The Model Kate Middleton Fit to Marry a Prince?

Some may say it was luck, but I like to think there was more to it than just good fortune. Credit should be given to her and her parents. She already had a great foundation before meeting the Prince, as you can see below:

Kate's personal attributes include:

- She had a very good education.
- She was accustomed to wealth, as her family runs very successful business.
- She was a high achiever and well accomplished.
- She excelled in sports in school, especially hockey and cross-country running. She was also proficient in tennis, hockey, swimming, netball, and rounders.
- She loved art, as Prince William does, and graduated with an art history degree.
- During middle school, Kate was a real golden girl, excelling at sports, drama, and music. She took part in plays, learned ballet and tap, and was a skilled flautist and singer.

- She was impeccably dressed at all times, and had unimpeachable taste.
- She has a solid, squeaky clean image, and was always well-behaved.
- She shows real integrity. Even though she and William broke up in 2007, she did not become a sell-out and refused to speak or explain anything to the media.
- She coped without complaining when she did not have access to royal protection before her official status.
- She has down-to-earth qualities. Apart from her gentle demeanor, she took public transport, bought high-street brands, and wore things over and over.
- She understood the pressures and the cruelty of the limelight, yet she was unfazed. She treated Prince William as a person, and as a man, even helping out with the cooking when he came home from work (something she didn't have to do).
- She volunteered for charity. (Great start to her royal duties as the new princess). After all, she was modeling at a charity event when she caught Prince William's eye.
- She took care of herself. It's evident that people don't get a body like hers without working out and eating healthily! This is important because men, often subconsciously, choose healthy and fit women.
- She had almost *all* the layers of class.

Personally, I think the royals are lucky to have her! That's what I mean when I say she is adaptable. She can fit into the royal social life with relative ease. The royals feel comfortable with her, and that means they can be themselves.

She is an inspiring tasteful and elegant woman, and I will always be rooting for her.

14. How to Be an Elegant Woman

Ashley Judd plays a wonderfully elegant woman in the movie *De-lovely*.

There are all sorts of theories on how to be a lady. There are two that particularly stand out for me. One is that you are not required to have wealth to be a lady, though there were more ladies in wealthy community, historically speaking. I also think that with wealth, it is easier to become a lady because of accessibility, but let's focus on the fact that you can become one without having riches.

The second theory is a Texan saying: *"It takes seven generations to make a lady"*.

Since one generation is equivalent roughly to 30 to 40 years, that means it would take over 200 years for anyone to become a 'proper' lady! Thanks largely to modern technology, along with libraries and videos we are able to find many examples and detailed studies to help speed up the process.

It is my goal on elegantwoman.org to minimize the 200 year time period, though I fully understand why the saying claims that it might take seven generations to make a lady. Yet, I feel the saying is rather outdated because we have much greater and easier access to education, media, and inspiring women than previous generations ever had.

Ladies Are Not Born, They Are Made

"Being a woman does not automatically make one a lady. – elegantwoman.org"

The sooner we understand this simple fact, the less hard we need to be on ourselves when making mistakes or etiquette faux pas.

The key to understanding the learning process of how to become a lady is this: Learn through reading, understanding, imitation, acting, and getting over your blunders as soon as you recognize them.

Many women tell me they often feel fake and unnatural when trying to develop ladylike behaviors. Their friends are often unfamiliar with their new conduct, even commenting that they have become, or are becoming, too formal.

When change happens, you'll often feel like *everything is thrown off balance*. You may feel uncertain at times, nervous, and even wobbly. That is simply the process of finding a new balance. Tweak it, adjust, and you'll find your equilibrium as you evolve into who you've always wanted to be.

What Does Being a Lady Mean to You?

So many images are conjured up in people's minds when they think about how to become a lady. Perhaps they think of Scarlett O'Hara from *Gone with the Wind*, and feel wearing that style of dress is important to looking ladylike and elegant. Quite often celebrities, and their movie/television characters, are mimicked as reference points for ladylike behavior, due mainly to their high visibility.

But being a lady is more than that. I believe it is best summarized by Candice Simpson, who wrote *How to Be a Lady: A Contemporary Guide to Common Courtesy.*

Here is my paraphrased and abridged version: *Manners, attitudes, appropriate dress, and social mores have changed so dramatically that the definition of being a lady has left everyone confused.*

A lady, by today's definition, knows that educating herself in every way possible, from higher education to common sense manners, empowers her to become a woman of accomplishment and poise. She knows it is not her dress size or the money she possess that brings her satisfaction in life.

A lady also knows that beauty and wealth can be fleeting, but her inner character is the measure by which others will ultimately judge her as a person.

*Her courtesies, the high esteem in which she holds herself and others, and her sincere words of praise and thoughtfulness will reflect her strong values and place her ahead in the minds and hearts of those who know her. **Being thought of as a 'lady' may be one of the highest compliments a woman can receive in her life**.*

The Modern Lady

In the past, women from all socioeconomic backgrounds wanted to be thought of as ladies. Peasant girls would treasure a hand-me-down bonnet and wear it on special occasions or when they went into town. Girls that were fortunate enough to be educated at home would pride themselves in learning. They also made great efforts to remember their manners. It was very common for girls to learn to read, write, draw, play piano, and sing, no matter how much money, connections, or status they lacked.

Servant girls worked with dignity and tried their best to mimic the way ladies spoke. Many devoted their time to read by candlelight when their duties were over.

Wanting to Be Ladies in Modern Times

I know that wanting to learn 'how to be a lady' in the twenty-first century may come across to many as unnecessary and uncool. You might even get laughed at. After all, it's more fashionable to be like our modern day superstars, the likes of Katy Perry, Rihanna, Fergie, and the list goes on. Learning how to be a lady, well, even the subject itself sounds old fashioned and grandmother-ish.

Call it what you like, but understanding the processes of how to be a lady is akin to pursuing a well-rounded education. These are the fruits of a studied life. Becoming a lady will produce greater happiness, fulfillment, real purpose, and genuine influence, depending of course, on what you would like out of life.

These studies of being a lady did not come without a price. They are the result of many years of trial and error, research and discovery, years of thought on the philosophy and the culture that was inherited, modified, and passed down to us through the years. I think we are sometimes too quick to discard the old and embrace the new. Yet, there are many benefits to living as a lady.

The World of a Lady

- Your world is generally a more pleasant place to live.
- People tend to treat you better.
- You'll start to feel more appreciated whenever you go.

(On a side note, I stumbled upon a blog of an ex-friend, and she complains about how people are rude to her all the time. I wish she could see that they are rude and mean to her because she has been rude and mean to them first.)

The more you act like a lady, the more you bring out the gentlemanly side of the men and boys in your life.

When you ask nicely and gently, you'll be surprised at the reaction it evokes in others. Your husband or son might initially think there's something wrong with you. Perhaps they will become suspicious at first, but you do not need to explain yourself. Just keep doing what you're doing, improving and adapting as you go.

People become relaxed around you and take an instant liking to you.

I know this might sound absurd, but you'll notice that even domestic pets will like you more. It is a great self-esteem booster!

When you feel like a lady, you'll feel more beautiful.

Eventually you'll stop feeling like a 'fake', because you really have become a lady, and you might even develop the courage to graciously stand up for something you believe in, or for someone who has no voice or power of their own.

You will gain a relaxed sense of confidence and notice a natural ease.

You will feel secure in yourself. You won't feel the need to impress others, or to respond to bad manners with the same tit-for-tat. You are gracious and have moved on from such behaviors.

Whether by conscious effort or by instinct alone, being a lady helps you become decisive and assured.

You will intuitively know how to go about your day, get around in life, and what to do in most situations. Being a lady is about being kind. And kindness is about choosing to see the best in others and yourself.

Misconceptions of Being a Lady

Today, what it means to 'be a lady' is lost amid a plethora of mixed messages. These might include: what she wears, what she talks about, who she hangs out with, where she dines, vacations, and the places she frequents, ad infinitum. None of this has any real validity.

Here are six common misconceptions of becoming a lady, or just who is a lady. Don't let any of what you read here put you off:

1. A lady has to know all the rules of etiquette.
2. A lady is boring and rarely says what she really thinks.

3. A lady can't be fashionable. She wears conservative clothes.

4. Being a lady means you're fogyish and uninteresting. It's the desire of grannies.

5. A lady is so feminine; she doesn't like anything to do with sport.

6. A lady is elegant but not sexy. She is not carefree or free-spirited.

Read more *misconceptions of being a Lady* and *myths about elegance* on www.elegantwoman.org

How Did Teachings of "How to Be a Lady" Develop?

Some say training women to become ladies originated from royal etiquette.

This is my interpretation, from what I've read thus far. It seems that it all began with a little set of rules. It is in human nature to prefer beauty over vulgarity. With some basic observations and adaptation of culture over time, a series of behaviors had been encouraged and others were eliminated (pretty much in favor of what is beautiful).

Etiquette developed alongside these advances. Back when kings and queens ruled, etiquette was written for people who lived in the royal courts. They were guidelines on how to behave appropriately.

Fun fact: A little bird told me that the first etiquette rule was in French, and it meant 'stay off the grass'!

Over the generations, the art of how to be a lady has been studied, polished, and refined. It most likely started in the royal courts and aristocratic circles. As time passed and societies evolved, these teachings trickled down to the masses, and then finally on to us. Our exposure came about mainly due to social and technological advancements, and the widespread availability of education for all.

The Essence of Being an Elegant Woman

A Kind Heart and a Conqueror

Being an elegant woman is simply having extended manners, such as always seeking ways to be kind and generous to all, as well as being a conqueror in life (meaning overcoming struggles and rising above difficulties).

She has usually given thought to her conduct, and likely developed a natural and organized way to go about her life.

Obviously she should engage in personal grooming, dress well, and learn etiquette. (However, if she is not a good person, people will see through the actions as being artificial). I've met many women who appear elegant, but they lose that appearance and impression quickly from the moment they speak. It doesn't matter if a woman looks sophisticated, if she does nothing but complain, criticize, or snipe then she is far from being truly elegant.

At the end of the day, we'd all rather be acquainted with someone who laughs a little too loud and heartily, or knocks tea cups over because of her clumsiness than someone who is negative, quick to accuse, or overly boastful. The latter person is one that possesses a mean spirit and lacks any real refinement.

An Elegant Woman Will Not Rush Around or Appear to Be in a Hurry

It is terribly hard not to rush, especially as lifestyles become ever busier. I've found that when I have to rush, it's because I have underestimated the time I need. If you have such tendencies, always allocate about 25 percent more time. I've found that I do not like to wait, which is why I subconsciously try to be perfect with my timing, but the feeling of rushing makes me feel desperate and ugly, which motivates me to be punctual.

Rushing around is also a sign that we are taking on TOO MUCH. When we are hurrying, we tend to neglect the upkeep of both our home and our appearance. That affects our peace and happiness. This is not what we want, so it's a good idea to sit down and assess whether you're over committed.

How to be an elegant woman? Never be in a hurry or rush around. It's usually unproductive anyway, or as the wise old adage goes: "More haste, less speed!"

She Is Gentle, She Is Not Rude and Has a Consistent Character

It does not matter if a person is perceived as a 'nobody'. She treats everyone with equal respect. She does not flatter, namedrop, or apple-polish anyone just because they might drive a flashy car or appear to be well connected.

She is kind to all people no matter what their social standing is. Although she treats everyone the same, she chooses her friends wisely. She will not tolerate someone who is unduly mean.

She Is Tasteful in Speech

She is tasteful and considerate in her conversations. Her words are full of grace. She handles discussions appropriately, whether it's a casual setting or a formal one.

She knows when to maintain a respectful distance of friendliness. She'll know not to ask inappropriate questions, such as when are you going to get married or when are you having children?

She also does not assume. She does not presume you know of her, or 'how important she is'. She'll not be cheeky and ask for a lift home, or for a favor. If she needs a favor, she will ask respectfully and politely, and without manipulating guilt. And if you can offer a professional service, she'll expect to pay you the same as any other client.

Is Always Presentable

An elegant woman makes an effort to present herself properly in her appearance. She employs good grooming in good taste. She has lovely posture. She is poised. She stands up straight, yet her shoulders are relaxed.

Is Beautiful Inside Out

Outside beauty does not go beyond the eyes. You can tell whether a person is internally beautiful by the look of their eyes. Do they wear a bored look? Do they appear proud?

A woman with elegance has kind eyes; eyes that smile. These eyes come from inner beauty. Inner beauty comes from kind thoughts and a genuine love and care for others.

How does she get to be this way? She invests in her mind and soul. She is careful not to harbor resentment, but forgives. She is able to let go and move on from any unpleasantness. She reads good books and probably goes to church.

It is important to invest in 'good food for the soul' DAILY! This is also what I mean when I talk about starting from within.

Takes Care of Herself

She makes an effort to be healthy, to eat and sleep well, and to exercise regularly. She doesn't take her health for granted. This is not vanity; this is disciplined character.

Keeps to Her Appointments

Remember the time when we did not have cell phones? If we had a lunch appointment at noon on Saturday, it happened as arranged. Folks generally arrived on time, too. It was expected that we turned up and were punctual, arriving at the exact location and at the agreed time.

With the convenience of emails, cellphones, and smartphones the integrity of socializing has been compromised.

Last minute cancellations, constant change of details (right up to the latest possible time) like, *"Let's meet at 2 pm.*

No, make it 2:15.Then again, how about 2:30?" Or "Let's meet at the Blackbird cafe. Hang on; let's change that to Gloria Jeans at Chadstone Shopping Mall", or, "Can you meet earlier?" or, "sorry I'm late, I'm on my way". And so it goes; a stream of confusing and never-ending excuses and letdowns.

It's not unusual to find ourselves waiting at one o'clock pm only to get a text message at 1:15 informing us that our party is going to be late, or worse, canceling altogether.

What's so appalling is that such disrespect has become common practice and people seem to accept it because it allows for reciprocal behavior.

It makes you wonder about the dependability of the other person to turn up when you make an appointment with her. A lady can be depended on to stick to her appointments and not cancel them at a whim. She is one who knows that changing times, places, and other arrangements just to suit her own convenience, is selfish, unladylike, and just plain wrong.

Is Meek but Not a Doormat

While she is meek, she stands up for her family and friends whenever a situation calls for it.

She does not shy away from objection, but she is not rude when doing so. She merely states her objections and protests respectfully.

If someone cuts in front of her in a queue, she is not afraid to say politely to that person, *"I'm sorry, but I believe I was here first."*

She is **self-controlled when she is angry**. She does not give into anger easily, but when she is upset, she handles herself with dignity and pride. She will raise her voice but speak firmly and assertively.

She will not give into ugly emotions and retort with unkind words, insult, and ridicule. She remains in control of her emotions at all times. She will be fair. If an issue is getting out of hand, she will walk away from it first, and then come back when both parties have cooled off a little.

Is Responsible

If entrusted with a secret, she keeps it in the strictest confidence. If it's a child, or a pet that she's looking after, she takes care of it to the best of her ability.

She stays at home if she has a cold or other spreadable illness. She will not drive if she suspects she has had a little too much to drink. If she borrows her friend's car, she returns it cleaned with the petrol tank full, or with the parking money topped off.

She always returns borrowed items in good order. If she breaks something, she replaces it immediately.

Refuses to Be Victimized

No matter what life throws at her, she never behaves like a victim.

She does not indulge in self-pity; neither does she drag dark clouds around, telling her sorry stories to everyone she meets. If she has to, she relates them in a matter-of-fact manner, downplaying the emotions and keeping the details short. She rises above pressure. She remains composed at all times. The character of an elegant woman is that she remains composed.

No matter what the situation, she tries her best to keep composed and calm at all times. She knows that freaking out will do nothing to help the matter. Keeping a cool head and being calm enable her to employ her best response.

She Does Not Steal Someone's Thunder

Upstaging the bride, turning a conversation onto oneself, talking over others, speaking incessantly about herself, or chattering non-stop (and without pausing for breath), are not the kinds of things she does.

She gives credit when credit is due, but better still, she may give away all the credit, and single out people who have made it a team effort.

She Does Not Have a Know-it-All Attitude

Despite her qualifications, she does not let her appearance communicate a sense of "I-know-better". She keeps this to herself and retains a humble attitude. In fact, the more one knows, the more likely they are to be humble about it, because they understand that it's impossible for anyone to know everything or achieve it all. She does not make anyone feel less-than or stupid.

She does not expect everyone to like her, think like her, agree with her, or be friends with her.

No matter how nice she is, she understands that about one in ten people she meets may not like her in the way she would like them to. She simply goes about her business, remaining friendly and polite. She'll not obsess over it, nor go the extra mile to make someone like her.

She also does not expect everyone to agree with her, share in her values, or her way of life. She accepts individuality and respects personal choice. She is comfortable with differences.

She Keeps Her Word

She respects deadlines and keeps to them. She also remembers that words, no matter how friendly they are, are not to be taken lightly. She acknowledges that words have power. She knows that she can refuse to talk about anything. She also means what she says and keeps her promises, even if the other party does not.

She's careful not to talk too much about a subject. For someone who divulges too much detail often seems to have slight regrets to bear afterwards.

How to Be Elegant at Work

She is formal in her emails at work. She writes in a respectful and business-like manner, knowing that it's important to keep it short, to the point, and unambiguous. She uses the subject in her email appropriately and concisely to allow the recipient(s) to identify it immediately. She also leaves adequate contact details in her signature.

Even though BlackBerry phones and 'email-on-the-go' are common these days, she does not assume that an email can replace a text message or a phone call.

She does not expect a reply immediately and will wait for a few days before sending a reminder. She also understands that if it is truly urgent, she will not depend on email, but will use the phone, make a trip to the office, or send a registered letter.

At work, she is respectful to those she works with, and does not treat people differently according to rank and position within the company.

She does not act like she works hard only when the boss walks by or into her space. She does not claim all the credit when she hands over a report if the workload has been shared. She humbly accepts praise. An elegant woman does not speak with excessive positivity, or use extra smiles and energy on those above her, nor is she rude and cold to those who work under her.

How to Be Elegant at a Party

She is a great guest at parties.

Proper Introductions

When meeting someone for the first time, stand up to shake his or her hand. When being introduced, politely stand so that everyone may see who you are.

How Does an Elegant Woman Become the Perfect Guest?

She never arrives too early or too late, and always brings a gift. She dresses appropriately for the party. She will not show up with, or as, an uninvited guest. She *always* asks permission if she hasn't been formally invited.

She socializes, gets acquainted with other guests, and engages in pleasant conversations. She does not hog any guest or monopolize the discussions. She keeps her conversations light and friendly.

She would not ask to be shown around the house unless she is offered a tour. She will avoid venturing into personal areas like a bedroom or bathroom, and remains in the rooms that have been allocated to the party.

She doesn't take or touch things that are not part of the gathering. Nor is she too friendly so as to help herself to items in the refrigerator or cupboards (unless requested to, or they have been allocated to the event). She sends a thank you note (either handwritten or via the phone or email) to the host after the party.

When Invited to a Party, She Does Not Ask the Question, "Who Will Be Going?"

This shows a conditional acceptance and is not particularly gracious. It exhibits a self-absorbed focus instead of a genuine appreciation for being invited. If you have some concerns, do find other ways to respond and be tactful about it. She also replies to the RSVP as quickly as possible, mindful that her host will have an easier time planning.

If she declines, she gives a straightforward answer instead of, "I'll let you know, I might be able to make it" (95% of ambiguous replies end up without any further response or attendance).

If you said you were coming, make sure that you turn up. I cannot count the number of times I've heard hosts complain about how they prepared food and drinks for 20, yet only 15 came. Worse still is when someone sends a lame text message to say they cannot come until 9pm when the party started at 8:00. Such behavior is inconsiderate.

Socializing Elegantly

She asks permission before giving out the phone number of a friend. She also never calls anyone after 10:30 pm or before 9:00 am, unless it is an absolute emergency or prearranged.

She Knows Her Boundaries and Does Not Overstep Them

She does not call people she barely knows by their first names unless asked. She does not turn up unannounced at someone's home. She never asks about what someone's property is worth, profit margin, or how much money they make or earn.

She never enquires about how many people another person in her company has dated, their sexual history, or goes into any intimate details whatsoever. She also never asks how much something costs, amount spent per head at a wedding, where they bought a thing from, or at least NOT directly or out of pure nosiness.

She knows that even if a certain person is her best friend, and calls her such, she cannot expect to gain that same 'title' in return, but is graciously happy if it is returned.

She does not expect her 'best friend' to tell her everything, or keep nothing from her, but simply respect her wishes.

She also makes her requests known clearly. For example, if she could have the price brought down due to a defect, but does not persist relentlessly or says something that might make the sales assistant feel uncomfortable or embarrassed, and thus avoid eye contact or cause her to blush.

Note: I know when you are very close to someone, all the above does not matter, but this is written only to encourage discretion and sensitivity.

An Elegant Woman and Her Phone

During dinner, or when having a meal with someone, she does not chat casually on her phone. Depending on the formality of the situation, she may put her phone into silent mode, and does not take calls during a formal dinner. If the dinner is casual, she answers only if the call seems urgent. If she does take the call, she offers immediately to call them back after her social engagement has ended, unless it's something that really cannot wait.

She certainly does not stay on the phone for a casual chat, or to resolve any issue etc. Such behavior is very disrespectful to the person or people she's dining with.

Traveling Elegantly

At a hotel or a friend's home, she leaves the place as she found it. She clears her rubbish, tidies the place up, and cleans the bathroom sink, bathtub, or shower areas if there are visible watermarks.

Integrity

She does not cancel on a whim. She is dependable when you make a social engagement with her.
I certainly enjoy meeting up with these people, and am very happy that most of my friends bear this trait. If they say they will turn up, they do, no matter how many people are already at a party. They show commitment, disciplined character, and real integrity.

An elegant woman never says what she doesn't mean to do or follow up on. For example, she doesn't say, let's do lunch or have coffee, and then never follows through with the suggestions. She does not take someone's phone number without the intention to call. She does not say, I'll call you later, and not call.

If someone says to her, *"Let's do lunch,"* she understands that it is their responsibility to contact her. She may make the first move, but she also understands that not everyone says what they mean.

An Elegant Woman Would Not Give a Thoughtless Gift.

If she receives one, or a gift she doesn't like too much, she smiles and bears it. She appreciates the fact that they thought of her.

Elegance in the Art of Conversation

She never interrupts someone mid-sentence. An elegant woman should never try to second-guess what someone is going to say before they finish speaking, and she never interrupts the person talking mid-sentence.

However, I do understand that it's hard to remain quiet when we enter into conversation with someone who talks incessantly. In situations like these, I try my very best to relax, and let the person continue chattering while I remain very quiet.

Sooner or later, the talkative one will note your patience, and eventually give you a chance to speak. I often notice that people who talk too much do not listen as well. So take extra care to ensure you have communicated clearly.

An Elegant Woman Refrains from Giving Unsolicited Explanations

If you have been offered something you don't want, simply say "no thank you" and perhaps ask for something else. It is really not necessary to explain your choice. Sometimes we tend to rant on a bit because we feel a little insecure. I had a humiliating experience once when I was in my teens. My mother insisted I carry a cellphone to school because she had bought one for me. But at that time, no one had cellphones except the 'rich kids'.

I was not rich (but had a generous mother), nor was I comfortable being labeled as someone who was 'well-off'. I just wanted to be like everyone else. I even kept my leather designer purse at home that my mother had purchased for me on a previous business trip. I bought an ordinary faux leather bag at the local mall to avoid embarrassing questions, such as how much it cost, can I see it, etc.

From a very young age, I never felt comfortable parading around with things that other kids didn't have. When some of my friends found out that I had a cell phone, they obviously asked to see it. I sheepishly handed it over and proceeded to explain how I got it, and how my mother had acquired it at a great discount. One guy looked me straight in the eye and said, *"Hey, I only asked to see it, not to get a full explanation"*.

From that moment onwards, I learned to shut up and not apologize for anything, while at the same time respond graciously.

How to Be Elegant in the Company of Others

An elegant woman makes an effort to remember people's names and pronounce them correctly.

She repeats a name after being introduced to make sure she got it right. She may use little tricks and ways to ensure that she remembers the name in the future. *"I'm so bad with names"* is a lame excuse and is used far too often. An elegant woman asks permission before giving out the phone number of a friend.

She also never calls anyone after 10:30 pm and before 9:00 am, unless it is an absolute emergency.

Proper Introduction

Introduce the younger to the older, the man to the woman. When there is rank, introduce the 'lower' rank to the 'higher' one. Though I do not feel that we have to strictly adhere to this rule, use your own discretion, and take this as a general guideline. And never assume that your friends know each other or have already introduced themselves.

Elegance

She makes light of her achievements when praised by others. She also quickly changes the topic after graciously saying her thank-yous. She never brags, especially about luxury items, and particularly if someone present might be struggling on a small income. She never says things to make other people feel small, neither does she says anything to make herself feel big.

She Never Laughs or Makes Jokes at Other People's Expense

Even though it has been many years now, I can still recollect the painful memories of being laughed at when I was a child, a teenager, and a young woman. Such mockery could be due to a small income, the absence of designer goods, lack of sophistication, and a lack of knowledge on intellectual matters, ad infinitum.

I don't want anyone to ever feel how I felt back then. Nor do I want anyone to participate in making individuals feel terrible about them and their lives. It's far better to encourage people than to put them down, plus it's more rewarding for both parties.

An Elegant Woman Refrains from Asking Uncomfortable Questions:

- "Have you lost/gained weight?"
- "Is it real?" (e.g., gold, diamond, designer goods, etc.)
- "How much did it cost?"
- "What grade/specs is your diamond?"
- "What happened to your face?"
- "What is that on your face?" (e.g., an unusually large pimple or rash)
- "You don't remember me, do you?"
- "Is that your boyfriend?"
- "When is it your turn?" (e.g., to get married, have a child, etc.)

- "Why did you get retrenched? What happened to your old job?"

If you really feel you have to ask, please try to be indirect or be as sensitive as you can. Be mindful of the fact that your friend might be uncomfortable about a probing question, or simply does not want to talk about it.

And please, whatever you do, refrain from using that age-old disclaimer, *"I don't mean to intrude,"* or *"I hope you don't mind me asking, but..."*

She Does Not Speak in another Language to another Person about Others

If there are others in the room who cannot understand the language, she never whispers or points at someone and laughs.

If you can't communicate in the general language of the party, try your very best to speak privately, or look at your other guests and say, "Excuse me for a bit, I need to explain what that means in Indonesian for her."
It's best to keep to topics where you can communicate in the common language, particularly if there is someone present who only understands the basics of the language being spoken. Do not let the party go on with a constant translation in progress, as this is inconsiderate and frustrating for the other guests.

Whispering, or cupping your hands over a person's ear, is also a big no-no. Looking at someone from a distance, then smiling and laughing out loud is also offensive. These are the kinds of actions that can make a person feel very insecure and uncomfortable.

If you need to speak privately, do it out of the view of others. Send an SMS message discreetly if you really must.

An Elegant Woman Is Not Afraid to Apologize When She Makes a Mistake

No one likes to do it, and it takes a humble spirit and strength of character to do so. I work on my character (or ask God to work on me!), grit my teeth, and keep my face calm when I do.

She does not bring it up again and again. When being apologized to, she accepts it as graciously as possible, and keeps her feelings under control, no matter how much she might want to lash out at the offense. She makes the effort to move on and put the incident behind her. She never apologizes if she's not in the wrong.

An Elegant Woman Does Not Raise Her Voice

She never allows her face to be contorted with rage, to seethe, or become incensed. When angry, she is still in control of her emotions and very smartly removes herself from a situation if she feels ready to snap, near her tipping point, or on the verge of losing control. She knows how to cool herself down, and knows it's best to deal with the situation in a calm manner, later on.

If she is having an intense discussion, and the other person is perhaps getting irritated, possibly enraged, she becomes affected and wisely excuses herself or changes the subject for the moment. She knows that there is no point in arguing about a thing that has no likely resolution, especially in the short term.

She can always come back to it later, if need be, when some time alone has passed for each party to calm down and reflect.

An Elegant Woman Does Not Get Embarrassed

When she uses a wrong word, makes a silly mistake, or is the subject of 'jokes', by an inconsiderate friend who proceeds to tell of her dating history at a dinner party, as an example, she does not allow herself to be embarrassed, and deals with the mishap in a composed and dignified manner.

She does not proceed to 'fake laugh' at her mistake, and go on and on about it in the hope of concealing her faux pas. But perhaps she'll afford herself a little laugh or a smile, and then move on.

She gives a generous grin at her offending guest, and says: *"Now enough of that, you embarrassed me!"* Show a bit of unconcern and disinterest, shift eye contact, then strategically change the subject.

When an Elegant Woman Calls First, She Ends the Call Too

If it is only a minute-long call, say, *"Do you have a spare minute?"* And do stick to that minute. Or if you need five minutes, make that request clear. You may also say, *"Is this a good time?"* Asking the question: *"When will be a good time to call?"* is also a good choice if the person is busy.

An Elegant Woman Will Not Put Anyone on the Spot

She never singles out a person and asks direct questions, especially in front of others. If she has to say something unpleasant, she does so privately.

She does not ask guests to pray, acknowledging the fact that not everyone is comfortable doing so. She also never insists that everyone must pray when she is hosting a dinner party or other event where praying is appropriate for some but not all.

She does not make guests play games at her parties, especially if those games involve speaking in front of everyone, running around the room, or sitting on the floor.

Some people might be wearing dresses, are concerned about dirt on the ground, or have fears of speaking publicly.

I personally prefer not to have those games where everyone stares at you in the room while you share something about yourself. Playing a game using any sort of intelligence is perhaps better for a mixed group (unless there are children participating of course!).

Although I have no qualms personally about public speaking, providing it is in English, I do recognize that we're all different, and some folks really don't want to do it for various reasons.

I simply state my observations here. I've noticed that, in general, at least half the guests are extremely uncomfortable, or are shy, or might feel insecure displaying their lack of grammar, quick wit or creativity, whether it be fancied or real. If all of you have been friends a long time, or it's a small group in an intimate setting, then speaking confidently in front of one another is more than likely to be perfectly all right.

I do not like to subject my guests to games (especially with larger gatherings), because I do not assume they all enjoy participating in games!

An Elegant Woman Does Not Complain or Whine or Nag

This can also be a result of cultural differences, but how many of us can actually say that we enjoy a conversation where someone is complaining, whining or nagging about someone, something, or some place?

An Elegant Woman Avoids Vulgarity

An elegant woman uses positive words and refrains from crudity in language. Spoken vulgarity in language does not simply apply to swear words; she does not use swear words in her speech and maintains composure in her vocabulary. Limiting what you say is the key here. It is vulgar to criticize, boast, or speak of other people's personal problems to everyone and anyone who lends an ear.

It is sometimes vulgar to be too direct, to the point where it is inappropriate. It's improper to assume as well. Steer clear of using "I", "me", and "my" too much. Learn how to avoid "intense words" like "angry"(use annoyed or irritated instead)."Ugly", "hate", or other rude words display a venomous tone as well.

Elegance with Personal Opinions

She does not voice strong opinions on her likes and dislikes, such as *"I can't stand poodles. They are so ugly."* She understands that her present company might actually like poodles, has a poodle, or intends to buy a poodle. She also does not preach about any subject or give strong comments on politics, business, different religions, various races, and so on, especially to people she doesn't know too well.

I understand we are all humans and that we have many strong opinions about various things. Do use great discretion when voicing them, or limit them as much as you can. Discuss them with your mother or your husband if you need to air your views. You could also write anonymously on a blog or an internet forum, as that helps to get things off one's chest.

She does not correct someone's grammar, pronunciation, or laugh at their mistakes. She does not say things like, *"Goodness, what is she wearing?"* or ask, *"What brand are your jeans?"*

An Elegant Woman Never Freeloads

She never asks for free help from professional friends, and only asks for assistance if she fully expects to pay. If a friend offers to help for free or at a discounted rate, she accepts them graciously if she feels comfortable doing so. But if she has the means to pay the 'going rate', then she may insist on paying the full price to support her friend. If the friend in question is already doing well financially, she might show her appreciation by recommending more friends or returning a favor of some kind.

After I ran my first business, I never found it very satisfying when a friend asked for a discount, even though I had every intention of offering them one at cost price or even free.

I also appreciate it greatly when a friend insists on paying full price to support my growing business. So, even though I'm open to giving discounts to close friends, I want the gesture to come from me and not to be asked for it.

When an elegant woman does a favor, she is quiet about it and tries not to let anyone know. She does not make an announcement or spectacle of it. She also does not try to make the person receiving the favor feel embarrassed or remind them of her generosity.

She does not tell anyone that she has sponsored her family's holiday, the costs involved, how much she paid for a new spa package, or who she's invited onto her yacht, etc.

If she allows a friend to use her restaurant for holding a party at a discounted rate, she does not tell her friend that the partygoers did not spend enough, or how she could have made more money that day if she'd not allowed Kelly to use her restaurant for a private get-together.

She does not tell her any of these things, no matter what inconveniences it may have cost or caused her at the time.

If her friend and her party of friends made an awful mess, or damaged some property but did not pay for the damage or help clean up afterwards, then she will have a quiet word with her on those issues, but will not mention any of the other matters above because they are separate concerns.

Obviously, she will not be invited again if she is inconsiderate, rude, or unappreciative of the favor.

She Is Aware of Social Debt

If she accepts favors, she knows the favor has to be repaid. She repays social invitations by giving social invitations. She understands that a friendship has to be a two-way thing. One invitation is reciprocated by another. She cannot expect to be constantly invited to parties and various functions without mutual goodwill.

An Elegant Woman Never Points the Finger

She never points out or discusses the mistakes, faults, or imperfections of her partner. This can be a difficult one, because we ladies like to seek solace in one another and complain and compare stuff to make ourselves feel better. Occasionally, within a light-hearted conversation, some degree of the above is acceptable. After all, it's good to talk and get stuff off our chest at times, right? However, no matter how lightly you treat the matter, be considerate and mindful of what we say and how we say it. Try to think of how your partner would feel if he could hear you, or how you would feel should you find out he was doing the same to you?.

An Elegant Woman Never Goes into Relationship Details

She avoids going into details about her break-ups or her past relationships. Leave the past in the past and try to move on. And do not inquire about others either. It is none of our business.

An Elegant Woman Doesn't Find Fault with Others

She never points out negative observations about someone's manners, the bad behavior of someone's child, the state of her house, car, or anything else.

She makes people feel at ease, never takes things personally, and does not get offended if they did not do or say something differently than she would have done.

She pretends not to notice small issues like a child's bad behavior, a person's unkempt appearance (thinking she might have had a bad time at home before leaving the house). She refrains from staring when someone chews with their mouth open, talks with their mouth full, spills, or knocks over a coffee cup, sneezes, coughs, or belches. She does not stare or point no matter what.

An Elegant Woman Does Not Make a Gossipy Fascinated Face

She avoids visually expressing curiosity, no matter how interested she might actually be in something or someone. She does not encourage gossip, nor does not she want to know. At least she wills herself to think that way!

She Does Not Eat Someone Else's Food

She never reaches over and takes food off of someone's plate and she *never* asks if she can have a taste. She refrains from doing eating other people's food, even when offered, unless under intimate circumstances.

Foot Etiquette

On the airplane, she does not remove her shoes unless she does so to wear the 'special slippers' the airline has provided for passengers. She is mindful of how feet can sometimes smell or be unsightly to others, so she is diligent to keep hers covered with footwear. She brings a pair of fresh socks to wear on the plane if she must remove her shoes. She also does not hog the adjacent armrests.

Eating Etiquette

She understands that eating is a private action and does not stare or look at someone as they consume their meals. When having a meal with someone, she focuses on the person's countenance, her/his eyes, and not how she/he eats.

She allocates proper time for her meals. She always sits down and eats at a table, and not in front of the television. She eats slowly and chews. She does not eat on the go, i.e., eat while walking, driving, on the bus, or in other public places, unless of course it's is a picnic.

She Does Apply Makeup in Public Places

A discreet quick application of lip gloss or lipstick is quite acceptable, though it is advisable to do so in a restroom whenever possible.

She Is Respectful Around Other People's Children

An elegant woman does not feed other people's children, touch them, or play with them, unless invited to do so. She does not reprimand other people's children or correct their manners. She also does not try to teach them how to behave.

One may give the occasional smile, or wave. Do not feed anyone's children with your food, or offer from a packet of candy you may have in your bag. Always check with a parent first.

I know many mothers are particular about the germs and diseases hands carry from other people, so do be considerate of the different standards of cleanliness that some ladies have.

When it comes to giving gifts to children, do check with the mother to ask if it's okay or not. Some mothers don't allow certain types of toys, or toys made of certain kinds of material.

All mothers have their own ways or philosophies of how their children should be brought up or what they should be taught. Do ask if you are in doubt. Feel free to give your compliments though.

Netiquette

On Facebook or other social networking sites, an elegant woman does not add every possible acquaintance as a 'friend', especially if she's only met that person for five seconds. That's unless, of course, she would genuinely like to be further acquainted with the individual for whatever reason(s).

She also does not feel obligated to approve every request she receives. She does not allow online social networks to replace her 'real-world' social life. Nor does she depend on it with the same confidence as email or phone communication. She does not expect her friends to log onto Facebook regularly or to read her messages and respond to them quickly.

She does not post embarrassing photos of herself or her friends on any social networks.

She adheres to her friend's requests as much as she can. If, for instance, they do not like their image in a photo and request it be deleted, she will do that. She may ignore them if they are too picky too often, and simply do not like various photos because they think they look unflattering in them.

There's always the option to un-tag herself, especially if it's a group photo.

An elegant woman does not upload vulgar photos on Facebook, photos of compromising positions, drunken faces (unless they are happy and tasteful), photos of a sexual nature used as jokes. If you really want to post things that are a little 'risky' shall we say, then put them in a private album. Be mindful of the fact that some photos of friends (even if taken many years ago), might get them into trouble with their partners or work associates.

Try to think of the "grandmother test:" If you wouldn't want her to see it, then don't share it publicly online! Such images or unladylike comments might just come back to haunt you one day, because once they're out there in cyberspace, they will be there forever.

She also does not use crudity freely or join groups that have vulgarities in their names or descriptions.
Though it is personal choice, she does not upload every single photo of her life. She chooses her photos wisely and sees Facebook albums as a way of sharing her best moments with her friends, rather than overwhelming them with never-ending photos of her model-make-over poses, her kids, her wedding, pointless videos of herself, or anything boastful.

It's sometimes quite easy to assume that other people are interested in the intricate details of our lives, but the fact of the matter is that most are not. The key here is to use social networks in moderation, or as one of my favorite sayings go:

"Everything is okay in moderation, including, moderation!"

An Elegant Woman Uses Designer Goods Subtly

While she enjoys and values the finer things in life, and appreciates designer goods, she does not adorn herself with upmarket logos displayed over her clothes, shoes, and bags; nor does she have brand name logos dangling from her ears.

She also knows when it is appropriate to wear or carry a certain type of bag, and when to wear specific types of jewelry for different occasions.

An Elegant Woman Is Well-Groomed

An elegant woman takes care of herself and her appearance at all times, and that includes after marriage and after having a baby. She will find a way to do this. It is as fundamental as brushing her teeth.

She Does Not Wear Clothes That Cause Others to Blush

She does not wear clothes that are too sloppy, too revealing, too high fashion, or too wild in expression, and anything else that draws negative attention to herself.
She also wears the right shoes for the appropriate situation. Not kitten heels for hiking, for example (which I have witnessed before in Hawaii). She also ensures her footwear is not dirty or scuffed.
She does not wear clothes that reveal hints of undergarments, for instance, a dark colored brassiere with a white blouse. If it is too translucent, she either wears a nude set or a camisole.
She does not adjust her bra straps in public other than a quick swipe to put it in place. In an unfortunate situation, she excuses herself to the bathroom and fixes her underclothing. If that option is not possible, she has little choice but to do a quick and discrete adjustment. If someone points out something revealing about her undergarments, she keeps a straight face, calmly says thank you, and excuses herself to the restroom.

An Elegant Woman Is Modest

She does not have excessive things and does not place too much value on the material belongings in life.
There is always something very frugal and sensible about an elegant lady. She does not go and spend money on every latest 'must have' item, or newest fashions, nor does she talk much about material things or personal possessions. There is something ethereal about her, and you can tell, or feel, where her true values lie.

When she buys new items, she always buys the highest quality she can afford at the time, and will only replace something if it is no longer of any use.

An Elegant Woman Does Not Behave Inappropriately

Behaviors change with age. When one is young, she may get away with certain things that would be totally inappropriate for a lady of more mature years. Running down hills, jumping up and down in delight, girly giggles and so on, are not the way a lady at, say, age 45 would behave.

How to Be Elegant with Appointments

An elegant woman makes the effort to call and check-in as soon as possible. Whether she's late for an appointment at the spa, needs to change the reservation at a restaurant, or to check on the appropriate attire for an opera, she always calls to be considerate.

She does not ask if she can bring a guest to someone's wedding. If her invitation says, 'guest', then the invite is loud and clear.

Understanding Dress Code Etiquette

She knows how to be an elegant woman at functions and to use a dress code. An elegant woman understands the meaning of a dress code. She does not wear anything to upstage a bride. She does not wear anything too revealing as if setting off for a nightclub (she does not wear anything too revealing, period).

She knows that 'formal' or 'black tie' mean long dresses and gowns. She would not wear a cocktail dress to a formal event. She also does not wear denim to a wedding.

Cell Phone Etiquette

An elegant woman knows when to turn off her cell phone. Examples are: At the movies, at dinner, at a meeting, at a wedding, etc. She does not take calls at a wedding or performance, not even discreetly.

Marks of an Accomplished Woman

Who is the accomplished lady? Jane Austen tells us it's whoever deserves the respect and praise of being educated, refined, and accomplished.

In fact, it can be quite inspiring to look to the past, to the era of Jane Austen for example, when people seemed to be educated and refined. It wasn't a time of constantly being hurried and dashing everywhere, as it is nowadays. People took their time. Women became ladies.

I suppose we are more educated in the times that we are living in now. However, there was a different spirit of elegance, or essence in how people lived their lives in those times, according to the writings of Jane Austen. Reading deeper into the writings of Jane Austen, one can discover how society viewed the quality and class of ladies.
Not dissimilar to today, men of status wanted to marry women of the highest quality. Such a woman is described in many words today: educated, beautiful, family oriented, intelligent, kind, elegant, and so the list goes on. But we can sum it up by saying she is an accomplished lady.

Like in Jane Austen's time, an accomplished lady commands the respect of society and everyone around her. She will probably have many eligible suitors.

What Are the Traits of an Accomplished Lady?

The following quotations from *Pride and Prejudice* illustrate past views on the accomplished lady:

"'It is amazing to me,' said Bingley, 'how young ladies can

have patience to be so very accomplished, as they all are.'

'All young ladies accomplished! My dear Charles, what do you mean?' (His sister's response)

'Yes all of them, I think. They all paint tables, cover skreens and net purses. I scarcely know anyone who cannot do all this and I am sure I never heard a young lady spoken of for the first time, without being informed that she was very accomplished.'"

Mr. Darcy, his friend, far from agrees with him. He goes on to state that he does not know more than six women whom he can consider to be an accomplished lady. And Mr. Bingley's sister heartily agrees with this.

"'Then,' observed Elizabeth, 'you must comprehend a great deal in your idea of an accomplished woman.'"

Bingley's sister, who probably had her eye on Mr. Darcy, eagerly agrees, as she was trying to impress him. She is sarcastically described as "his faithful assistant". I'm sure! (See below):

"'Oh! certainly,' cried his faithful assistant, 'no one can really esteemed accomplished, who does not greatly surpass what is usually met with. A woman must have a thorough knowledge of music, singing, drawing, dancing and the modern languages to deserve the word; and besides all this, she must possess a certain something in her air and manner of walking, the tone of her voice, her address and expressions, or the word will be but half deserved.'

'All this she must possess,' added Darcy, *'and to all this she must yet add something more substantial, in the improvement of her mind by extensive reading.'"*

Thus, we can draw these conclusions from Mr. Darcy, and representatively at that time, on the **description of the ideal woman**.

Traits of an Accomplished Lady

To summarize, a woman must have a thorough knowledge of the following :

- Music
- Singing
- Drawing
- Dancing
- Modern languages
- Possess a certain something in her air
- Manner of walking (and I suppose her gestures)
- The tone of her voice
- Her address and expressions
- She must yet add something more substantial in the improvement of her mind by extensive reading.

These are the characteristics that **respectable men of that day wanted in their wives**. They certainly did not want silly partners.

How Does That Apply in Today's Society?

What really astounded me was how little has changed from 200 years ago.
The descriptions are of how one defines traits of class today. The more traits you have, the 'classier' the world views you.
        If a young woman pursued the above list, then we can refer to her what we call today as "classically educated".

She will have her original character, but it has been shaped through the discipline of her mind, from hard work, acquisition of knowledge, and esteem for the arts and language.
Her confidence will soar with her education, allowing her to develop poise, manners, and the ability to socialize elegantly and at complete ease.

15. The Art of Elegant Living

An Elegant Life and the Art of Elegant Living

To acquire an elegant life, you first have to 'choose' to want it.

So just how do we live an elegant lifestyle? In my opinion, it is one that is uncluttered. It is simple yet filled with meaning, love, family, and friends. It includes a selection of hobbies that are practiced with passion. Know what it is that makes you smile and seek the pleasures of a simple lifestyle.

An elegant woman is never in a rush, nor is she flustered. She may be occupied, but not busy. She makes time for her family and leisure activities, but lives with only her family in her life. She does not dread her fate and tries to find meaning in her work. She is thrilled when she has found a vocation that inspires and energizes her. One wonders: "How has she managed to put it all together so well?" It all boils down to one simple principle: **careful selection**.

First of all, some degree of self-reflection is a must. Think about what is MOST important to you in life, and then work to **ensure your daily choices** reflect that.

For instance, if you want to spend more time with your children, opt for a lesser paying job that allows you to work fewer hours or from home. Time with family is one of the best investments of your time.

If you decide that you no longer want to be in a toxic relationship, reduce the amount of time spent with that person, and then slowly withdraw yourself altogether.

"Elegance is refusal." ~ Coco Chanel

With this "framework" in mind, we eliminate choices that are not healthy, and we no longer compromise on our priorities.

There are also some general principles of an elegant life you can follow:

- Choose quality. Always go for the best that you can afford. Learn to assess value of the item. Once you can do so, you can pick out good quality goods for less money. Leave all that cheap, poorly made stuff behind. It ends up costing you more in the long run anyway,

- Minimize stuff. Have only one of everything. Do not buy anything until you have completely exhausted its use, or at least give it away before you buy something new.

- Keep your house in order at all times.

- Do not overload your schedule.

- Do things that make you happy as often as possible.

- Be selective in the activities and hobbies you pursue. Limit them to less than five.

- Don't give more attention to fashion than you need to. It is fickle, fleeting, and high fashion styles only suit very specific body types. It's okay to be inspired by fashion, but develop your own style.

- Learn to enjoy the simple most authentic pleasures in life, like: a good book, cuisine made from the freshest and finest ingredients, riding a bicycle, and so on.

- Choose your friends wisely. Look for friends with similar values as you.

- Go to church and grow spiritually. It does wonders for your heart.

- Learn something new. Take an online class. A new language, a skill of some description. Pursue that nagging interest.
- Dance: Take up ballet or ballroom dancing, or any other type of dance that takes your fancy. It does wonders for your posture and health.
- Travel: Traveling opens up mindsets and exposes us to different cultures. It causes us to reflect on ourselves as well. Many great ideas for life are derived from travel!
- Keep your finances healthy. Learn the art of good stewardship. Be financially educated and fiscally savvy.
- Appreciate the arts. Learn to see the beauty in the world around you. In children's art too, and in plays, musicals, etc.
- Throw a party! If you are intimidated, throw a small dinner party for a few close friends. Jot down some tips from my *Elegant Entertaining* page.
- You don't need to know everything in this life, but pick a few subjects you love and passionately pursue a deeper knowledge of them.
- Cultivate a relationship with yourself. Spend some 'me-time'. Always seek self-knowledge. It is easy to get lost, especially when we wear many hats.

So, therein lays the art of refinement. Despite the greater understanding and knowledge we obtain, we still have to make a conscious effort to simplify and weed out that which is unnecessary.

Elegant Decorating and How to Make Your Home Elegant

I wrote the piece below for wikiHow some time back. Enjoy!

Elegant Decorating for an Elegant Home

While we differ in our tastes and styles for elegant decorating, there are some basic principles of elegance where we can all identify and differentiate a level of stylishness within our homes. A beautiful space that you reside in is a reflection and extension of you, what you represent, and what you love.

Making your residence elegant does not necessarily mean you have to spend large amounts of money, if any all, as there will undoubtedly be some cohesive elements already, which simply need tweaking. Naturally, if you have a fair budget, there are always ways to spend it!

Elegant Decorating Basics

1. Choose a color scheme.

Select two to three main colors for the principal color palette, followed by a couple of complimentary colors. For example, you might choose cream, brown, and green as the key colors. The complimentary colors could be a few shades lighter or darker from the cream, brown, and green, such as champagne, ivory, beige, and pastel green.
Stay away from harsh colors or any color that heavily contrasts with other colors, unless of course you are aiming for contrast for a particular feature.

2. Include the main items of the rooms in the chosen color palette.

Main items include major furnishings, such as a sofa and shelves, plus the room itself, in the form of paint and carpet or flooring.

3. Add elegant home enhancements

Elegant home enhancements include such things as green leafy plants, framed artwork or photographs, curtains or drapes, décor items, etc.

4. Create a main focal point in the room.

This central point, or feature, should be the thing that draws the eye or starts conversations when visitors enter. It might be a very elaborately framed mirror, an eye-catching painting or wall hanging of some kind, an unusual couch perhaps, or a beautiful fireplace, to name a few. Only one thing should be the sole attraction and everything else should complement it in a stylish way.

Point to note: When there is too much going on in a room, it becomes busy, creating a stressful, rather than a relaxing and unified environment.

Elegant Decorating Tip: If in doubt, leave it out!

5. Keep clutter out of sight.

Clutter includes the mail, shopping catalogs, kid's toys, clothes, and anything else that is neither pleasing to look at, nor serves any purpose to the space. Set rules about how there should only be five items on a table or any counter. Don't let anything dangle or display too many items and trinkets in your elegant home.

6. For things that you regularly use, still make an effort to keep them out of sight as much as possible.

Elegant Decorating Tip: The principle of 'group' and 'hide'.

Try to group things together. For example, keep remote controls in a beautiful basket so that only one item will be seen on the coffee table. Keep magazines in an opaque holder where one can easily access them from the sofa. You should only see the number of magazines when looking down from the top. On your makeup table, only display favorite perfumes and gather all your other cosmetics into a single cosmetic bag or basket.

The elegant home concept is one where you have easy access to things, but maintain a unified, simple look. Choose cabinets, bins, or baskets that cover and contain items. If you choose glass cabinets, plan to keep the contents in order. Clutter only interrupts the flow of the space.

7. Select beautiful, meaningful things, and use them to give the elegant home some soul.

A beautiful, elegant home is one that shows that it is loved and well planned out. Stay away from Zen looks, or overly minimalistic kinds of decorating unless that is truly your personal style. Those types of looks typically belong in corporate offices where there is a very sharp, 'switched on' feel as opposed to a relaxed, cozy, warm environment.

Elegant Decorating Tip: The Principle of Being Stringent

The key to an elegant home is stringent selection. Depending on how much space you have, select a couple of favorite things that represent lovely memories. They might turn out to be great conversation starters, and items that you'll love to share with others.

Perhaps you might display a beautiful vase full of freshly picked flowers from your garden. Such an item could serve as the centerpiece of your dining table. Maybe you have some unique treasures that you collected on your travels, or works of art that you or a friend have created.

Elegant Decorating Tip: Cleanliness is next to Godliness

8. Keep things clean.

Draw up a system for housekeeping and refer to it until it becomes habitual. Write down daily, weekly, bi-weekly, and monthly tasks, and stick to them.

Pay attention to rubbish; never leave it till it's overflowing or reeking.

If you cook a lot, ensure that the smells don't stray and spill out into the other rooms. Have your home smelling nice at all times. This also contributes towards a relaxing atmosphere.

Avoid getting stains and remove the ones you do get promptly. With clutter out of the way, you will be astonished at how much easier housework and home maintenance become.

9. Keep it simple.

Stick to a few selected styles. Avoid anything that looks too opinionated, complicated, or might be considered rude.

Elegant Decorating Tip: Things to Avoid

Avoid posters, such as posters of celebrities or movies. (Use posters only if they are elegant and can be elegantly framed.) Use joke and novelty items sparingly, if at all. This includes things like joke calendars and novelty appliances (telephones, kettles, etc.). Avoid items emblazoned with advertising or brand names.

10. Ensure your elegant home is always airy and well-lit.

Preferably your home is filled with natural light, and in the evening with a soft warm glow. Lighting in a home can either make or break the quality of elegance. In reading areas, make sure that there is enough light. Choose lamps that make sense, fit your style and theme, and aren't too gimmicky.

Elegant Decorating Tip: If in doubt, choose simple designs.

Pay attention to wires and ensure they are hidden as much as possible. Otherwise, place the wired items near sockets in order to prevent someone tripping over them.

11. Do without wires.

Nowadays, we use more electrical and electronic appliances than at any time in history. The wires and connections are often unsightly, to say the least. Here are a few suggestions on tidying up your cables:

- Go wireless wherever possible.
- Choose items with inbuilt wires and places to wrap up cords neatly.
- Conceal cords (being careful to handle electrical wiring safely).
- Run wires and cables as neatly as possible by bundling them, perhaps tying them along the underside of furnishings, etc. Never coil or tangle electrical wires. If in doubt, seek the advice of a professional on how to best manage your electric cables.

You may wish to check out my *Elegant Decorating Ideas* page on www.elegantwoman.org

Table Etiquette

The way we eat gives away a great deal about us as women. This very public exhibition is impossible to hide, and says more about our elegance in a single mouthful than the clothes we wear.
Eating is as necessary as breathing. Good manners while eating is an act of kindness. It puts people at ease and

enhances the dining experience. A sloppy eater is distracting and she draws unnecessary attention to herself. It also turns off those eating with her.

Some table etiquette faux pas:

- Eating with the mouth open
- Making noises; slurping, chewing loudly, burping
- Talking and gesticulating while eating
- Elbows stuck out in a flapping-like-a-chicken position
- Holding the fork or knife in a stabbing position
- Hunching over the food like a dog

Taking a Seat

If you have invited a friend to dinner, you're the host, and as the host, it is a nice gesture to offer seats facing a more interesting view, one which is pleasing to the eyes. If you are a gentleman, be sure to do so for the ladies. It will be nice to help with her chair too, especially if she is wearing a long gown.

If you're at a dinner party, women and men should be seated next to each other, but preferably not next to their own husband and wife. This practice is not as common as it once was, as I presume most modern husbands and wives prefer to sit next to each other.

In some traditional clubs (formally gentleman's clubs), male dinner companions were asked nicely to keep their dinner jackets on, so please do not remove your dinner jacket, especially if you are dining in the finest hotels and restaurants.

The Art of Dinner Conversation

Though most people say anything goes with regards to dinner conversation these days, there are six sensitive topics you should be wary of discussing.

Taboo topics include:

1. Money
2. Politics
3. Religion
4. Sex
5. Inappropriate jokes about race, gender, and religion
6. Sinister gossip

Boasting, bragging, name-dropping, or incessant talking are also surefire ways to make someone unpopular.

Proper Manners at the Table

Beverages, such as wine, water, coffee, etc., are usually served from your right, and another waiter usually serves plates to your left.

Point to note: It is only necessary to thank your waiter once.

Excusing yourself to use the bathroom: Okay, *if you have to go, then you have to go,* that's all there is to it! But be mindful of the fact that it is also is a conversation breaker and unsavory. It is therefore a good idea to use the bathroom before dinner to minimize this occurrence.

A good waiter should refill your glass when he sees it is half empty. Try not to raise your tumbler mid-air to 'help' while he is pouring. If he fails to see your drink is getting low, make your requests known and simply leave the glass on the table.

At a buffet, don't overload the plate if you're not going to eat everything that's stacked up on it. This just looks greedy and will guarantee to get you some unwanted attention from other diners.

Practice cutlery etiquette: Hold your utensils the right way. If you are leaving the table temporarily, set your cutlery in 'I'm-coming-back' position (just leave your cutlery separated from each other, instead of side-by-side on your plate) and leave your napkin on the seat.

It is common practice to taste the wine before accepting it. Please don't be afraid to refuse it if you can taste the cork or it is not to your liking. Of course, feel free to ask the sommelier (pronounced *somel-lee-ay*) for recommendations.

If there is a speech going on, it is rude to speak to the person beside you, no matter what!

Be aware of differences in **American table manners** and **continental style**. Always pass salt and pepper together, even if only pepper is asked for. Start with cutlery on the outside. Always break bread into a piece before buttering and eating it (refers to the bread plate at dinner). Be punctual. Do not add salt and pepper to your food before tasting it, as you might insult your host. Do not put used cutlery back onto the table.

Planning a Dinner Party

Choosing China
You would typically need 18 pieces for a dinner of 6 people.

- 6 main plates
- 6 sides
- 6 dessert plates

Glassware

This section is especially important if you love cocktail parties and plan on hosting one soon.

It is elegant to have some uniformity of glassware at the table. Traditionally, says Royal Butler Paul Burrell, *"Each drink should be served in a different style and a different size glass"*. Essential glasses for lunch and dinner are: A **water glass** and a **wine glass**. If you are serving both red and white wine, then you should have a different glass for each.

The **white wine glass is smaller** and narrower than the one used for red wine.

Champagne should be served in a flute (a tall narrow wineglass), which is designed to hold the bubbles for longer. Glasses should not be filled more than two-thirds full. Normally, **a red wine** glass is only filled one-third full.

Setting the Glassware

The general rule of thumb here is to place short in front, tall in the back. You may set the red wine, white wine, champagne, and water glasses as suggested below.

BRANDY

Brandy is served in a balloon glass (a wine glass with a larger-than-average bowl).

PORT

Port is served after dinner in a small glass (miniature looking wine glass).

Cutlery

Note that knives are always facing to the left and never to the right.

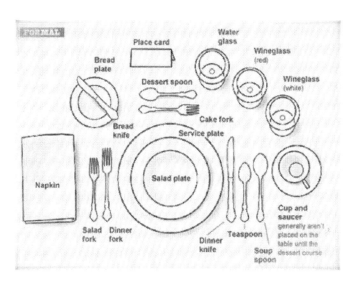

FORMAL

Water glass

Wineglass (red)

Wineglass (white)

Place card

Bread plate

Dessert spoon

Cake fork

Bread knife

Service plate

Salad plate

Napkin

Salad fork

Dinner fork

Teaspoon

Dinner knife

Soup spoon

Cup and saucer
generally aren't placed on the table until the dessert course

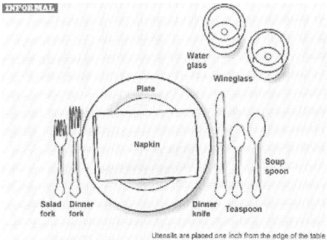

INFORMAL

Water glass

Wineglass

Plate

Napkin

Soup spoon

Salad fork

Dinner fork

Dinner knife

Teaspoon

Utensils are placed one inch from the edge of the table

Elegant Entertaining

An introduction to Elegant Entertaining: How to be a gracious host.

"Any excuse for a party!" ~ elegantwoman.org
"Celebrate life, or it will pass you by." ~ Unknown

One of the most refined traits of an elegant woman is her ability to be a gracious host. Being a gracious host is all about serving others, being generous, and investing time in relationships with family and friends.

A good party does not happen by chance. It requires planning, a bit of legwork, along with plenty of cooking and cleaning. It takes considerable effort to make a guest list, follow up, and organize the RSVPs. It also costs money! Not all parties are equally entertaining.

The Marks of a Good Party

The marks of a good party include things like, everyone is comfortable and at ease; all are well fed, and there is sufficient space to mingle after the meal. There will also be plenty of interesting conversation flowing, the lighting is flattering, and there is easy access to more drinks, etc. These are just some of the things that contribute to a great party atmosphere.

Elegant Entertaining Inspirations

Why should we learn how to entertain? Firstly, it's an elegant skill. Secondly, we are creating memories. A life fulfilled is a life shared.

Spend time, not money on materials or holiday traditions. Quality time is more precious.
Cook, eat, drink, and gather your loved ones together. Create rituals of celebration. Pass them on. It is the tradition of celebration!

I agree that it seems commercial, all these birthdays, anniversaries, Valentine's Day, Christmas, and so on. I once asked myself, if I did not have these little celebration dates, would I have made the effort to honor all the important people in my life? Probably, but celebrations are just an organized way of making sure you lavish all your attention on loved ones at least once or twice a year.

Fun Trivia
There is a call for celebrating life. If you look up the word "celebrate" in a thesaurus, you will that it also means to honor, mark, make merry, memorialize, remember, have fun, have a good time, paint the town red, make whoopee (I'm serious!), live it up, have a ball.

The Benefits of Elegant Entertaining

If you have moved to a new town, entertaining is a great way to meet new people and introduce yourself to the local community. It is also a way to enrich your business networks and relationships. That is why companies set aside an entertaining budget for team building exercises and events.
　　　　You will leverage your time by meeting all your friends at once. You will also create a memory. I remember *all* my parties. They give an excuse to take those fabulous snaps for posterity too!
It is also a good motivator to get you tidying up the house. As your dinner party looms ever close, you'll find yourself going that extra mile to prepare your home as you'd like it to be on the day.
　　　　As Debra Ollivier says, "There need not be any logical reason to celebrate - to clink glasses in a simple fete!"

Elegant Parties

When you host a party it is also about presenting yourself to your guests. You want to do it in a tasteful way. Look past the big packet of chips and bottles of soda and beer. Try to get something that looks better than the economy plastic cutlery and paper plates. Remember to do up the place a little to make it more conducive for a party! Most of all, forget effortless, sloppy parties! Make a commitment to present your party as a welcoming event.

What Type of Elegant Entertaining Do You Prefer?

Different types of parties suit different kinds of people. See the list below on the common party types:

Types of Elegant Entertaining
- Elegant Coffees
- Tea Parties
- Brunches
- Garden Parties
- Dinner Parties
- Cocktail Parties
- Dinner and Dance
- A ball
- Charity events
- Theme Parties

See more *Elegant Party Types & Ideas* on www.elegantwoman.org

How to Be an Elegant Host

- A great party has good planning
- Create a guest list
- Extend elegant invitations
- Create an elegant atmosphere
- Serve yummy food and a good variety of drinks.
- Set elegant table decorations

- Graciously handle embarrassing situations.
- Be an elegant and fabulous host and don't forget to dress up!

16. Sophisticated Elegance, Casual Elegance, and Style Elements

Being a sophisticated woman is a lifestyle choice. In everything that we dream and desire of becoming, there are usually some hard choices to make in order to achieve our goals.

Sometimes you'll need change the direction in your life. You may need to move location, change your job, and even your friends.

Characteristics of Sophisticated Women

How does one learn to be sophisticated?

First of all, we need to understand the makings of a sophisticated woman.

You will find the following characteristics in all of them:

- Self-love and a rich self-esteem
- Excellent posture and good grooming
- A contained facial expression
- A walk that has energy and purpose
- Social skills — at ease in all situations (comes with experience)
- Experience and exposure to new people, places, and things
- Comfortable with imperfections

- Never intimidated

- Dressed up (well presented at all times)

- Possessing a 'millionaire's' confidence

- Comfortable talking to just about anyone

- Educated: Hungry in the pursuit of knowledge

- Well-read and well-traveled

- Comfortable with luxury

- Discriminating taste and an awareness of quality

Self-Love and Self-Esteem

It is a kind of personal confidence, an assurance that allows her to know intuitively how to act in any given situation. That might be dining in a traditional Japanese restaurant, or meeting someone from a different 'world' than her own. While she may not know everything, nothing really surprises or intimidates her. She does not feel stupid and engage in negative self-talk, nor does she often feel embarrassed. She is herself at all times, a lady who is evidently comfortable in her own skin.

She loves herself in a way that allows her to give love and receive it in return. She takes pride in what she is given, invests in herself, and counts her blessings.

Excellent Posture and Grooming

Just as she has awareness for her manners and consideration of others, she is also aware of how she presents herself to the world.

She is well groomed and develops good habits for posture. Posture is not just vanity but contributes to good overall health too. She is also keenly aware of her womanly gestures. These are the motions that make her a vision of elegance.

A Contained Facial Expression

Just like her elegant gestures, she is acutely aware that certain facial expressions can ruin her elegant appearance. She refrains from harsh expressions and tries to maintain a peaceful appearance at all times.

The smiles of simply sophisticated women are 'just enough', and are neither tight nor cause her to squint. She laughs gently and does not roar. If she does have to frown, or is annoyed over something or someone, those facial expressions are slight. She takes silent deep breaths, and does not make a show of it.

A Walk with Energy and Purpose

You'll never find simply sophisticated women dragging their feet. They walk with feet straight and close together. You'll hardly ever find them wandering around aimlessly in shopping malls either. Their walk is of purpose, yet gentle. They never rush, not even when hurried.

Social Skills

Universal social skills come with lots of experience. You won't find her at every party in town, but when she does attend an event (usually one with great purpose), she will be at total ease wherever she is, talking to whoever is there. She is light-hearted and speaks with an easy friendliness. She will not cross conversational boundaries, and does not talk about herself in a personal or boastful way. She will be able to engage in good conversation, thus making her the perfect guest at every social function. She has acquired social ease.

Experience and Exposure

She values experiences over material goods, knowing that experience is a better educator. She derives exposure from her experiences, as she is curious about the world around her, its people, and their cultures.

Comfortable with Imperfections

Simply sophisticated women are comfortable with their imperfections. While they attempt to learn and improve, they do it unhurriedly and unabashedly. Simply sophisticated women know they are human after all.

Never Intimidated

They just don't know how to be! They employ manners, good taste and are consistently cultivating themselves. They are aware of the art of conversation, knowing they don't have to keep talking. They also recognize that it is impossible to know everything. They are at social ease. If someone tries to intimidate them, they know that they can always graciously excuse themselves and re-direct their attention to somewhere or something else.

Dressed Up

Simply sophisticated women are always elegantly dressed in the finest materials they can afford. They also know dressing etiquette, wearing only what is appropriate to fit the occasion. You'll never find them wearing flip-flops downtown. They also adhere strictly to dress codes.

Possessing a 'Millionaire's' Confidence

Have you ever met a millionaire that is not confident?

Being Able to Talk to Anyone

The more you study and celebrate the differences in people, the easier it is to understand and accept those who are unlike you. That is an act of refinement. Not liking someone because she/he is unlike you only breeds shallow thinking.

Hungry in Her Pursuit of Knowledge

Simply sophisticated women seek education and knowledge. Read more about how the study of liberal arts can shape your thinking.

If you are considering going to college, I highly recommend it. I also think that pursuing a classical education, at home on your own, is very useful and highly recommended for elegant women.

Well-read and Well-travelled

As above, she seeks knowledge and pursues experiences, including travel, as a form of education, understanding, and fulfillment.

Comfortable with Luxury

She enjoys it for what it is, but never places luxury above the feelings of others. She will never brag or boast about her luxurious experiences. She uses words like 'car' instead of limo, the Jaguar, or the Mercedes, etc.

Discriminating Taste and an Awareness of Quality

Simply sophisticated women need not depend on labels to have discriminating, elegant taste, or to differentiate quality.

The Elegant Sophisticated Woman

Who is the elegant sophisticated woman? People often mistake sophistication for elegance. While it is possible to be both, you can be sophisticated without being elegant and elegant without being sophisticated.

Elegance, as we know, is graciousness in action, and possesses a certain confident simplicity. Sophistication, on the other hand, derives from a great deal of worldly experience and knowledge of fashion and culture.

A Sophisticated woman will display wisdom, good taste, and subtlety, but that alone does not necessarily make her gracious. She will possess an in-depth understanding of her surroundings, and have a refined awareness and appreciation for different cultures. She will also be comfortable with luxury.

Yet to become 'simply sophisticated', she must find her way into elegance. That means it's vital to make good choices if she's to experience and enjoy elegant living, and so become a truly and simply sophisticated woman.

The Word 'Select'

If you study Old English, you'll find that the root word of "elegance" is "select". To become elegant, you must select. Select can also mean the following:

Pick out, single out, sort out, opt for, decide on, settle on, determine, hand-picked, prime, first rate, first class, superior, finest, best, top-class, superb, excellent, elite, favored, privileged, and wealthy.

Isn't that most interesting?

Put Together Your Own Chic List

So, to select you must be choosy! Putting considerable thought into choices are the foundations of an elegant sophisticated woman.

I know there are some of us who do not like change or making new decisions (that includes me). Nevertheless, no matter how indecisive you might be, you had better get savvy at making good choices, because the decisions we make shape our lives. Making the right choices is a life skill that affects the quality of our life!

Making good choices is the art of living well. We cannot simply expect everything to be handed to us on a plate. We should not passively accept whatever life or circumstances throw at us. We must know we have the power to change and have the courage to follow through on our decisions. After all, faith without works is meaningless.

Why Put Together Your Own Chic List?

We cannot afford the time to go searching and evaluating every given opportunity, choice of education, job, friendships, or single items in the mall etc., (more on this later).

In fact, sometimes sophistication can be quite vulgar. We've all seen it before, especially when there is an over-emphasis on materials and luxury goods, not to mention the braggarts and snobs that are sometimes found living among this high-profile, high-lifestyle culture.

Other examples are those women who dress up in too much bling and overdo the monogrammed designer goods. Then there are those who balk at flying economy class, pretending to hop off their private jet and are routinely inconsiderate and rude to service staff, often refusing to make eye contact with those they consider beneath them. Such pretentious women often attempt to be sophisticated by rattling off their knowledge on cuisine and fine dining at exclusive restaurants. They like to be noticed browsing the pages of certain books and magazines, hoping to give the impression that they're well-read and therefore 'oh-so-literary and sophisticated'. Yet, as previously discussed, true elegance embodies an inner grace that extends to all those a true lady encounters.

A Sophisticated Confidence

The elegant, sophisticated woman has a kind of sophisticated confidence about her. What this means is that she can be confident and comfortable in a sophisticated situation, say dining in a traditional Japanese restaurant, in Japan, with the locals.

She's comfortable talking and gently debating politics or other topics of interest. She's not afraid to choose the wines from a wine list, discuss Italian art history, or have her say on just about any conversational topic that comes up.

On subjects she knows little or nothing about, she listens and learns intently, and will not be afraid to join in the conversation later by way of questions or statements. The only failure in her life would be the failure to try new things, adapt to new situations; and a lady with sophisticated confidence does not shy away from new and unfamiliar circumstances.

While she may not know everything, nothing really surprises or intimidates her. She is open to venturing into the unknown, and will expose her taste buds to new and unfamiliar foods, and learn new behaviors when appropriate. She listens attentively and is engaged in learning about other cultures. She is not self-conscious, meaning she's detached from the 'self', i.e., this is not a woman who constantly thinks, frets, and sweats about herself or what others think of her.

You will feel more beautiful and comfortable in your own skin when you train and develop this sophisticated sense of confidence within yourself.

Gold Chains & Necklaces

It has been said that confidence (not to be confused with arrogance), is next to beauty when it comes to making a woman genuinely appealing in the eyes of others. There is no greater gift than that of confidence. Those who have it know how to act in any given situation, and are able to proceed with careful thought and without becoming flustered.
How do we get confident in _____ (you fill in the blanks)?

It could be, for example:
- Playing tennis
- Being comfortable on a first date
- Speaking French
- Dressing up
- Doing your hair

- Being financially free
- Attending a gathering with strangers

The Secret to Elegant Sophisticated Confidence:

Confidence only comes when you've done something over and over, and have made enough mistakes to finally learn how to do a thing right. Don't be afraid to make errors because we learn far more from failure than we ever do from success.

"Mistakes are part of the dues one pays for a full life." ~ Sophia Loren

Once you can do something, go somewhere, or perform some task automatically, that is you don't have to think about it anymore, then you have achieved confidence.
   Whatever it is that you want to accomplish: practice, practice, and practice some more! Keep at it no matter how frustrated you become, because you CAN realize that which you are striving for. Negative belief is the only thing that can potentially get in your way, or as Henry Ford once said:

"Whether you think you can, or you think you can't - you're right."

Start by Looking Confident

While you are practicing and establishing your sophisticated confidence, you might as well work on looking confident.
No matter what you hear about inner beauty, your first impression communicates who you are to the world. If you don't create a confident impression, people will never know whether or not you have inner beauty.

Below are three simple suggestions to work on, all of which portray confidence:

1. Work on the perfect posture.
2. Pay attention to your grooming.
3. Practice making eye contact.

Posture

Your posture tells the world how to treat you from sight alone. You can either look like winner or a loser. Posture is the single most important form of body language. Erectness is confident-looking. People will believe what your posture tells them about you.

For instance, if you tell a little boy to 'act like a king', instantly you'll see him straighten his back and his neck as though he were wearing a crown. You wonder who teaches them these things! Seriously, your posture communicates far more than you probably know. Having good posture also makes you feel better about yourself as it lifts the spirit and instills energy.

Personal Grooming

Psychologists say that the first indications that a woman's morale is dropping is when her daily grooming habits begin to slip.

Haven't we all seen, or experienced ourselves, girlfriends who have had their hearts broken and soon after the breakup they stop bothering with makeup and hair? And more generally they start letting themselves go by putting on weight and developing a negative attitude and outlook on life? We've all watched television shows that depict people in real life who have been told they've lost all their money. Even the most educated and well-groomed men can start to resemble the beggar on the street. When personal grooming takes a backseat, self-respect and confidence leave us.

Eye Contact

Making good eye contact is another indicator of confidence. Practice looking people directly in the eye as it will help you establish a position of poise in the minds of others, but try not to stare or gaze at people as you practice being comfortable with eye-to-eye contact. Look into their eyes when speaking (don't forget to blink), and just be natural.

Remember this, if you are opening your eyes more than normal, you're gazing! If you're listening, the eyes are your nonverbal communication with the one speaking, and good natural contact will portray your confidence. Furthermore, it's easier to listen attentively when looking directly into someone's eyes while they're talking.

How to Be Sophisticatedly Interesting

An interesting person is someone who is interested. Do not worry about being interesting or TRYING to be interesting. Tastefully engage in conversation with others, learn about someone else's culture. Remember, the best conversationalists are those who speak less and listen more.

Have an avid social life. Take part in charities, serve in church, or throw dinner parties. The point is to get involved in life outside of your own. Take an interest in your gifts and talents. Seek personal growth, refine your knowledge, and pursue your passions with confidence. Don't run from change but embrace it. Learn about things that increase your sophistication levels.

Here are some suggestions:

- Art - drawing, painting, museums
- Literature/history
- Languages and culture
- Theater, plays, musicals
- Dance – the ballet, waltz, etc.
- Music - symphonies, musicals, learning an instrument
- Sports - skiing, tennis, golf, etc.

- Water sports - sailing, speed boating, swimming
- Travel & adventure

One Genuine Manner

The elegant sophisticated woman has one genuine manner.

So what does it mean to have one genuine manner? Well, it simply suggests you treat everybody the same, from the very important or famous, to the waitress that just served you dinner. This will give you freedom from pretentiousness, phoniness, and self-consciousness.

People that have no manners save their best behavior for the VIPs, or those they need to impress for whatever reason(s). They then change back to their old mannerisms once they feel there is no longer any need for airs and graces.

Raise Your Comfort with Luxury

The elegant sophisticated woman is at home with luxury. Your confidence level can only rise to what you are comfortable with. For example, do fancy stores and high-end restaurants intimidate you? Does a certain kind of highly accomplished person or wealthy individual make you feel embarrassed or inferior?

These are just a few typical examples, but they can be stumbling blocks unless you tackle them head on. To do this, you have to confront your fears and reservations and remove them! Learn how to be comfortable in ANY place, circumstance, or situation, no matter where you go or what you do. All these so-called fears only exist in your head.

FEAR can be seen as an acronym to mean:
- False Emotions Appearing Real
- Failure Expected And Received
- Forgetting Everything's All Right
- Forget Everything and Run

But the two below are perhaps the ones you might want to focus on:

- Forget Everything and Relax
- Face Everything and Recover

With the last one in mind, here are six suggestions that will surely help you to push through some of the common things that hinder the growth of so many women:

1. Eating at different restaurants
2. Traveling to unknown places
3. Talking to strangers
4. Being around people who normally intimidate you
5. Public speaking
6. Attending a fancy ball or event with important guests

The idea is to step out of your comfort zones until you become comfortable. Let's go a little further. Say, for example, you are not comfortable with dressing up — then just dress up and go out! Or practice dressing up in the privacy of your own home. Get away with a little at a time. If you are always in flip flops, wear sandals, then move on to little ballet flats, and when you're comfortable with them, try on kitten heels, and so on and so forth. When you look as good as you possibly can, it makes you feel better and that helps to strengthen your self-confidence and esteem.

Not all of us are fully conscious of our fears and uncertainties though, which is why it's always a good idea to write them down. So, on that note, write down as many situations as you can think of that are uncomfortable for you personally.

Here are a few ideas to get you started:
1. A party where I don't know anyone.

2. When people ask me about ...

3. When I have to speak about ...

4. _____

Work out a response in your mind, write it down, memorize it, and practice it in the mirror if that helps.

Study the Art of Conversation

I'll say it again, you will only rise as high as your comfort level, so you want to begin elevating those levels until you become at ease in many types of situations and events. All you need to know is that it can be done.

For instance, when you first got your job and earned $100 a week, you only shopped in stores that sold shoes at $20 or less. To buy $150 shoes was out of this world for you, and was something that other people got to do. Then you earned $500 a week and suddenly, that $150 footwear seemed more affordable and so became the new norm, and your confidence with luxury items increased as a result.

Let us take another example. You could only ever afford 300 thread count Egyptian cotton sheets, then there was a sale at Bloomingdale's and you decided to upgrade and buy 700 thread count bed sheets. So you changed them out when you got home and slept on them for a week. It was time to wash the sheets and you replaced them with your previous 300 thread count, and instantly you could tell the difference. Again, your comfort with luxury just got elevated and you developed a discriminating taste for quality.

The same principle applied to raising your comfort level to luxury applies to people who intimidate you as well. It's hard to justify, but different kinds of people make each of us nervous. They seem to be able to push our buttons every time we're in their company. Talking to a celebrity might make you nervous, but perhaps not your sister. But talking to a highly-educated person might make her feel inferior, but not you. Sometimes, the reasons we feel ill at ease in the company of certain people can be quite latent, but we must identify the root cause if we're to grow. The types of people who intimidate us can be very individualistic.

Examples may be:

- Beautiful people

- Famous people

- Influential people

- Intelligent people

- People with heavy accents

- The well-connected

- The fashionista (devoted follower of fashion)

- The knowledgeable

- The materialistic

- The religious

- The savvy

- The snobby

- The sophisticated

- The wealthy

- The widely traveled

- Those financially savvy

- Those from certain schools

- Those who speak many languages

The more intimidating people that you meet, the more you get to practice and increase your quiet self-confidence. It won't be too long before you realize that they are just like you and me, and you will be wondering what all the fuss was about. Best of all, you will no longer be intimidated, and once again will have acquired yet even more elegance.

Embrace Luxury — Don't Fight It

The elegant, sophisticated woman embraces luxury. She appreciates the finer things in life.

Contrary to popular belief, luxury is not just for the rich and famous. Luxury can be, and is, for the likes of you and me too. Luxury and luxurious items did not just appear overnight. The finer things in life result from a passion for studying and improvement. Whether it's a fine vase, a pair of shoes, or a handbag, all quality items underwent certain processes. The master artists devote substantial time to perfecting their works and true craftsmanship for all of us to enjoy.

I used to scoff at high prices, but when I raised my luxury level, I became amazed at the difference. If you can afford some luxury, why not enjoy it? Initial costs aside, such items are far better value for money in the long run anyway!

Treat Yourself First Class

The elegant and sophisticated woman treats herself first-class. If only for fun, try on clothing that costs double what you would normally spend. Test-drive a luxury car. Learn how to differentiate quality. Get to know the labels that have high prices. Try to touch, feel, carry, wear, and find out why it is that they command such prices.

Whenever you can, treat yourself to some luxury items. That means you should pamper yourself with something nice. Get used to using fine creams, good cosmetics, wearing a pair of really decent shoes, even if they're the ONLY pair you have.

Even if it is just a single piece, try to purchase one of the most excellent Egyptian cotton towels for your bathroom, and one set of the finest silk bed sheets for the master bedroom. In short, buy yourself some small (or large) luxury items that represent the lifestyle you so desire.

Sometimes we are too quick to slam the finer things in life, and call other people materialistic or commercial for buying them. It's all too easy to forget, or simply not be aware of the kind of devotion, passion, and hard work that's gone into developing these finer things in life. While it's not my life goal, I do make an effort to understand and to be comfortable with luxury. Most importantly, I get to enjoy and appreciate it! By doing so, I also develop what is known as discriminating taste.

Developing Discriminating Taste

"Choosing on the tiniest level to position yourself, bodily next to only the best develops what is called discriminating taste." ~ Ginie Sayles

Discriminating taste means that you are "aware" of quality, aware of the best in life. You are constantly reflecting a stronger sense of self-worth. People think that by doing so, one becomes more materialistic, yet that couldn't be further from the truth. When you've become increasingly comfortable with materials, you'll realize that they are not as important to you as they used to be. You'll learn to enjoy them without placing an over-emphasis on things, thus becoming that elegant and sophisticated woman you always wanted to be.

How to Look Chic

Here we look at how to be chic and the mystery of casual elegance. For a long while, I've wondered what 'chic' exactly meant, let alone how to look it.

Definition of Chic

Somewhere along the way, it dawned upon me that to be chic is to be casually elegant. It also means to have style with a bit of attitude. It is also original and a little unexpected.

There are many definitions or interpretations of chic, as many style advocates will tell you. But my definition is that chic style is casual elegance with a bit of an attitude and independence included (from fashion trends).

Since some others may not define chic the same way as I do, I would also like to say that not everything chic is casually elegant (or elegant at all), and not everything casually elegant is chic.

How to Be Chic

As much as I prefer classic and traditional elegant styles, I've come to realize that most of them are on the formal side, by today's standards anyway.

If you consider the history of fashion, our way of dress has become increasingly casual. Take travel for instance. Not too long ago, men wore suits and women wore tailored dresses and fitted jackets to travel by air. These days, you'll see many people travelling in camisoles and shorts, pajamas, tracksuits with flip-flops, and no makeup at all!

So, the real question we face is this: How do we adapt to the casual modern society without compromising on elegance?

I believe that one of the ways is to learn **how to be casually elegant**. Having a little fun with casual elegance is to be chic. To inject a bit of personality into the 'expected', or cliché styles shows an independent spirit. First, we have to understand what casual elegance actually is:

Casual Elegance Is Dressing in a Relaxed Way

- Sometimes, an elegant woman wants to leave all her bling at home, kick off her heels, lean back, and enjoy a cup of coffee in her garden.

- She wears her husband's watch to achieve a 'smart casual' look; a break from her usual ladylike outfits.

- She also decides to wear ballet flats with her tailored dress because she will be going into the city and doing lots of walking.

- She may run out of time, so decides to wear a beret masking her untidy hair.
- She loves her elegant bag, and decides to use it everywhere, for special occasions, to work, and even to the supermarket.

Chic Is Casual Elegance with a Bit of the Unexpected

A person who has chic style is someone who thinks independently about fashion. She is confident and self-aware to know what looks good on her and what doesn't. She adapts fashion to meet her style, not the other way around. She is somewhat of a free spirit. She doesn't like to be showy or obvious; she likes to keep a little mystery, and that way, she unknowingly keeps everyone guessing!

She embraces change at the right time, and is not one to sport the same hairstyle for the next couple of decades. She is fresh, exciting, and passionate, and most importantly, comfortable in her own skin. She likes to reinvent herself when she feels the need for change.

How to Look Chic

- She is not a fashion victim. This does not mean she is not modern or out of date. She keeps an eye on fashion, but only takes what is appropriate to her personally.
- She doesn't like to be too obvious. She avoids clichés and expected coordination. For instance, to match white dresses with turquoise earrings, polka dots with red shoes, and so forth. She might just sport a French

bob hairstyle when everyone else is leaving their hair long and curling it at the ends, like Kate Middleton.

- She does not buy popular designer labels. The more obscure the better as far as she's concerned, but with exceptional quality, of course. She prides herself on discovering secrets and new ideas.
- She prefers chic boutiques to chain-stores, whether luxury or not, although she will still get her basics, like tank tops and camisoles, in departmental stores. She is not one of those people who want to be different just for the sake of it.
- She buys from a wide selection of price ranges, from low end to high end, but always with quality in mind.
- She will not wear what she is not confident or comfortable in.
- She likes reinvention. Sometimes she moves her furniture around in the house to add a new feel to the space, or learns a new makeup technique.
- She is more concerned about real life than superficial things. For example, she prefers talking about interesting topics more so than idle chit-chat on the latest 'IT bag' or 'celebrity gossip'.
- Her look and style appears effortless. It looks layered, thrown on, relaxed, not fussy, yet maintains a certain class. This is opposite of 'try-too-hard' styles. Her look says: "I've got more important things to think about than mimicking the catwalk. I love many other things

passionately, like my work, children, and my love of life, than to spend two hours sitting in front of a mirror getting ready to face the world outside". Her look also says: "I don't know if I'm seen as beautiful, but I know I look presentable, and that is a sign of respect of other people and society". And probably, "I'm an individual. I'm my own woman".

- She'd rather you not know where she gets her things from, be it clothes, shoes, or furniture etc. She definitely doesn't want conversations on how much a thing costs.
- She is unpretentious.
- She doesn't aim to impress anyone.
- Balance is her thing. That is the secret of her poise. She embraces the new, but treasures the old. She finds equilibrium in most things. Chic and poise go together.
- She doesn't try to be who she is not. She has a very clear view of exactly who she is.
- She enjoys a good mix-and-match using both masculine and feminine clothes.

I heard about this from a designer when I was working for a fashion magazine. Vivien told me that she likes a little clash in her outfits. A lacy top perhaps, but with her boyfriend's jeans instead of the predictable pencil skirt.

The actual terms 'masculine and feminine' is from Ines de la Fressange, in her fabulously chic book: *Parisian Chic: A Style Guide by Ines de la Fressange.*

Parisian Chic **Review**

I loved this book for its beautiful presentation and 'chic pointers', but I have read her chic tips from other French style books before. Some areas I don't quite agree on because I felt it clashed with elegance. I felt that Ines's way of being chic is heavily emphasized on making a statement, or being different (sometimes for the sake of it), and many of the stores that she recommends in her book are not what you might call elegant. Her book is also more like a flip-through publication, rather than a book you would read intensely.

Don't get me wrong, it is VERY, VERY GOOD and gives some great basic pointers and reminders that we don't have to LIVE LIFE and follow the pack, and it also dares the reader to be different.

Her tips are useful, practical, and very chic! It will stay on my favorite bookshelf for future reference, there for those times when I'm feeling a little predictable and in need of inspiration and ideas. After all, though we may be a bit different, Ines de la Fressange is one of my favorite style inspirations. She is the epitome of French chicness.

The Chic Wardrobe
Sophisticated Elegant Style Elements - an Overview

Purses, bags, and everything else! The following will cover how to acquire elegance with items other than clothes.

Handbags

While designer bags are an obsession with many women the world over, choosing the right one for your outfit still remains a skill to be honed over time. A great looking bag and a chic looking outfit might not look so impressive if they don't go well together.

It doesn't matter how expensive your bag is, or what label it sports, the fact of the matter is that there's is no such thing as a stylish bag for all occasions. You don't have to possess a large number of bags, so long as you are mindful of your lifestyle, your needs, and your wardrobe. Understanding these things is the first step to editing and building an effective and elegant wardrobe that is befitting to you.

Quick Tips

- For the morning bag, keep it very simple.
- For the evening, you can go a little dressier, shinier, and much smaller.

When buying a new bag it's very important to check the quality of the leather or fabric. A fake leather or pseudo leather may completely cheapen your outfit (this applies to shoes as well). Try to buy the best quality (note: not necessarily designer) that you can afford. Take some time to study the finishing, the leather (and how it endures scratches), and also the inside of the bag, the zips, the lining, and stitching.

There was a time when I used to buy very cheap fashion bags, but I always got bored of them very quickly. I assumed this was because I got tired of the fashion, but I later realized why I lost interest so quickly and discarded them without a second thought. There were three main reasons for this:

1. They were bought on a whim and failed to fulfill my needs specifically.
2. Material and construction were poor, so they soon became tatty and embarrassing.
3. These bags didn't cost much to buy, so I didn't really value them.

If I added up the cost of ten cheap fashion bags, I could have afforded a really nice one. Instead of buying a bag every month, I could buy one, say, every eight months, or even longer, and still be perfectly satisfied with it.

Not to mention that having too many bags clutters up your wardrobe and frustrates the process of getting dressed. Bags are no different than any other item in your elegant collection, in that less really is more.

The size of the bag also matters. Put your usual bits and pieces into a bag and stand at the mirror. Does it make you look a little silly? Perhaps you look as though you're going away for the weekend. If you're not happy with the visual relationship between you and your bag, then something's got to change.

I'm all for de-cluttering and carrying only the bare essentials. Get rid of extra cards in your wallet, mints and gum, brochures, receipts, and anything else that's unlikely to get used. Try and get into the habit of clearing out your bag every day, or at the very least, once a week.

To see a woman frantically rummaging around in her bag is painful to watch. To avoid too much digging around, group things together and place them in little cosmetic bags. For example, put makeup into one bag, sanitary items and tissue papers into another, and so forth. You should only need one pen and a diary or notebook. With a little imagination and organization, a jumbled bag containing all sorts of non-essential items will become a thing of the past.

Scarves

There is something quite elegant about scarves, and there are many ways to wear them too. You can experiment and see how a scarf best suits you. If you get stuck for ideas, then search through some new and old magazines or fashion websites to see how they can be worn.

Perfume

Personally, I think it's subtly sexy to have a signature scent. It's wonderful to use perfume based on your mood and character. I know the old saying goes, "Spray in the air and walk into it," but I don't think we should do that anymore because perfume is not made anywhere near as concentrated as it once was.

A better approach is to hold the bottle at some distance from you and spray. Apply a little onto your wrists, and then put some on your fingers so that you can dab behind the ears and neck. If you feel like it, you can also spray a little onto your hair! But you don't have confine perfume only to your body; you can spray it into your purse, on your pillows, and around your room.

The downside to a lot of today's perfumes is that they never last more than a couple of hours. If it's possible, keep a miniature in your purse and spritz a little throughout the day so as to maintain your scent.

Hats

Too bad that in modern society we have neglected the use of hats. It's a shame because they can be so elegant and can save us time when having a less-than-ideal hair day. Most of what we see nowadays is trucker hats and baseball caps.

When I travel in some countries, I often see the more mature folks still hanging on to their hats whenever they are in town or attending various events. How I pay tribute to them!

If you can, try to make the move and start using hats, and wear them with pride. Who knows, maybe we'll be the leaders in making them comeback as an elegant part of modern fashion. Putting the beauty of hats to one side for a moment, let's not forget that they also act as good protection for the hair, scalp, and go some way to shield the face from a harsh sun!

Umbrellas

We can never stop the rain so this is a classic accessory. They are so cheap these days too, but that often means we find ourselves buying rather silly looking umbrellas, many of which are totally useless in a storm anyway.

If you can only buy one umbrella, opt for a small portable one for modern convenience, but pay the bit extra and invest in quality. The best colors to go for are black or beige. Black will last longer because the beige will soon have rain water stains and begin to look shabby, though it goes without saying that beige is a touch more feminine.

My advice is to stay away from silly colorful umbrellas, as they almost never match our outfits unless you are wearing a white top. To take elegance up to another level, get an umbrella with lace trimmings or embroidery. Be sure to pay attention to the quality at the end where you hold the strap.

When in London once, I was inspired by this wonderful vision. It was raining quite heavily and there was this very elegant lady wearing black low-heel boots and a beige coat with a misty gray scarf. Her umbrella was beige and brown — very simple in style and no visible logo. She was huddling under her umbrella, walking briskly along the street. She looked poised, in control, unflustered, and elegant as she went on her way.

From that exact moment, I told myself, never again will I buy silly looking cutesy umbrellas adorned with patterns or visible logos. The days of holding up a brolly that displays brand names, store names, or promotional messages were gone.

Now I choose to have umbrellas that match my outfit, though not too obviously. Simple colors or lines in cream, black, or navy blue all work well.

Jewelry

If you have the real thing, then use it! Do not be too precious with it otherwise it serves no practical purpose. For example, don't lock your jewelry away at home and only take it out once a year for some special event. If it's appropriate, wear your jewels daily. Take care of them and remember to send some of the items for regular cleaning. Become accustomed to a little luxury and learn to enjoy and appreciate what is rightfully yours.

If you're thinking about buying some precious jewelry, go for the finest instead of the biggest. Wearing a large diamond on your finger is a status symbol, telling everyone that you have lots of money. This is far from elegant behavior; in fact it's almost vulgar.

I think it's better to buy jewelry that is proportionate to the size of your finger, wrist, neck, and torso. But there are other considerations too. You also have to think about how it will look on you and against your skin-color and type. Generally speaking though, it is not wrong to wear big expensive jewelry if it does genuinely reflect your taste and circumstances. This is also a reflection of your personality, lifestyle, and daily activities. It is something you have to think about personally, and know how you want to be viewed by others.

Rings

Rings subtly accent to the outfits we wear. It's recommended that we don't have more than one ring on each hand, with the exception of an engagement and wedding ring in a set together.

Traditionally speaking, it's tasteful to wear diamonds mainly in the evening and at night time as this is when they sparkle at their best, which was the basis of why diamonds are so precious. The only diamond ring that is perfectly acceptable to wear all day, every day is, of course, a diamond engagement ring.

Since your wedding band and engagement ring are often worn together, and with the expectation of wearing them for life, then it is vital that you choose with great care and not compromise on anything.

Necklaces

- A silver pendant, classic length (a staple in every wardrobe)
- A silver necklace that is thicker and longer (to give that elongated neck impression)
- A single strand of pearls
- A double or triple strand of pearls

Lingerie

When we mention lingerie, people tend to think of nightclothes, but of course it also refers more generally to a women's underwear. Invest in good lingerie, both in quality and fit. Well-made lingerie will not only hold your body well, but also make your clothes look better on you. You can always tell when someone is not wearing an appropriate set, because you see things like lines, weird body shapes that don't move, or look as stiff as an armor plate. Poor quality, or badly fitting lingerie may have straps don't hold as they should and therefore keep slipping, or the strapless variety causes the top to sag. Get your lingerie wrong, and the he body can suffer and look out of shape.

It is important to have different sets of undergarments that are appropriate for the types of clothes you wear. The basics should include: lingerie in pale nude and black colors; one to wear under tight fitting tops (this should be seamless) a good strapless bra for evening wear, and panties that use flat-seam technology so as to prevent visible panty lines (VPL).

Watch out for those constructed brassieres that look as solid as egg cartons. They do not look natural and can in fact be quite distasteful. While the Wonderbra can be used to correct body proportions, it seems that elegant women are determined to not fake as much as possible, so use only it if you feel it is necessary.

How to Travel Elegantly

If you travel a lot, it is important that you identify some clothes that you can single out as 'very travel-worthy'. These garments are usually lightweight and require no ironing. They also need to be versatile, meaning you can dress the items up or down for day or evening, casual or cocktail. They have to match the most classic shoes, as well as mix and mix with various accessories and scarves. Clothes that do very well with layering are also excellent choices.

Obviously your travel wear has to be comfortable as well, because you will be hardly sitting around if you are traveling to and from various places (apart from when you're in transit of course).

Elegant Luggage

I love luggage! It is probably because of what it represents. I do realize that travel bags are getting cheaper, and you can find really good bargains at lower-priced stores such as Walmart, Target, and sometimes at Asian bargain stores and outdoor markets as well. But before you go buying very cheap luggage, you might want to consider these four points first:

1. How often you travel?
2. Where do you travel to?
3. How much do you usually need or pack?
4. Will you have to travel by car/train once you get to your destination?

If you don't yet have your travel bags, then try to get a coordinating set that matches your style. Think also about choosing luggage that will go well with your usual travel outfit(s).

How Often Do You Travel?

If you make many short trips, then invest in a good small- to medium-sized trolley bag. To go even further, get the cabin size one and train yourself to survive with less. This way, you never have to wait in long lines at baggage claim areas, and that means you will be able to jet in and out much more quickly.

If you do a lot of long flights, larger options make more sense. Go for bags with wheels that turn 180 degrees, as you probably will have to do more lugging around more often. Therefore, it's wise to make carting your stuff around as easy as possible.

Where do You Travel?

In very big cities, you can be sure there will be trolleys, convenient buses, trains, or taxi stands for you to hop right into the minute you step out of the airport.

However, not everyone is ready to depart as soon as they touch down. Some airports even require that you take all your bags out and check them in again at the counter if you're in transit. This can be a bit of a mad hassle at times, depending on the time of your connecting flight. Unless you are familiar with all the transit procedures at an airport, you really do need to be well-prepared and make sure your luggage is practical, easily identifiable, as well as elegant.

To recap, play it safe and choose the lightest, most durable wheels that turn full circle. Have your luggage match your personality and outfit, and personalize your signature on it so that you can spot it a mile away.

What Does Your Luggage Say About You?

It has been rumored that the kind of luggage you bear actually reveals more about your social situation than what you are wearing at the airport. While you shouldn't be embarrassed of any social situation, it is a good idea to choose the best you can afford with whatever budget you have. Let us travel with pride and dignity.

I say this because numerous times in the past I've bought something less-than-par, only to later find myself embarrassed to use the thing because it looked ugly, cheap, or both. I bought it because, yes, it was cheap, and I needed something quickly at the time. But such hasty decision making means you will likely end up with a bag that only ever gets used once or used begrudgingly, and that's just a waste of money and effort.

Matching Your Bags

It does not matter if your bags are bought from different places so long as you know what you're buying and why. It is quite elegant to see a kind of coherence in your outfit. Thus, some reasonable effort should be made to matching luggage in accordance with your travel wear.

The Color of the Bag(s)

What colors you opt for depends on personality and style. I've seen some people do well with green bags or orangey-brown luggage, and they can look very elegant. If it is patterned, best to keep it all the same, or at least have the same base color. If in doubt, simply go for all black or all pieces in one solid color. Make sure you have a different colored tag though!

I've personally chosen red for my luggage in the past, but more recently I've decided on chocolate brown. I chose red before because it was a bright and not-an overly common color. Chocolate brown is my favorite choice now and it goes very well with my favorite duffel that I take everywhere.

My new bag has wheels that turn in all directions. It makes things so much easier! Chocolate brown goes with almost every outfit I own, too, and it definitely goes with my duffel bag! Since I've always matched my travel bags together, such as my duffel bag to the luggage, I now always attempt to try to:

- Pick an outfit that goes with my luggage

- Pick a handbag or purse that goes with my outfit

Elegant Packing

The way you pack your bag reveals something about your character and habits. While I'm not for packing everything into little rolled buns, or having airtight Ziplocs, there are certain standards to good packing.

Usually I try to pack fast, and I've honed my skills to do this without a list. However, for unseasoned travelers, or those of you just getting started, then I highly recommend making a list, for no other reason than it saves you valuable time.

Packing Lightly and Quickly

Packing is never fun, unless you revel in it of course. So this is how I pack my bag the day before I travel.

I put aside items that are travel-specific. These are things like my travel case, which contains toothbrush, facial wash, and other essentials. As my daily makeup case is comprised of the simplest day and evening makeup, I just empty its contents into my cosmetics case. I have another bag that is specific for wires, chargers, and cables. I also carry a multi-country adapter so that I never have to worry about how to use my electronic devices abroad.   Next, shoes go into special shoe bags, and if I have very specific events to attend, I carry clothes into outfits and place them into large Ziplocs. That's one outfit per Ziploc, including the inner garments. That way I know exactly how many outfits I have. It is smart to know which ones to pick so that you can mix-and-match the item(s) to get more use out of it/them. By the way, I also carry an empty laundry bag.

If I don't have time, I wear pearl earrings and a silver bracelet with two rings, and that is all the jewelry I wear throughout the entire trip.

When packing, place all the heavy things at the bottom and lighter items on top. I prefer to keep my expensive shoes in boxes or bags, and store them in separate luggage. Otherwise, I try to cushion the footwear by wrapping some clothes around them to soften any impact.

By packing in this way, you keep your clothes and shoes clean, as well as keeping makeup and facial products away from each other. There's nothing worse than having bottles pop open, making a mess of other stuff inside your luggage.

The Feminine Toilet Case

The most beautiful and elegant ones (and those which make the most sense), are the cases that sit up by themselves and open from the top. They can contain everything pretty much like a basket does. They are much better options than those with a hook that you dangle off the door (they can be quite cumbersome too). The sit-up toilet case is also better than those which lay flat and may take up too much space, because these types have to be quite big to fit everything.

Travel Tips

- Pack solid, neutral colors for clothes.
- Pack more tops than bottoms.
- Try to determine the activity of your trip and pack accordingly.

Inspiration for Travel!

Being at ease in other cultures is a trademark of elegance. The credo of sophisticated travelers is that your home is wherever you happen to be at any given time.

This means you can easily adapt to the customs of the land you are visiting without making negative comparisons to the way you do things back home (a common mistake made by so many of us).

If you are in university, try to participate in an exchange program. After university, see if you can take some time off 'serious career work', and do a year or so of vocation abroad and travel. If you are single (or if your family is willing and able) attempt to get work overseas. This way you can attain that ease among fellow travelers and locals alike as you get to meet many people across numerous cultures. Be sure to make travel a priority in your budgeting.

To develop the travel layer of class, your first foreign trips should be to classic locales. These include cities such as London, Paris, Monte Carlo, Venice, Rome, Amsterdam, Singapore, and New York City.

What's important here is experiencing new cultures, meeting local people, acquiring knowledge about other places, and feeling at ease with global cuisine. Try to learn a little bit of other languages too, as this helps to develop travel sophistication.

17. How to Be Lovely: Examples of Elegant Women

How to Be Lovely

"The most effective kind of education is that a child should play amongst lovely things." ~ Plato

Elegance must be combined with loveliness, because one usually doesn't just desire to be elegant purely for oneself, but to shed a little joy around for others too.
        If you look up the word "loveliness" in a dictionary, you'll find that it's defined as "an exquisite beauty". Researching still deeper, I've found that the intrinsic meaning of beauty is **natural**, **internal**, and it comes from all the goodness and **love** of the heart. So how does one become absolutely lovely?

Cultivate Loveliness

I've found that it is easier to **be the right person** rather than ***trying* to be the right person.** So, what is the difference? Well, if I know in my mind that I should not be late, I try very hard not to be late. I do this by setting a timer or an alarm if I have to. It is hard work, very hard for me indeed. However, if I have reverence for other people's time, I WILL NOT be late. It is easy to do after some practice. For instance, if I were meeting the Queen of England, as a once in a lifetime opportunity, I wouldn't dream of being late. I might be two hours early! It all boils down to what I value most. Do I value other people's time? Or do I assume that it will be alright for them to wait for me? A lovely person is thoughtful at all times, and without having to think about it.

She Is Always on T.

When she has an appo
on time and usually a litt.
    If she foresees th
late for a hair appointment,
before to inform the salon. ᴗ
potential time-hazards when ᵢ
As mentioned earlier, she has
only her own, but that of others.
    She sticks to her appoinᵗ
She is dependable to turn up for h.   ᵤgreed.
She hardly cancels, unless it is a rᴇ   ᵧ. She is not
the sort of person to call something ᵥ   ᵢₑ last minute due
to some petty, selfish reason. She knows others have cleared
their schedules for her. Time is one of the most valued
currencies. While money can be lost, it may be earned back.
But when time is lost, it's gone forever.
She shows her respect for time by the way she lives her life,
settling into an unrushed, quality lifestyle where she has time
for church, family, and friends.

How to Be As Lovely As Audrey Hepburn

Audrey Hepburn was always generous with her smile. Hearts
warmed quickly when she smiled. It is bighearted to be the one
who smiles first because it takes a sort of admirable courage
and lack of self-consciousness to do so. She who smiles first
either believes a smile will be returned, but isn't fussed if it's
not. Her smile encourages other smiles. Her pleasant
countenance exudes from her.

She Is Kind

A lovely woman asks if you and your family are well. She
listens and refrains from talking about herself, unless she is
asked to do so.
    If you have an embarrassing moment, she will look as
though she hadn't noticed. That is her way of not

. If it is impossible to pretend that
g, say you spilled soup over yourself,
she will make light of it and assure you
all the time.
words are kind and thoughtful. Her gestures and
reflect this too. Say a little pat on the head for
someone's tiny dog perhaps, listening with delight when
children attempt to have a conversation with her. She will
always offer a helping hand to the elderly.

She Believes Others Come First

She stirs her tea quietly so she doesn't draw attention to
herself or bother those around her. She speaks softly in public
places to avoid disturbing others.
She respects the wishes and personal choices that others
have, and will not ask intruding or potentially embarrassing
questions. While she may not agree with differing opinions,
she will be gracious about it.

She Is Disciplined in Mind and Heart

She will not assume she is well-known and popular, even
though she may be. She does not consider herself important to
the point where people have nothing better to do than idolize
her in their thoughts or conversations. She will also not
assume that someone will give her a ride home, or bend over
backwards to help her in any given situation.
        If she finds herself in any of the aforementioned
situations, she graciously accepts and expresses her
appreciation. She will not say to someone such things as, *"Do
you know who I am?"*, *"I don't deserve this"*, or "I deserve
better". She is not the sort to 'steal the thunder' by turning a
conversational topic towards herself. For example, if someone
was talking about their trip to Italy, she'll not take over the
conversation to tell them what happened when she went to
Italy. She is a good listener and shows genuine interest in the
one talking.

If something embarrassing happened to her, she will not torture herself with that bad memory by repeatedly going over the incident in her mind. She disciplines herself not to fuss over such things, and just gets on with life. She is not one to get embarrassed easily.

"She is disciplined in her lifestyle, not allowing herself to become drunk with wine, be addicted to bad habits of eating junk food, shop incessantly, be overridden with debt, have too many possessions, or have disorder in her life and home." ~ Quote unknown

She also knows that being disciplined in both heart and mind means taking efforts to 'protect it'. In Proverbs 4:23, it says "Above all, guard your heart, for it is the wellspring of life".

Guarding one's heart is reading, watching, and listening to good, wholesome things that will inspire the fruits of life. Such things may include love, patience, and kindness.

Personally, I find it helpful to keep this mental discipline by attending church on a regular basis. I get involved in good causes within the community, and read decent books. I also practice a daily devotional.

She Is Impeccable in Her Appearance

To be lovely is also to be impeccable in appearance. I was once told that, in France, it is considered rude to go and buy bread at the bakery in home-clothes and with an unmade face. This is because you force others to look at you in your less-than-presentable appearance. What great food for thought!

Good posture is important as well. A beautiful impeccable appearance is ruined by poor posture. Stand and sit straight at all times. Do not fold your arms, slouch, or lean on anything. Do not put your hands on your hips! Learn to feel graceful with good posture. If need be, see a professional health provider, such as a physiotherapist or a chiropractor, to assess the health of your posture. Working with these health specialists to regain and rebuild posture has many benefits for wellbeing and self-esteem. I would highly recommend it if your posture is less than it could be. Good posture leads to good poise.

A lovely person does not need to spend excessive time getting dressed. She achieves a timeless style by a sense of thoughtfulness, and in an organized manner.

She Has a Good Work Ethic

She shows us how to be lovely based on values of hard work and diligence. Just as she is always on time, she also exercises a strong work ethic.

She does whatever is required of her without complaining. She works hard and doesn't give in, not even when she's tired. If she has a big client meeting the following day, she prepares for it beforehand. She doesn't go out the night before if she has to handle a big project the next day.

"I adored my work and did my best.' ~ Audrey Hepburn

She Has a Balanced Life with the Right Values Intact

She will not put herself in a situation where she is too busy to spend time with her family and loved ones. She prioritizes her life and keeps things simple.

She is passionate about her work, but not to the point where it will cause her to compromise her priorities. Her priorities are set based on the right values. Even though she is devoted to her work and family, she is careful not to neglect herself. She also believes in cultivating herself in order to have something to give to others.

She knows when she is overstretched and says "no" to that which is not necessary. Due to her disciplined approach for living, she enjoys what she has chosen to do; the path she has taken. She is unhurried yet still gets things done.

She Loves

She loves her husband, her children, and her mother-in-law. Maybe not in equal intensity, but she is able to love naturally nonetheless. She loves animals, beautiful gardens, books, and other fine things. She takes time to get to know the world around her.

Whenever she comes across those folks who are unlovely, she tries her best to love them by first understanding them. If her attempts to show love and compassion are not welcome, she keeps a polite and respectable distance, and leaves it at that.

She does not merely express her love with words, but through her actions as well. She employs qualities and thoughtfulness through the continual observation of her surroundings. She notices things about little children, and remembers their favorite toy. She sends birthday gifts, flowers, or thoughtful cards for various occasions. She loves to decorate her house beautifully and keep it to the best of her ability.

She Treats Everyone Equally

She does not think she is better or more important than anyone and, vice versa. She speaks in more or less the same manner to the janitor as she would to the vice president of her husband's company. She does not respond to rude comments with nastiness.

She Is Gracious

She assumes the best in people. She likes to believe that everyone has capabilities and talents to offer. She never dishes out unsolicited advice. She'll say something like, "I'm sure you'll be able to make the right choice". When complimented on something, she accepts it kindly but gives away the credit, praising someone who has helped with her hair, for example.

She Is Authentic and Unpretentious

She is unafraid to confess when she doesn't know something, and she never pretends to know when she doesn't.
She does not fake her youth, wealth, accomplishments, or her age. She tries to be as authentic as possible, respectful and humble. She always invests in the best quality items she can afford, and will use whatever it is until it needs to be replaced.

She Is a Giver

A giving woman is not merely generous with finances. She is also generous with her time, words, possessions, affection, compliments, and her encouragement and praises.
Ultimately, being lovely comes when one is inspired for the love of people, which is something that comes from God. It is when you realize how much God loves you (in spite of yourself), that the wonderful sense of loveliness comes to pass. This is how we can bestow the same love God gave us onto others.

She who is altogether lovely is:
- Generous with her smile
- Kind
- On time, if not a little early
- Believes others come first
- Disciplined in her mind and heart
- Impeccable in appearance
- Has a good work ethic
- Has a balanced life with her values intact
- Loves
- Respects others equally
- Gracious
- Authentic and never puts on pretenses

- A giver

While achieving elegance may be a long journey as you progress forward losing bad habits, unhealthy ideas, along with that old and uneasy way of life, here are some quick tips that allow you to understand the concepts of elegance rather instantly.

Elegant Women: Beautiful Women Who Inspire Me

I'm a thousand times more inspired by elegant women than the beauty of beautiful things (though many 'things' are very lovely).

I like to archive biographies and pictures of women who inspire me. It is sort a visualization exercise. **(Visualization: Putting before my eyes and in my mind what I love, so that I can become what I love.)** I am continually inspired by how they live magnificently through the tumbles and rumbles of life. They are role models by the way they carry themselves (elegant carriage), the manner in which they speak, what they say, how they say it, and their style of dress.

They have all the qualities necessary for authentic refinement. **Point to Note:** These featured women serve to give us encouragement, ideas, and inspirations, whether they are fictional characters or not. They are not meant to be put on a pedestal and worshiped, as they are, like all humans, imperfect.

More on Audrey Hepburn

My elegant woman inspiration is Audrey Hepburn. I wrote about her in the first couple of chapters. A large part of my study about achieving elegance was devoted to studying this one lady. I love what she says about life. Read the *Biography of Audrey Hepburn. Audrey Hepburn: A Life in Pictures.* She also had the most impeccable style. I even devoted an entire section talking only about her elegant hairstyle!

"Audrey Hepburn, Audrey Hepburn, now won't you reveal your fabulous secrets of grace and poise and teach us how to grow old as wonderfully as you have?" ~ Unknown quote

Natalie Portman

I'm just really inspired by her. She is an intelligent beauty and down to earth. Enough said.

Kate Middleton

She is an excellent example that an ordinary woman can assimilate into royalty.

Michelle Obama

A constant source of inspiration in the way she speaks, her values, and the way she raises her children. She is an elegant wife and mother.

Barbara Bush

Elegant woman Barbara Bush. I shared one of my favorite examples of her elegant and fine behavior in the article: "*Elegant Sophisticated Bearing*" – on elegantwoman.org.

Linda Porter

Played by Ashley Judd from the movie *De-Lovely: The Cole Porter Story*. This movie is based on the true story of Cole Porter. Linda Porter was the wife of Cole Porter, musician, songwriter and gallivanting socialite. She is also known as Linda Lee Thomas. She was a noted beauty in her youth and a descendant of the Lee family of Virginia (a prominent family in

American history). She grew up in a life of luxury. However, she did not have happy marriages nor was she ever loved in the way she had hoped. She was gracious to the end, and loved with all her heart.

In the movie, Linda had excellent taste and carriage. The way she moved, sat, and walked was simply lovely. The way she spoke was noticeably elegant, whether she was happy or angry. I felt sorrow for her when I watched her try so hard, always gracious and elegant as she went about her life. I wanted to wring Cole Porter's neck (played by Kevin Kline)! To his credit, he was extremely talented and wrote many of my favorite songs.

For some reason, the movie was not well received, but I loved it. It has to be one of my favorite movies of all time, and with many great Cole Porter songs worked in too!

Lily van der Woodsen

She is played by Kelly Rutherford in the popular television series, *Gossip Girl*. I particularly loved her in season one, as she was always immaculately dressed, whether it was for an elegant event, casual day wear, or a themed party. She was flawless and always appropriate and elegant. At first, she seems cold and sarcastic at times, but you soon warm up to her with each passing episode.

Cece van der Woodsen

She is proof one can be elegant at any age! The actress who plays her is Caroline Lagerfelt (descended from Swedish nobility in real life). Read about being an *elegant, mature woman* –where there's a page I devoted to writing about her. There are some pictures of her styles too, along with a few videos.

Charlotte York

My next elegant woman is Charlotte York from the television series, *Sex and the City: The Complete Series.* I featured her elegant Park Avenue home in my article, "*Elegant Decorating*." I love everything about her. She is sweet, kind, and appropriate, yet we see a very human side in her that all of us can relate to.

Bree van de Kamp

The next elegant woman is Bree van de Kamp. She has excellent posture and carriage. Her gestures are very elegant. One of the best I've seen so far.

She is a little uptight and sometimes too self-righteous, but she's still elegant nevertheless. I'll encourage you to watch her in the series, even just to watch the way she carries herself in television series *Desperate Housewives: The Complete Seasons* 1-5. She is played wonderfully by Marcia Cross.

Taylor Townsend (played by Autumn Reeser)

From the television series, *The O.C.* - The Complete First Season. She is a little bit crazy but you'll love her. Her articulation is beautiful and elegant. In terms of dress, she is preppy on casual days, but elegant for evening occasions. She has excellent posture. There are several 'schools of thought' on preppy dressing. Some feel that preppy is not elegant, others do. Personally, I think classic preppy styles can be elegant if the 'preppiness' is toned down a few notches.

Cheung Wing-sing as Ip-man's Wife

Cheung Wing-sing is played by Lynn Hung in the film *Ip Man* [Blu-ray]. It's a 2008 semi-biographical martial arts film based on the life of Ip Man, a grandmaster of the martial art Wing Chun, and the first person to teach Wing Chun openly.

Though quite grouchy, she is elegantly dressed always, and was quite the elegant mother. So far, I do not know whether she was wealthy by birth or by marriage to the legendary martial arts master Yip Man (I have not read up her history). But she seemed very comfortable with herself and her child. Later on, when they became very poor (because of second Sino-Japanese war), she was still able to be happy, despite having lost everything.

How many of us can remain content and happy when everything is stripped from us? See also *The Elegant Wife* on www.elegantwoman.org.

Jessica Alba and Katherine Heigl

I don't know much about them other than watching their movies and reading their biographies on Wikipedia. I've noticed they've always got excellent carriage, posture, and casually elegant dressing. They both seem appropriately elegant. They are all such wonderful women, though imperfect, they are elegant nonetheless.

18. Elegant with or without Money

You can be elegant with not much money.

I've had lots of people ask, "Can I be elegant even though I don't have much money?"
Personally, I understand this. Unlike several authors of elegance and stylish living, I did not come from money. However, as the world progressed and several opportunities become more accessible and affordable, I was able to be exposed to some things that traditionally only the wealthy have access to.

Luxury Does Not Always Equate to Elegance

The belief that you have to have money to be elegant bothers me. It seems like from what some people are saying about elegance, there is a trend to need expensive beautiful things. The message is like this: Your home has to somewhat resemble *Vogue* magazine to be elegant. The elegant crowd dresses in stylish outfits, of good fit and quality of certain labels such as << insert designer label >>.
        Usually, these websites are filled with lots of beautiful visuals with beautiful things that are way beyond our budget! Then there are the cultured folks who feel that you need to know in detail of writer/poet/artist and read ABC type of books and speak XYZ language and dine at EFG restaurants to gain approval to socialize with them and be on par with their sophisticated tastes.
        There is also the wealthy mother who is profusely elegant and makes the rest of us cash-strapped folks feel inadequate for our lack of finances. Perhaps you feel that you need to do this-and-that for your children; sign them up for all these so called 'designer' classes, and only then will they be adequately and elegantly educated.

While those things may indeed be elegant, they're not truly defining yardsticks of what elegance actually is. You can be genuinely elegant without all these things.

Principles of Elegance are More Important

On elegantwoman.org, there are several reasons why I prefer to write down words as opposed to focusing on perfection and displaying beautiful pictures (and by the way, my writing isn't particularly elegant).

While I love all those elegant stylish pictures and blogs, I try to express my thoughts on the topic of elegance as straight-forward as possible, and in an accessible way where my readers can pick and choose those areas that best suit their own style. I also don't want to write in elegant language because making it sound too stylish is impersonal and unrelatable to ordinary women like me.

Non-Material Elegance Fosters a Confident Elegance

Everyone has a right to express their beliefs and style of elegance. I'm grateful to all those who create beautiful things for us to enjoy, but right now I believe women with tight budgets can **live their lives with absolute dignity and style regardless**, and not feel inferior to their wealthier counterparts.

I also prefer to subscribe to a non-materialistic sort of elegance. This way, I am less dependent on 'things' to make me feel secure, and so I have a healthy self-esteem as a consequence. Everyone should be encouraged to form their own style/brand of elegance. That simply is a carefully thought out way of life.

.

Genteel Poverty

Actually, being elegant without money occurs more often than many of us know. There are lots of stories about people who used to be rich, and who suddenly found themselves poor due to a family tragedy, failure in business, or the loss of a job. However, those who were internally elegant carry on their lives with respect and pride, and continue living in a state of genteel poverty.

Poor but Genteel Kimono Makers

I first stumbled upon that term, **genteel poverty**, when I was reading about Japanese culture, particularly the tradition of Geishas. Specifically, I read about a way of life where you tried your best to live as respectably as possible, despite your change in financial status. The traditional kimono-makers, who became poor yet still kept their homes neat and as beautiful as possible, spoke respectfully to one another, continued to encourage the arts and books, and served tea as much as they could.

Cultural Elegance of Kazakhstan

One of the biggest patrons of the Singapore Symphony Orchestra, Mr. GK GOH and his wife, told me how inspiring the Eastern European country of Kazakhstan is with regards to supporting the classical music scene.
 In most developed countries, classical music concerts have trouble selling tickets. The reasons are not because of the lack of money, but rather a lack of arts appreciation. However in Kazakhstan, where the disposable income is just 1/5 of most developed countries, such as the USA, Australia or Singapore, it still spends more on the arts and music than the affluent West, be it symphony orchestra or The Black Eyed Peas. Elegance there is cultural. Music and art are as important to them as food and water.

Malay Culture of Living Well

Singapore is a prosperous, multi-racial country where I've spent more than half my life. Here, there is a Malay culture that prides elegance over money.

They speak well, are immaculately dressed and groomed (and in style too!), work at their jobs dutifully, smile a lot, and respect their elders. And even though they may have humble dwellings, their homes are decorated to the best that they can afford.

The Malays are warm, family orientated people who cook a lot, and pursue inexpensive activities such as camping, walking along the beach, gathering around a guitar, visiting family, and watching television together. They treat themselves to a trip to the zoo or an oceanarium on special occasions, and enjoy celebrating birthdays and other family functions. They are always tastefully elegant and happy.

They don't seem to need to dine at expensive restaurants, nor gawk into the windows of luxury boutiques. They are down-to-earth and friendly.

For these reasons and more, I find the Malays to be an inspiring group of people that I highly respect and draw lessons from as much as I can.

Elegant without Much Money

Here are some suggestions on how you may be elegant without money. The main idea is to have pride in yourself and your home, but stopping there makes it a superficial sort of elegance. That is why getting outside of your world is essential to becoming a well-rounded, authentically elegant person, whether you have money or not.
Pick and choose or do all!

1. Immaculate Grooming

This is something I believe you *can* do without much money.

Skincare

Buy drugstore brands. Research has proven that our belief in thinking expensive skincare products work better is simply not true. It might be that you haven't found the one that works for you.

Makeup

There are so many beauty bloggers and beauty YouTube videos to show you how drugstore brands can help women look a million dollars! Of course, whether you have money or not, you have to put in the work and learn the art of makeup, which you can do for little money by using inexpensive brands and by watching YouTube video tutorials.

Elegant Hair

If you can't afford the hundred dollar haircut, then go for a simple classic style of shoulder length hair, either with bangs or a long fringe. Lily Van Der Woodsen of *Gossip Girl* looks incredibly elegant with that hairstyle. You can learn to tie your hair elegantly as well.

Classic Clothes

Choose your clothes wisely and stick to the classics. If you're on a budget, express your style using accessories.

2. Immaculate Home

I'm constantly at war with clutter. There are tons of websites that help you deal with this, but deal with it you must! This is for the peace of mind and heart, both of which are essential for attaining elegance.

Neat and Tidiness

I'm not naturally neat. I find myself revisiting Flylady.net from time to time to get a refresher on her housekeeping systems.

Elegant Design

In my home, the walls are all varying shades of white, the furniture and coverings are creams and grays, punctuated with browns, gold, silver, and grays. My plates are all white, both the fine china and the regular everyday stuff. It was all done very inexpensively. I don't think my home reeks of luxurious elegance.

In fact, a friend whose family business is in retailing high-end designer furniture (e.g. a single arm chair = $25,000) said that my house looks like a cozy farm house! Ha! I choose to take those remarks in a good way. Most visitors to my house have said they feel very peaceful and warm. I guess some people must have liked it because my house was used for filming a movie and a TV series. I've not watched the TV series yet, but you can see bits of my home in this Asian movie (Link: http://youtu.be/AtJSfJajdwg).

There are various ways to style your home beautifully and elegantly. A couple of years ago, a style called shabby chic became very popular because it made old cheap things look very chic. Shabby chic is a type of interior decoration where the room's furniture and furnishings appear to look old and show signs of wear and tear. The idea is to give an overall vintage appearance.

Here's a pictures of Audrey Hepburn's Home http://www.flickr.com/photos/monkeyscrews/3687387313/ I'm pleased to add that even Audrey Hepburn decorated her home in a relaxed way. She was completely unpretentious. In the above photo, you can just picture her home, with modest furniture in happy colors like sunny yellow. She always had fresh flowers in her house too, which were taken from her own garden.

3. Immaculate Speech

Speak as properly as you can. That means clearly, audibly, and at a reasonable pace. Try to express yourself as concisely as possible (which I understand can sometimes be hard for us women!). Try to avoid using slang. If you have friends who you consider to speak better than you, take note of their elocution and use this as a guide to help improve your own speech.

4. Read the News

This is just so that you don't live in your own tiny world and become self-absorbed. Current news is often used as popular conversational topics. You might like to join Twitter and follow the accounts of newspapers or reputable news channels. This is a good way to browse through headlines and stay in touch with current events.

5. Have a Hobby, Play a Sport, Adopt an Art

What you pursue will depend on the amount of free time you have and your budget. Try to find a hobby, sport, or art that can fit into your routine. Ideally, you would pursue something from all three if possible. The main reason for participating in sports and hobbies is for you to develop a side of yourself that contributes towards an elegant way of life. It is more beneficial to engage in something outside of yourself than it is to waste time mindlessly flicking through TV channels. If you are very involved with taking care of your family, you may find a way to integrate something into family time.

Sports

Playing a sport is great for your fitness and overall wellbeing. It also gives you an opportunity to get acquainted with other communities of people. Is there a local community club nearby that organizes inexpensive sporting activities? If not, do the work yourself; put the word out and organize some of your own.

Hobby

Find a hobby you're interested in and that you can easily afford. For instance, maybe you can take up bird watching, or birding as it's also called. You can perhaps find places nearby to go to on the weekends, read more about the birds in your area, and their habits, etc. Birding is also one of those recreational activities that involve a great community of like-minded folks.

Adopt an Art Form

You can pick a style of art that you like, and then continue to learn more about it. You can also do some research and find out what others have to say on the subject. Maybe you could study the art of one particular artist, say Andy Warhol, if he and his work interest you. This will help you to develop an appreciation of other artists. The same goes for music too. You may even study films, film making, acting or directing. With access to libraries and the Internet, many art forms are accessible.

6. Volunteer

If you go to church, volunteer and get involved in some way. If church isn't your thing, you can become a helper for a local charity. Giving freely of yourself by volunteering will not only provide you with a priceless sense of perspective, but with a better appreciation of life. This is thoroughly elegant living, and something that can't be achieved from buying and accumulating things.

7. Inexpensive Education

There is so much you can learn for free or certainly with very little money! My favorite choice is to make use of the library. Here you can borrow books, videos, and CD-ROMs. You can also learn from websites or by YouTube videos, and even sign up for online courses.

There are also inexpensive classes in community colleges where you can learn a new skill, such as cooking, jewelry making, the art of makeup, and so on. This was how I got started on expressionism oil painting some years ago.

There are also many free or inexpensive exhibitions and concerts in lots of areas (hopefully in your region too). You can learn a language by setting aside a weekly budget for lessons, and then supplement it with free stuff from websites, or books from the library, and perhaps find inexpensive language CDs on Amazon.

You can also simply pick a topic of interest and start reading up on it with a passion. If you can't think of a topic, just go to the library and browse around until something catches your attention. I've discovered many interesting topics this way.

Conclusions on Elegance without Money

In conclusion, you don't have to have lots of money to live well and elegantly. If you find yourself a little strapped for cash, don't despair! You can still be an elegant person and gain respect from those around you. You also don't have to be cheap to be elegant.

If you have plenty of money, well that's okay, too. Being well-off is not a bad thing when it's respected. There are elegant attitudes towards money that can often be improved upon.

An Elegant Attitude towards Money

How does one develop an elegant outlook on money and gain an understanding of wealth? It's just one of those things that are assumed as becoming in an elegant woman.

We have all been taught that talking about money is rude, especially when it comes to asking about people's salaries, or trying to get others to divulge their mortgage details and loan amounts. This includes our commonly experienced conversation question of "How much did you pay for that?"

So, what are some of the attitudes and outlooks regarding the money and finance of an elegant woman? First of all, it is inevitable that a woman has to deal with money and wealth. It might be about choosing how she ought to spend her cash, or informal conversations on world affairs during cocktail hour.

Naturally, the world believes that you need money to be elegant or classy. I've written that this isn't necessarily so. However, I can't deny the fact that it is easier to be elegant with some wealth. Why? While this list is not exhaustive, here are some reasons:

With wealth:

- You are more generous and giving.
- You have access to the finer things in life that contribute to elegant taste and an elegant look.
- You are often in a better mood when money worries are absent from your life.
- It is easier to have an elegant countenance.
- Without being bogged down with money problems, it is easier to take the focus off yourself and think more about others.
- You are in a better position to help and to influence people.
- Education is expensive, and is easier to afford, which in turn can propel you to become the fine woman you strive to be.

Thus, I think it is important to be financially secure on your own.

Elegant Sense of Being Financially Secure

To be financially secure, you must have:

- A habit of saving and a healthy savings account
- A good understanding of wealth - how it comes about and how to elegantly manage it
- General knowledge on the world of money - basic education of investments, such as property, stocks,

businesses, interests rates, and some understanding of economics

- Access to extra cash (after putting some savings away), but not by spending over your limit

A habit of saving and a healthy savings account will give you a certain sense of poise, knowing that you have the ability to take care of yourself and others if you need to. You will also gain self-respect for being diligent and disciplined.

To understand wealth and to gain knowledge about the world of money is a form of self-improvement. Taking charge of your future independently is to obtain a healthy sense of self-reliance. It gives a woman a quiet sense of confidence; something that is very beautiful. There is a certain elegance of quiet authority that comes from within. She will not be pushed around nor easily impressed. Money, or people who use money to impress, will have no hold on her.

Learning all these financial cues also helps you in social hour. You'll be able to **speak the subtle 'language of money'** especially if you find yourself socializing in more elegant circles. For example, **portfolio income** is from paper assets, which include dividends from corporations, plus income from real estate investments and interest. What is an asset and liability? What is the meaning of earned income and passive income?

To have extra cash after putting some away **enables you to be in a position to give**, to help others, promote a worthy cause, or to invest in your own self-improvement, such as taking a literature class, for example.

An Elegant Woman and Her Money

Now let's talk about some elegant attitudes about money.

An elegant woman generally has the following beliefs about money. Please understand that these are my viewpoints and you are free to disagree with me.

Spends Wisely, but Is Not Cheap

She spends her money wisely, but she does not practice frugality. In other words, she considers the value of her purchase, but she does not deliberately go out and buy the cheapest of everything. She handles her money with great respect, but she is not miserly.

Generous

She will not calculate to the last penny what you owe her. She is generous. This is also cultural, but I do believe that a truly elegant woman is usually generous.

Enjoys Finer Things, Is Willing to Spend

There is a delicate balance here, but she eats, wears, and uses fine things to the best of what she can afford. She takes pride in herself and she believes she's worth it. She treats herself well. However, she is not the sort of person that spends money only on herself while being cheap with others.

Perhaps Uncommon Outlook towards Money

Here are some of my favorite quotes from the author of the *Rich Dad Poor Dad* series:

"I love spending money, but Kim and I are not foolish with ours. I love having the finer things in life. I love having the choice of flying first class or economy. I love tipping people well, if they have given great service. I love making my friends rich when our investments do well. I love the freedom that money buys. I love working if I want to and not working if I don't. So for me, money is fun, money buys me more choices and most importantly, it has bought Kim and me the freedom from the drudgery of earning a living."

"I don't understand people who said, 'Money does not make happy.' I often wonder what they do for fun."

"One of the main reasons people spend money is to make themselves happy."

"In my opinion, it's not money that makes you unhappy. It's not being able to pay your bills or not having the money to do the things you would love to do that tends to make people unhappy. "

"You spend less if you buy what you desire. I am very happy with my car and my wife is happy with hers. We may have spent more initially by being clear on satisfying our material standards, which includes our house and clothing, but we actually spend less in the long run."

*"Some people believe that God wants us to live frugally and to avoid the temptations of the finer things in life. There are other people who believe that **God created these wonderful creations for us to enjoy**. It is up to you to choose what kind of God you want to believe in."*

What do you think?

Elegance towards Money Matters

To develop elegance on matters of money, you will first have to face any concerns you have with it. Most of us all have something!

A good place to start is by making a commitment to become financially educated. Only then can you really become comfortable with finance and money-related issues. Some of us over-spend and then hide our credit card bills, hoping against hope that they will somehow disappear! For others, money has such a stronghold over them that they can never give up being cheap or let go and be more generous with their loved ones.

There are tons of courses out there that can teach us how to be more financially savvy. Not all are good though, and some are way too risky in their approach. But being educated on financial matters is a must for women who want to be more financially confident, and thus be able to take care of their finances properly. Learning how to better manage money will certainly help any woman grow in self-reliance and elegance. Even though you may not necessarily want to become the next Oprah Winfrey, understanding how to make your money work for you is invaluable.

I suggest you start by reading a few books on the topic, just to gain a general knowledge and some sophistication in speaking the language of money (subtly of course).

I would recommend the *Rich Dad Poor Dad* series to anyone. Treat it like a financial immersion course. You might get them all at your local library! Read them with a mindset of increasing your financial language for the sake of elegance. It is up to you how far you would like to take this financial education. Whatever you do though, remember to get proper, sound advice from professionals or trusted advisors.

19. Tips on Elegance, Quick and Easy Ways to Become Elegant

Here we look at simple daily reminders about the choices you make and how to choose the elegant way of life on a daily basis.

Start With Your Heart

Elegance starts with the heart. It shows in your eyes, your face, and your smile. It is present in your speech. There's something about you. People gravitate towards you because of that *special something* you possess.
To develop your heart, spend a little time every day with God. Sing a song, read a page of the Bible, or a good book with inspiration and words of wisdom. I find it helpful have a daily reading sent to my email entitled 'Daily Devotional'. There are plenty of websites with an option to subscribe for free daily devotional emails.

Appearance

Elegant Keywords: **Clean**, **Neat**, **Simple**
- Posture: Always stand up straight. Do not slouch, or sit with your legs crossed, or with folded arms.
- Clothing: Ensure your shoes are not dirty or scuffed and that your clothes are ironed nicely and void of stains or grubby marks.

- Positive thinking: Think about positive things. An optimistic outlook on life will have you wearing a warm expression on your face.
- Hairstyle: Keep hair away from your face. Wear it in a neat chignon or ponytail.
- Dress sense: Dress appropriately according to the occasion. If in doubt, wear a classic-styled dress in a neutral color with small, elegant accessories. That always works best.

Speech

- Bad Language: Refrain from using vulgarities.
- Cheery: Remain positive and speak about only good things.
- Tactful: Be gracious when you encounter someone rude. If insulted, hold your head up in self-respect and walk away.
- Affable: Be friendly and remain light-hearted in conversation. Pour your sorrows only to a very close friend.
- Clarity: Without sounding stiff, speak as properly as you can manage. Pronounce your words with clarity and avoid using slang.
- Emotions: Downplay your emotions, or any problems you might have, unless you are talking with a close friend.

- Hyperbole: Exaggeration is not pretty. *"I've been to Paris a million times!"* vs *"Yes, I try to go there as often as I'm able, because it's one of my favorite vacation spots"*.
- Boastful: Never praise yourself or draw attention to yourself.

The Elegant Home

- Minimal: Keep it simple, clean, and add soft decorative elements.
- Disorder: Keep clutter out of sight! Be mindful of the 'a place for everything and everything in its place' concept.
- Knick-knacks: Avoid novelty items, dangling trinkets, too many photos or art work on the walls.
- Décor: Avoid harsh colors, sharp-edged looking furniture. For a more in-depth commentary on an elegant home, click the "Home" title of this section.

Shopping for Elegant Things

- Appeal: Learn to cultivate an eye for beauty. Appreciate good design, flowers, beautiful places, books.
- Restraint: Discipline yourself to keep your possessions as sparse as possible. Have only one of everything

whenever possible. One car, one watch, one camera, etc.

- Worth: Train yourself to decipher value instead of going for the cheapest or most expensive items. Learn what item is the most value for the money.
- Quality: Develop a shopping habit to only purchase things of the highest quality that you can afford.
- Outfits: Before you shop for clothes, spend about five minutes looking through your wardrobe. This will help you buy things that you really need and pieces that complement the items of clothing you already have.

Pursue Education

- Learning: Take pride in getting educated. Do not undermine the value of education.
- Investment: Continually invest in your education.
- Subjects: Pick an area of interest and develop it. Take classes, read, write about it. Become elite!

Adopt a Sport

- Get active: Learn a sport or two and pursue it passionately.
- Commit: Make time for that sport. Devote once a week, a month, and stick with your commitment.

- Team up: Find friends and pursue sporting activities together if you can! Teaming up is great for increasing motivation levels and adding a little fun into a pastime.

Travel and Culture

- Educate: Develop a more in-depth knowledge of different cultures. This will give you an appreciation of the differences in people, their countries, and lifestyles.
- Voyage: Travel as much as you can. It expands your mind and broadens your horizons.
- Food: Learn about the cuisine of different cultures. At least know one or two famous dishes from every country or culture.
- Appreciation: It is very flattering to those of other of cultures if you've made the effort to lean about them and their ways. To get out of our comfort zone is to be sophisticated.
- Awareness: Knowledge increases your elegant self-confidence.

Acquire Social Ease

- Etiquette: Always remember your greetings. Introduce yourself or introduce others to each other.
- Priority: At a party, find the host/hostess to offer your greetings and your gift if you've brought one.

- Socialize: Keep it light-hearted and mingle. Do not talk to any one person longer than five to ten minutes. Make your way around the room!
- Attire: Dress your best (appropriately). You'll be a lot more at ease with yourself wearing the right attire. Smile with confidence.
- Gratitude: Say goodbye to your host before you leave. Thank them for a lovely time.

Elegant Entertaining

- Learn: As you go to parties, learn how to throw one! It's returning the social favor.
- Assist: Start by taking the initiative to organize dinner for your friends. Organize the emails, text messages, book the restaurant, and send out reminders.
- Host: As you gain more confidence playing the hostess, you can start by throwing teas, coffees at your own house or in your garden. It is more elegant to throw and fund the event.
- Discretion: It's not elegant to expect your guests to split the cost or mention anything about how much you've paid for the food and wine.

An Elegant Mind

- Dutiful: Focus on filling your mind and heart with love, kindness, and compassion. My personal suggestion is to attend a good church or volunteer to help a worthy cause.

- Thoughtful: Be considerate and never rude. Always think about others before yourself, which is not really a natural trait in most humans. So I'll do so with the grace of God!
- Attentive: Be interested in others within the world around you.
- Grateful: If you are feeling a tad sour, look around you and tell yourself 10 things that you like about a room in your home, or that day, or a person, your work, etc.
- Value: Appreciate beauty, quality, perfection, and fine workmanship.
- Virtue: See past the faults of others, see the good in them. See them through Jesus' eyes.
- Anxiety: Never ever rush or panic. Ask yourself: What is the worst that can happen? In most cases, it's not a life emergency.

Time-Tested Beauty Tips

As recommended by your elegant ambassador, Audrey Hepburn:

- For attractive lips, speak words of kindness.
- For lovely eyes, seek out the good in people.
- For a slim figure, share your food with the hungry.
- For beautiful hair, let a child run his fingers through it once a day.

- For poise, walk with knowledge, you'll never walk alone.
- We leave you a tradition with a future.
- The tender loving care of human beings will never become obsolete.
- People, even more than things, have to be restored, renewed, revived, reclaimed, and redeemed, and redeemed, and redeemed!
- Never throw out anybody.
- Remember, if you ever need a helping hand, you'll find one at the end of your arm.
- As you grow older, you will discover that you have two hands: one for helping yourself, the other for helping others.
- Your "good old days" are still ahead of you, may you have many of them.

My References and Recommended Reading

A Guide to Elegance: For Every Woman Who Wants to Be Well and Properly Dressed on All Occasions
By Geneviève Antoine Dariaux

Entre Nous: A Woman's Guide to Finding Her Inner French Girl
By Debra Ollivier, Debra Olliver

Parisian Chic: A Style Guide
By Inès de La Fressange, Sophie Gachet

The Little Dictionary of Fashion: A Guide to Dress Sense for Every Woman
By Christian Dior

Audrey Hepburn, An Elegant Spirit
By Sean Hepburn Ferrer

The Little Pink Book of Elegance
By Jodi Kahn, Kerren Barbas

How to be Lovely: The Audrey Hepburn Way of Life
By Melissa Hellstern

Pride and Prejudice
By Jane Austen

How to Be a Lady: A Contemporary Guide to Common Courtesy
By Candace Simpson-Giles

Emily Post's Etiquette
By Peggy Post, Emily Post

The New Rules of Posture: *How to Sit, Stand, and Move in the Modern World*
By Mary Bond

The Art of Speech and Deportment
By Anna Morgan

All about Raising Children
By Helen Andelin

The Well-Trained Mind: *A Guide to Classical Education at Home* (Third Edition)
By Susan Wise Bauer and Jessie Wise

Geisha of Gion: *The True Story of Japan's Foremost Geisha*
By Mineko Iwasaki and Rande Brown

Secrets of Elegance
By Eunice Leong

Becoming a Woman of the Finest Class
By Eunice Leong

How to Meet the Rich: *For Business, Friendship, or Romance*
By Ginie Sayles

Rich Dad, Poor Dad
By Robert T. Kiyosaki